D1284481

THE IMMEDIATE EXPERIENCE

ROBERT WARSHOW

The Immediate Experience

MOVIES, COMICS, THEATRE
& OTHER ASPECTS
OF POPULAR CULTURE

Enlarged Edition

Now with "Robert Warshow: Life and Works,"
by David Denby
and "Epilogue: After Half a Century,"
by Stanley Cavell

HARVARD UNIVERSITY PRESS

Cambridge, Massachusetts, and London, England
2001

First Harvard University Press paperback edition, 2001

Library of Congress Cataloging-in-Publication Data

Warshow, Robert, 1917–1955.
   The immediate experience : movies, comics, theatre & other aspects
      of popular culture / Robert Warshow.—Enlarged ed.
      p.   cm.
   Originally published: Garden City, N. Y. : Doubleday, 1962. With new
      chapters "Robert Warshow: life and works" / David Denby and
      "Epilogue: after half a century" / Stanley Cavell.
   ISBN 0-674-00726-3
   1. Motion pictures—United States.   2. United States—Popular
      culture.   I. Title.
   PN1993.5.U6 W34   2001
   791.43′0973—dc21   2001039782

THIS BOOK IS FOR
MY SON PAUL

CONTENTS

ROBERT WARSHOW: LIFE AND WORKS

ONE OF THE most beautiful film reviews ever written begins as follows:

> Beneath all the social meanings of Chaplin's art there is one insistent personal message that he is conveying to us all the time. It is the message of most entertainers, maybe, but his especially because he is so great an entertainer. "Love me"—he has asked this from the beginning, buttering us up with his sweet ways and his calculated graceful misadventures, with those exquisite manners so perfectly beside the point, with that honeyed glance he casts at us so often, lips pursed in an outrageous simper, eyebrows and mustache moving in frantic invitation. Love me. And we have, apparently, loved him, though with such undercurrents of revulsion as might be expected in response to so naked a demand.
>
> Does he love us? This is a strange question to ask of an artist. But it is Chaplin himself who puts it in our mouths, harping on love until we are forced almost in self-defense to say: what about you? He does not love us; and maybe he doesn't love anything. Even in his most genial moments we get now and then a glimpse of how cold a heart has gone into his great blaze. Consider the scene in *City Lights* when he

tactfully permits the Blind Girl to unravel his underwear in the belief that she is rolling up her knitting wool; the delicacy of feeling is wonderful, all right—who else could have conceived the need for this particular kindness?—but it is he, that contriving artist there, who has created the occasion for the delicacy in the first place. No, the warmth that comes from his image on the screen is only our happy opportunity to love him. He has no love to spare, he is too busy pushing his own demand: love *me*, love *me*, poor Charlie, sweet Charlie. Probably he even despises us because we have responded so readily to his blandishments, and also because we can never respond enough.

Notice that the author of this prose, Robert Warshow, achieves both precision and a vivid emotional connection to the subject without a moment of insistence, without a phrase of punched-up writing, or even an unusual adjective. The tone is mild, the language unremarkable, and yet the passage has a definite lilt and a steady, even pressing, forward movement. On the basis of exactly eleven such review-essays devoted to movies, Robert Warshow, who died in 1955 at the age of thirty-seven, has long been considered one of the best of all American film critics. I have no difficulty placing him in the small journalistic pantheon that includes Gilbert Seldes, Otis Ferguson, James Agee, Manny Farber, Pauline Kael, and Andrew Sarris. Seven years after Warshow's death, the eleven pieces, along with Warshow's articles on literature, theater, the culture of liberalism, and the comics, were gathered into a short volume, *The Immediate Experience.* At various times in the last forty years, the collection has been out of print, but Warshow himself has never been forgotten: rarely has anyone who has written so little been quoted and anthologized so much. The current edition adds to the original text eight previously uncollected pieces on books. We now have a moving Warshow article on Kafka's diaries, trenchant remarks about Gertrude Stein and Ernest Hemingway, and, in a piece on Scholem Aleichem, a brief but enormously useful definition of Jewish humor.

As the passage makes clear, Robert Warshow loved fables, even "simple" fables—the bruising encounters of Chaplin's Tramp with the society around him, the gloriously redundant adventures of Krazy Kat, the resonant moral outlines of the gangster and Western movies. Yet Warshow's appreciation of fables—his love of movies in general—was wrested from a historical and, later, a personal background of considerable stress. Warshow wrote the latter of these pieces knowing that his young wife was grievously ill. The suffering that was his own merged with a rather gloomy mood shared by many American intellectuals of the 1940s and 1950s. Warshow and his colleagues had lived through the destruction of the European Jews and the murderous betrayal of idealism by the Soviet state. Perhaps only a man writing at mid-century could celebrate illusion in so powerfully an un-illusioned way. In a passing comment on the failure of the Bolshevik Revolution, and on the "irony" of utopias souring into dictatorships, Warshow wrote, "I would have given up all ironies and the sense of tragedy and the sense of history along with them, just to have stupid, handsome Nicholas grinding his heel once more into the face of unhappy Russia." This bitterly funny sentence from Warshow's piece on the Soviet silent cinema is both heartrending and (to our ears in 2001) a little strange. Warshow's seriousness now reaches out to us from across a considerable historical divide.

In the late nineteenth century, at the age of twenty, Warshow's father, Adolph, arrived from Russia and settled in New York, where he made his way in the wholesale paper business and became something of a figure in the Socialist Party. (Having a career in both business and left-wing politics was not then considered a contradiction; Adolph Warshow even ran for Congress once on the Socialist ticket.) Robert, his sole child from a second marriage, was born in 1917, and grew up in New York, surrounded by children of both his father's and mother's earlier marriages. Robert Warshow graduated from Dewitt Clinton High School and went on to the University of Michigan, and in 1938, at the age of twenty, received a master's degree in English from the university. He worked briefly as a salesman at his father's paper business before taking a job as associate editor and writer for the social-democratic, anti-Stalinist magazine *The New Leader*, to which he had contributed pieces from before the age of twenty. During World War II, Warshow worked as a code-breaker for the Army Signal Corps, performing secret work on Japanese military communication. Before the war, in 1939, he had married his college sweetheart, the intellectually gifted Edith Folkoff, with whom he shared a love of literature and a passion for modernism in the arts. Their son, Paul, was born in 1943.

At the end of thw war, in 1946, Robert Warshow became an editor at *Commentary*, where he was admired and loved for his literary skill, his patience, and his willingness to bring out the best in such writers as James Baldwin, Bernard Malamud, and Isaac Rosenfeld. It was a heady time for him: he began publishing regularly in *Commentary* and in *Partisan Review* at a time when they were both central to American intellectual life. But as Warshow gained in strength as a writer, his personal difficulties grew severe. In college, Edith Folkoff, had had occasional unexplained symptoms. But for more than a decade of the Warshows' marriage, the symptoms were neither too frequent nor too worrisome. By around 1951, though, it was clear that she had multiple sclerosis, and she soon became severely disabled. And Warshow himself, under stress, an inveterate smoker (it was the characteristic vice of the era), and always of delicate constitution, died of a heart attack in 1955. Edith died in 1958.

Robert Warshow belongs to film criticism and to the criticism of popular culture—he was one of the inventors of the latter genre—but it's only natural to see him at the same time as a member of what came to be known as "The New York Intellectuals." In recent decades, the aging warriors of that group have written memoirs of one sort or another, and studies of the individual figures and the group as a whole continue to come out. But for any reader under forty, for whom the phrase "New York Intellectuals" seems distant, vague, or menacing, a short summing-up may be necessary.

Such Gentiles as Dwight Macdonald, Mary McCarthy, and Elizabeth Hardwick were among the New York writers, and Edmund Wilson, from an earlier generation, was a universally admired figure, but the group was largely Jewish—mainly children of Eastern European or Russian immigrants. The New York writers inherited from the past a devotion to bookishness and a style of disputation acquired in earlier generations through close study of sacred texts and commentary. Growing up in the 1930s, however, these young men and women were largely indifferent to religion; they were schooled in Marx and Freud, and they excelled at aggressive strategies of interpretation whose purpose, often enough, was to take the ostensible significance of some phenomenon (political event, cultural formation, book, play, movie) and to find, within its core, a quite different or hidden meaning, sometimes the reverse of what appeared on the surface. Warshow's talent for decoding may have come into play here; in general, the New York group prided themselves on the act of unmasking. In some ways, they were lucky—they had been cast into a wealthy and optimistic country untouched by the worst disasters of the century. Yet lucky or not, they were eager to live with full knowledge of what Max Weber called the "disenchantment" of the modern world. Disenchantment, one might say, became not only their mood but their sword and shield. They cultivated a modulated wariness, a sense of humor tending toward grim irony, a general distrust of appearances. Robert Warshow embodied all of these attitudes, but with a considerable grace often lacking in the writing of his colleagues. In the excerpt from the Chaplin essay quoted earlier, Warshow surely and simply interrogates Chaplin's persona and the audience's response to it. His gifts were temperamental as well as literary.

The critical essay was the group's favorite way of addressing both the world and one another, and among the leading talents were such literary critics as Lionel Trilling, Philip Rahv, Alfred Kazin, and Irving Howe. The group also included the sociologists Daniel Bell and Nathan Glazer; the philosopher Sidney Hook, who became a leading anti-Communist writer; the German-born political theorist Hannah Arendt; the art critics Clement Greenberg, Harold Rosenberg, and Meyer Schapiro. The group's poets and novelists included Delmore Schwartz, Saul Bellow, and (somewhat late in the game and always rebelliously) Norman Mailer. As undergraduates, many of them attended City College in New York. They prided themselves on their bohemianism and independence, and though any accommodation to the university was difficult, even testy, several spent their careers at Columbia, and in middle age, a few others taught at the University of Chicago, Brandeis, and Harvard. The radical fervor most of them possessed when young modulated in the years after World War II into democratic socialism or a fairly conventional liberalism (in some cases, it kept on modulating into neo-conservatism). Radical or not, they are widely considered the only intelligentsia (in the European sense of the word) ever produced here—a political-intellectual class, immersed in both history and the tensions of the moment.

One of the personal tasks (or, as a later generation would say, "projects") of the New York group was to complete the break with the immigrant past. By "break," I do not mean an occasion marked by violence or derision. In his essay on Clifford Odets and in his severely restrained expression of grief at his father's death ("An Old Man Gone"), Warshow captures the generational struggle between immigrants and their children with the greatest delicacy and respect. The point of the break for the New York writers was to leave the ghetto intellectually, to enter an international culture—what Václav Havel would later call (without irony) the "universal culture." This break was accompanied by a sense of gratitude to America, the country which, by protecting the Jews, and by affording its citizens a free choice of cultural destiny, had made the break possible in the first place. The New York intellectuals' love of high modernism, its "European-ness," was accompanied by an amazed and delighted discovery of the American turf—its classic texts, its real and mythic landscapes, the vitality of its cities and popular arts.

There were cultural projects as well, two in particular. The first was to complete the work of explaining and defending modernism. As Irving Howe and others have pointed out, the serious struggle on behalf of Joyce, Proust, Kafka, Picasso, Stravinsky, Schoenberg, and the rest had been successfully waged earlier, in the 1920s, so perhaps it would be more appropriate to say that the New York intellectuals were a generation that came to maturity with the work of these artists fully alive in their souls and minds—

that they were unapologetic highbrows who felt that not to know something, and not to read or see something good, was a kind of crime. They were moralists of culture, almost unimaginable now—erudite, forbidding, intolerant of any breach in the highest standards.

The second project was to destroy any remaining doubts among liberals that Communism represented a political and moral disaster almost as complete in its awfulness as Nazism. That this task was required at all may now surprise younger Americans, who often have trouble understanding the appeal that Communism had for many liberals in the 1930s. And after the recent comic-pathetic collapse of the Soviet state, it may be hard to imagine that Communism was ever a genuine political threat in Europe and a genuine philistine threat here—that it wasn't merely a delusion of an overzealous FBI and the American Right. But for Warshow's generation, Communism, precisely because it made its appeal to idealism, was a dominating obsession. After a faltering beginning, *Partisan Review* broke with the American Communist Party in 1936 and embraced the modern movements in the arts. Denunciation of Stalinism in all its forms—the purges and trials, the forced labor camps, the ominipresent secret police in the Soviet bloc, the centralization of the economy—continued in *Partisan* and in *Commentary* (and later in the socialist quarterly *Dissent*) for years. But the New York group eventually fell into a bizarre trap mostly not of their own making. When McCarthyism began to hound American leftists—many of them patently innocent of anything more serious than bad judgment—the members of the group suffered the chagrin of seeing their anti-communist position overtaken by an extreme, even toxic version of everything they had believed. Thereafter, they were forced, in effect, to fight a two-front war—against Stalinism and against McCarthyism at the same time. This

xvi

painful (and at times painfully absurd) dilemma helped to impose a certain bleakness of outlook among the New York writers. As late as the 1950s, many liberals remained sympathetic to the Communist "experiment" and were infuriatingly slow to comprehend that they were supporting the cause of murder; at the same time, the anti-Communists of the Right were so rabid and punitive that it became hard to view American Communists as anything but victims. Out of such contradictions, Warshow constructed his brilliant 1953 essay "The 'Idealism' of Julius and Ethel Rosenberg" and his review of Leo McCarey's film *My Son John*.

In recent decades, "The 'Idealism' of Julius and Ethel Rosenberg" has struck a number of readers as unfair, even cruel, for here is a critic attacking two people who have been executed, and attacking them for the mawkishness and ungainliness of their prison letters to each other. One certainly wishes that Warshow had not accepted the execution of the Rosenbergs uncritically; and that further he had shown some awareness of the excesses of the trial judge in the case. But, at the same time, it's clear that Warshow is not entirely unsympathetic to the Rosenbergs; nor is he simply jeering at bad prose. The horror of American Stalinism, he says again and again, is that it prevents its adherents from having any kind of direct and honest relationship to experience. Thus the peculiar intensity of the passage in which Warshow quotes Julius Rosenberg on the Declaration of Independence. Julius claimed that having taped the document to the wall of his cell, he was inspired by what it said of free speech and other freedoms. The Declaration, of course, says nothing about such freedoms, and Warshow's point is that Julius's mistake is more than a mere slip, more than a garden variety lie: it's the result of a habitual practice of misrepresentation in which one's actual experience no longer mattered. Julius Rosenberg was prevented by will and by habit from knowing that he was lying, and for Warshow his failure had implications for a broad swath of liberal culture. In "The Legacy of the 30s," Warshow insists that the radicalism of that decade, the period of the Popular Front, engendered an "organized mass disingenuousness, when every act and every idea had behind it some 'larger consideration' which destroyed its honesty and meaning." The culture that resulted from this effort—a spreading rot of liberal middlebrow kitsch—was also prevented by will and by habit from knowing that it was lying.

Stalinism was Warshow's model for how dishonesty might work ("falsity" was perhaps his favorite word as a critic). The theater audience crying "Bravo!" at performances of Arthur Miller's *Crucible* was signaling its own participation in a vague community of dissent rather than any virtues of the play. The Soviet filmmakers, with their famous editing techniques, made an aesthetically satisfying but morally frivolous montage of corpses—"if they had got the chance, they would have made a handsome montage of my corpse too, and given it a meaning—their meaning and not mine." By contrast, the photographic record of events and personalities in the documentary *Tsar to Lenin* offered a gratifying sense of actuality—the faces and bodies of historical actors seen plain, without the imposed interpretive context that destroyed reality with "meaning." In some of these pieces, particularly the articles on *Paisan* and *The Illegals*— Warshow responds warmly and with a sense of gratitude to the semi-documentary image, unvarnished by ideology or by the treacheries of art.

Like James Agee, who died in the same year—1955— Warshow wanted an uncontaminated audience. American pop culture, at its best, was vigorous and crude. Moviegoing, Warshow said, was still a "a kind of 'pure' culture, a little like fishing or drinking or playing baseball." Left alone, the democratic ethos in art was sufficient—certainly the corruptions of middlebrow sentimentality were a greater threat than violence or vulgarity. For all Warshow's highbrowism, and despite the beautiful gravity of his style, one can hear in such sentiments a ready enjoyment of the life of the streets, the corner drugstore, the newspapers, and the ballpark. As Lionel Trilling and others have said, Warshow wrote about pop culture without the kind of distance or self-consciousness that crippled most intellectuals—but without losing his mind, either. He was eager to judge. He would never have understood the dissolution of standards encouraged by many of today's academics, who embrace sitcoms, music videos, advertising, and every other product under the rubric "cultural studies." Warshow was trained to discriminate, and he was fortunate in his timing. Fifty years ago, mass culture was still a series of specfic energies, outlets, and works. It was not yet a total environment conditioning everything we do—an infinite replication of images, sounds, moods and attitudes that reduces so many of us to a state of complete acceptance or constant exasperation. "A whole literature cannot be built on irony," Warshow wrote in 1947. Ah, but in the period of pervasive pop, it has—uneasily, even guiltily. Warshow, I imagine, would not have admired today's American literature or the more cynical varieties of smart journalism that celebrate a play of surfaces without ever acknowledging that a serious cultural value might be at stake. In the age of the conglomerate, moviegoing has lost its "purity," and criticism, often enough, has become facetious and defensive. The superb composure of that passage on *Limelight* would now be very hard to achieve.

Back in the 1940s, the issue for intellectual critics was not irony but authenticity. "A man watches a movie, and the critic must acknowledge that he is that man," Warshow wrote. This famous sentence is simple enough, but for critics its implications remain enormous. It means, among other things, that if you are drawn to something "low," you must acknowledge your connection to it. You must be willing to understand that saying a movie is not a work of art doesn't necessarily end your participation in whatever strength the movie has. It means acknowledging your attraction to the actors, to movement, to crude excitement. However well armed mentally, you cannot force the experience of seeing the movie through six intellectual filters—at least, not at first. First you must establish an image, you must put some flesh on the screen, some movement, a few colors, a tone, a landscape of emotion, all the elements of the medium itself. Only then can you exercise your learning. It is a lesson that Pauline Kael absorbed, brilliantly practiced throughout her career, and then passed on to the next generation. It was not a lesson that, in the 1960s and 1970s, a variety of intellectual film critics with traditional aesthetics ever quite understood.

Warshow was an essayist, not a regular reviewer, and probably couldn't have functioned as a reviewer. As a film critic, he lacked spontaneity and gaiety; praise did not come easily to him; he did not seek out new talent. But no film critic ever expressed the complex temperament of a modern skeptical mind with any greater power or delicacy than he did. The final paragraph of the piece on *Limelight* attains an eloquence extremely rare in film criticism—a happiness, one might say, wrung from all the unhappiness associated with modern life, modern history, modern art. One of the essays that followed, "Re-Viewing the Russian Movies," left unfinished and unedited at Warshow's death, offers a new, more flexible style, the words circling back on themselves with increasing suavity. It's a marvelous fragment, contemplative, angry, and witty, and it ends with a beautiful evocation of a scene from Dovzhenko's *Earth*—a passage that makes one believe that Warshow, having disposed of his political disgust, would have finished the essay with a renewed celebration of the aesthetic triumphs of the Soviet cinema. One feels more than a sharp pang of regret for the unfinished essay, the incomplete career. There is nothing for us to do now but to gather in these essays and fragments, and to read them again and again.

DAVID DENBY

EDITOR'S FOREWORD

IN WHAT NOW stands as the Author's Preface to this volume, Robert Warshow had set down the theme of a book on the movies that he was planning to write. He had already published several major essays on this subject which had won him an enthusiastic following, both here and in England. Scarcely had he begun working on one of the new sections of his intended book, a study of the Russian movies, when he was stricken with a heart attack and died. He was thirty-seven years old.

This present volume collects all the movie pieces, together with other essays ranging over related aspects of popular American culture, written between 1946 and 1955. Robert Warshow was fascinated by those forms of cultural experience in American life which, as he wrote, were "not yet assimilated to the world of traditional art," but whose meanings were so central to our contemporary life that the serious critic had a special responsibility to deal with them, as seriously and as truthfully as he knew how.

Robert Warshow was born in New York City in 1917, and went to the University of Michigan. From 1942 to 1946 he worked with the Army Security Agency in Washington as a translator and research analyst. After the war, he returned to New York and became an editor of *Commentary* magazine. And he was working on *Commentary* when he died, March 18, 1955. He had been hoping to go abroad, and to Hollywood, too. He had not been to so very many places, but wherever he went, he always went to the movies.

SHERRY ABEL

INTRODUCTION

ROBERT WARSHOW died in the spring of 1955. He was thirty-seven years old. In the circle of his friends the shock of his death was extreme—I have never known a death so intensely and openly grieved over. No one was inclined, in the modern way, to "accept" it. No one was reasonable or philosophical about it. It did not seem a fact in nature but against nature. It was *mourned:* the beautiful lost word, which survives only in the language of newspapers and of psychoanalysis, had, on this occasion, its old availability.

In this primitive directness of feeling, Warshow's youth and the entire unexpectedness of his death played their part. And those who were at all close to Warshow were aware that he died just at the moment when he was beginning to claim a degree of happiness after a period of great pain; just at the moment, too, when his intellectual powers were showing themselves with a new confidence. Yet these circumstances would not have saddened us so greatly had we not set a peculiarly high valuation upon the man himself as he lived, had we not known him to stand for, and to give, things of peculiar worth.

If I try to say what these things are, I must ultimately rely

on Warshow's published work as it is collected, virtually in
its entirety, in this volume. Yet I should like to suggest something of his personal quality. My view of Warshow will be
inadequate through lack of sufficient knowledge. I did not
know him intimately—it was an element in my own sense of
loss that he died only a little while after we discovered that
we liked and trusted each other; before that there had been
antagonism between us. Other friends, who knew him far
better than I did, have talked with me about him, and they
have spoken of aspects of his temperament that I had no
awareness of. But I am putting aside what they have told me,
choosing to speak only of what I actually perceived.

I first met Robert Warshow at the time when, on the invitation of my old friend Elliot Cohen, he joined the staff
of *Commentary*. I recall him as a slim, rather tall young man
of wry, quiet, prepossessing manner. He spoke in a voice that
even now, in my recollection of its flatness and dryness, seems
to me of the rural Middle West, although in fact he was reared
in New York, in a Jewish family of the middle class. He attended the University of Michigan, but I can scarcely think
that he had picked up a regional tone there—the quality of
his speech must have been only idiosyncratic, an expression
of his temperament, and certainly his speaking voice was con-
sonant with, I might almost say definitive of, his personal
style in general, which was one of avowed *plainness,* of an
insistence, gravely and quietly made, upon actuality. Some
English writers have lately taken to comparing the intellectual temperament of the provinces with that of the metropo-
lis, all to the advantage of the former. They describe it as
naturally inclined to seriousness, as stubborn in dissidence,
rooted in the circumstantialities of family and class, un-
deceived by what in culture is merely *chic* and graceful.
Warshow, for all his metropolitan origins, had something of
the temperament of the provinces as thus described, except

that he did not have what in England so often goes with it, a degree of dourness and suspiciousness.

Yet for a time I thought him dour and suspicious enough. On our first meeting I must have seen some of the happy charm that I later knew he had, for I invited him to visit me, but on the evening he paid the visit I found him anything but attractive. Although I came to think of him as notable for his social ease, he seemed under more strain than anything in the occasion called for, and even to be hostile, saying little and seeming to direct what he did say to someone or something not in the room. He sat on one of those chairs which consist of a wooden frame with webbing stretched across it, and so hard did he thrust back against it that the frame broke with a loud crack. I remember being annoyed because he was so much more determined than I was not to take any account of the mishap, and so I presume that the reason for the hostility was one of those undefined but powerful antagonisms between members of different literary and cultural generations. These emotions lie outside the province of the historian of culture, and no novelist I know of has ever given them the accurate notice they deserve. They can go very deep and be quite intense. In general, they are set in motion and made overt by the younger man, but no doubt they are reciprocal, and the older man, although it is usually his part to keep them out of his consciousness, probably has feelings as strong as his antagonist's. On both sides it needs considerable grace to compound the difference, or, better, to express it in a way that shall be creditable, and even instructive, to both.

In addition to the unvoiced generational dispute, there was, I believe, another element in Warshow's antagonism. When Elliot Cohen founded *Commentary,* he had asked me to serve as a member of an advisory board which he wished to organize. This I had refused to do, setting forth my reasons in a letter to Cohen. My earliest published work had appeared in *The Menorah Journal*, of which Cohen had been the managing editor and the presiding genius, and I had served for a time as a member of the editorial staff of the magazine—I had had my experience of the intellectual life lived in reference to what Cohen called the Jewish community, and I had no wish to renew it by associating myself with a Jewish magazine. Whatever such an association was for others, and I could understand that it might be anything from a help to a necessity, for me it could now only be a posture and a falsehood. I cannot speak with anything like certitude about the relation to the Jewish community that Warshow felt he had during his years on *Commentary*. If I consult my impressions of the time when we were friendly, I should say that it was essentially not very different from my own. That is, he acknowledged, and with pleasure, the effect that a Jewish rearing had had upon his temperament and mind, he was aware of, and perhaps surprised by, his sense of connection with Jews everywhere—and found that the impulses of his intellectual life came from sources that were anything but Jewish, that the chief objects of his thought and feeling were anything but Jewish. At the same time, he had, and thought he should have, a very considerable awareness of the life of "the Jewish community" and a genuine if detached interest in it; and I think that during the early part of his connection with *Commentary* his interest was not detached but was charged with a certain ardor. Elliot Cohen told me that the letter in which I refused to involve myself with *Commentary* had been read angrily and contemptuously by his younger colleagues; Warshow had not yet joined the staff of the magazine, but when he did, he shared in the general adverse feelings about my position.

The failure of our relations that first evening was consolidated by Warshow's expressed opinion of a novel that I published shortly after. I was uneasy about the book, being aware of all sorts of things that were wrong with it, and of course it was my uneasiness that made me especially sensitive to adverse criticism, but I thought that Warshow was captious and inaccurate in the particular objections he made —I still think so—and I took his review personally. My resentment apparently went quite deep, for it several times happened that, when we encountered each other, my usual uncertainty about recognizing people got out of hand at the behest of my unconscious and I quite failed to know Warshow. His way of dealing with this does him great credit and was the beginning of my personal admiration of him—on one occasion he came up to me and said in a manner that was both angry and good-natured, "Look here, I think it's about time you knew who I was."

If our first alienation from each other was in part a matter of generations, of, as it were, the cultural family, I must find it especially charming that we began to come together on a matter of the actual family. My very young son had an aversion to haircuts and I had brought him from the West Side to Madison Avenue (which has, we must remember, its domestic reaches) where there was a special children's barbershop which might make the ordeal less terrible. But the boy refused to be reassured—stormily, desperately, he refused to go in, and I stood on the street in the peculiar humiliation of a father who cannot manage his child. It was at this moment that Warshow appeared, and, despite the strain between us, he addressed himself to the situation. Although he was so much younger than I, he was older as a father. Far from being prepared to make an ultimate diagnosis, he seemed to think that a phobic attitude to haircuts might be within the range of normality. From his own experience, he took a dim view of the sincerity of the advertised child-orientation of this barbershop and recommended another which he believed to be more truly sympathetic. He went so far as to question whether the boy's shagginess had reached the point where a haircut was imperative; his opinion was that it might wait.

And when at last we began to see each other by design, the relation between us, my wife being included, was curiously based on a common concern with child-rearing. As a rule, nothing is more destructive to civilized discourse than conversation about children and how to bring them up. But Warshow provided the exception. He was the more involved in the problematical aspects of the enterprise because, his wife having become incurably ill, he had the sole care of his young son. He brought to these conversations nothing of what most people bring, the sense of guilt or of personal failure, or some unformed, dimly apprehended wish to reject the very idea of society. He spoke about children with his whole instructed awareness of culture, its good possibilities and its benign necessities as well as its traps and lies. He on his side and we on ours were in articulate revolt against the dominant "progressive" ideas of child-rearing. We felt them to be charged with a scarcely concealed animosity to parents and an essential malice toward children which lay hidden under the manifest child-partisanship, an impulse to deprive children of their dignity by underestimating their powers. The three of us joined in repudiating the conception of life—safe, simplified, unimpassioned—that was implicit in almost everything that the experts were saying. We confessed to the most retrograde desires for our sons, that they should become men of firm and responsible character; and adventurous, even heroic, in their quest for happiness and even for pleasure; and, into the bargain, intellectually distinguished. We went so far as to think that we had the right to influence them to have such intentions for themselves; we were willing, God forgive us, to commit the ultimate sin of "putting pressure" on them. One conversation that I especially remember occurred in the company of others, of whom some expressed surprise and dismay at the line that Warshow was taking, and he, with great fervor made an appeal to history, choosing an example that would have quite confounded almost any truly progressive mind. He said: "When Charles I was in prison, awaiting execution, he had his youngest son, Henry, brought to him. The boy was nine years old. The father told the son what was going to happen, and explained that when he was dead there would be some people who would want to make Henry king, but that the boy must never consent to this because his oldest brother was rightfully the father's successor. Then he kissed the boy and sent him away. *That* was how a father once expected he could talk to his nine-year-old son!"

The last time I saw Warshow was when he came to dinner, bringing with him, as he had said he would, a toy that had been outgrown by his own son and that he now wanted to give to mine. It was a magnificent fortress, with battlements and a drawbridge and a considerable complement of rather splendid lead soldiers. Everything was in excellent condition, nothing was lacking to make it a fine present. But to it Warshow had added a brand-new box of grenadiers or guardsmen which he had stopped on his way to buy. He explained, when we protested this extravagance, that to a boy it would not have been a present unless there was something new—it would have been a thing given but not a present. He said this with an especial gravity and it seemed to me that in his action and its enunciated principle there was something more than the sweet wish to insure the perfection of a child's pleasure. I thought I understood what this was when, a few months after Warshow's death, I read one of Isaac Babel's stories about his boyhood and came on the passage in which Babel speaks of children's passion for a new thing. "Children," he says, "shudder at the smell of newness as a dog does when it scents a hare, expressing the madness which later, when we grow up, is called inspiration." Warshow, it seemed to me, had meant his gift not only for a boy but for a man.

In his own case the connection between his boyhood and his manhood was one of the notable things about him. I have spoken of him in his paternal role, which was chiefly how he showed himself to me. But the qualities which marked his behavior as a father, the vivid consciousness, delicacy, and respect (of which the reader will find evidence in the essay, "Paul, the Horror Comics, and Dr. Wertham"), derived from his continuing connection with his own boyhood. This constituted a considerable part of his personal charm, by which I do not mean that he was "boyish" but that he had certain traits which we expect boys to have, and which they really do have, at least in greater degree than grown men—directness, a chivalrous sense of fairness, a commitment to the ideal of courage, and a felt intimacy with reason, with the way things ought to be.

And his connection with his boyhood played a decisive part in Warshow's intellectual life and goes far toward explaining, among other things, why the movies were a chief object of his critical intention and why he wrote about them so well. What serves as the preface to the present volume was, as the editor has noted, originally part of an application to the Guggenheim Foundation for a fellowship to complete a book about film. Such "statements of project" are difficult to write and it is perhaps worth saying that, of the many I have read, this is quite the best, the most communicative, the least troubled by that embarrassment that overtakes a literary person when he has to explain and justify what he wants to do in order to get money to do it. In this document Warshow speaks of his relation to the movies with an intelligent simplicity which derives from his never having repudiated the passion for the screen that he had felt in boyhood. In this he was like the other remarkable film critic of our time, who also died untimely, James Agee. There are great differences in the work of the two men, for Agee experienced the movies in an almost wholly unmediated way, while Warshow came to them with the questions of an avowed intellectual and a highly politicalized intellectual at that. But the two men are at one in their unabashed response to the charm that the art had for them, not merely in special instances of high success but entirely, in all its range. In describing his own mode of criticism, Warshow speaks, with all due admiration, of those critics who deal seriously with film either in the aesthetic way or in the sociological and psychological way and who, by one intellectual means or another, forbid themselves "the immediate experience of seeing and responding to the movies as most of us see and respond to them." "A man watches a movie," he says, "and the critic must acknowledge that he is that man." He meant, of course, that the man watches the movie with some degree of involvement and pleasure in it, responding to the personal charm of the actors and actresses, finding that the fantasy of the screen suits to some extent, perhaps to a great extent, with his own fantasy. And of himself as the man who watches the movie, Warshow says that in some way he takes "all that nonsense" seriously.

The ability to take all that nonsense seriously was what made Warshow the remarkable critic of film that he is. From it he derived his special accuracy in perceiving when the nonsense was artful and charming nonsense, or vulgar and lying nonsense, or nonsense with some odd sense to it, and when, as sometimes happens, it stopped being nonsense at all. And by extension the ability to take the nonsense seriously made him a remarkable critic in general. His work seen whole and in retrospect has a fineness of temper and tone and a degree of actuality which make it unique in its time. When we pass this judgment what we are responding to is the dialogue between reason and fact which is sustained throughout the work, giving it a complexity which makes it analogous with life. This dialogue is initiated by Warshow's willingness to implicate himself in what he wrote about, even when he knew it to be faulty or vulgar or without dignity. In the course of a review of a volume of E. B. White's essays, Warshow remarks of the *New Yorker* that "it has always dealt with experience not by trying to understand it but by prescribing the attitude to be adopted to it." This is, of course, a way of dealing with experience which is common enough. It marks much intellectual effort that is far more ambitious than the *New Yorker's*. It was not Warshow's way. Anyone who wants to press literally upon the sentence I have quoted can say that it isn't possible for the critic to free himself from attitude, nor from the impulse to bring about in his readers the adoption of one attitude or another. But in the sense that Warshow was using the word, attitude means mere attitude, unearned attitude, eventually the attitude of dissociation from experience. If we make criticism itself the object of investigation into the personal motives it may serve, we might say that one of the uses to which it can be put, both by the reader and by the critic himself, is to keep experience at a comfortable distance. But the principle by which Warshow worked was never to separate himself from the matter in hand, always to implicate himself in it. His criticism begins with the recognition of the human relevance of even the patently unworthy objects of his attention. He understands their deficiencies as being perhaps capable of making an appeal to some presumed deficiency in himself. And, since he was not a self-denigrating person, he could even entertain the possibility that the deficiency in himself might be connected in some vital way with a virtue. It is this self-implication, as against the quick readiness of many critics to hold themselves immune from all deficiency, that accounts for the tone of honesty that we hear in Warshow's work, what I have called the quality of *plainness*, the rejection of attitude in

xxxiv

favor of understanding. The word attitude still carries some of the histrionic meaning it used to have, and what I speak of as Warshow's plainness implies his (perhaps conscious) avoidance of all the histrionism that can find its way into the intellectual life. The categories of history and politics were essential to his thought, but he never, in his idea of himself as an intellectual, conceived of himself as being "on the stage of history," as having a "role" assigned to him by the *Zeitgeist*. He thought and felt, so far as a man can, *in propria persona*. That is why he is remembered so vividly.

His plainness, we must see, was very elegant. Nothing was so characteristic of Warshow as his feeling for English prose. He is to be read as something more than a good critic, he is to be read as a good writer—that is to say, the pleasure in reading him comes not merely from the cogency of his thought but also from his manner of presenting it, ultimately from his relation to the things he wrote about. I have the sense that it has become old-fashioned, almost quaint, to praise, as if it were a moral quality, the style of a writer of expository prose. But Warshow's style demands such praise, of the kind that used to be given to, say, Hazlitt, and indeed I believe that certain of his pieces—I would mention especially "The 'Idealism' of Julius and Ethel Rosenberg" and "The Westerner"—establish themselves in the line of Hazlitt, a tradition in which I would place only one other writer of our time, George Orwell, with whose feeling for the language Warshow's had much in common. Everything Warshow wrote—we see this the more clearly now that the various pieces are brought together—is marked by a tone of authority which is as firm as it is modest. I have been told that he composed by a method which is unusual; he formed each sentence slowly in his mind, and, when it was satisfactory, wrote it down as irrevocable. It is a method which is beyond my practical comprehension, but I can see that it might help to account for the way the prose moves, with a deliberate energy, a spirited gravity, refusing to be hurried as it makes its patient qualifications and witty distinctions, yet always pressing forward and taking us securely with it.

LIONEL TRILLING

AUTHOR'S PREFACE*

THE MOVIES—and American movies in particular—stand at the center of that unresolved problem of "popular culture" which has come to be a kind of nagging embarrassment to criticism, intruding itself on all our efforts to understand the special qualities of our culture and to define our own relation to it. That this relation should require definition at all is the heart of the problem. We are all "self-made men" culturally, establishing ourselves in terms of the particular choices we make from among the confusing multitude of stimuli that present themselves to us. Something more than the pleasures of personal cultivation is at stake when one chooses to respond to Proust rather than Mickey Spillane, to Laurence Olivier in *Oedipus Rex* rather than Sterling Hayden in *The Asphalt Jungle*. And when one has made the "right" choice, Mickey Spillane and Sterling Hayden do not disappear; perhaps no one gets quite out of sight of them. There is great

* This Preface originally formed the Statement of Project submitted with the application for a Guggenheim Fellowship, October 1954. Several paragraphs at the end, relevant only to the application, have been deleted.

need, I think, for a criticism of "popular culture" which can acknowledge its pervasive and disturbing power without ceasing to be aware of the superior claims of the higher arts, and yet without a bad conscience. Such a criticism finds its best opportunity in the movies, which are the most highly developed and most engrossing of the popular arts, and which seem to have an almost unlimited power to absorb and transform the discordant elements of our fragmented culture.

Serious film criticism has tended to fall into two general types. The first is that criticism which seeks to validate the film's claim to a position of "equality" among the older arts, emphasizing in one way or another the formal qualities of the medium and the self-consciousness of the film artist. Such criticism is likely to base itself on some fairly clear concept of the "cinematic" and to use this as a standard of judgment. Depending on the critic's predilections, he may think of the "cinematic" as residing primarily in visual patterns (a view which leads toward abstract films) or as residing primarily in the medium's power of "truthful" representation (a view which leads toward documentary films). In either case, it is typical of this criticism to place great stress on matters of technique, to minimize the importance of film actors in favor of directors (who are regarded as the artists of the medium), and, very often, to deplore the introduction of sound, and especially of dialogue, as having impaired the purity of the medium. In this category of criticism are such well-known works as Rudolf Arnheim's *Film als Kunst* (1931) and Sergei Eisenstein's *The Film Sense* (1942) and *Film Form* (1949).

More recently there has developed a second type of criticism which either minimizes the aesthetic problem or ignores it altogether, treating the films (along with other forms of popular culture) as indexes to mass psychology or, sometimes, the "folk spirit." Criticism of this sort ranges from the discovery of direct correspondences between the movies and life (e.g., the prevalence of themes of violence in American movies either reflects or encourages violence in American life) to the complex and "deep" interpretations of psychoanalysis (e.g., the relegation of women to a minor role in Western movies, and the supposedly "phallic" character of the Western hero's gun, indicate a latent homosexuality in the movie audience). Ideas of film aesthetics need not be excluded, but they are subordinate to the primary aim of sociological analysis. Thus, the sociological critic who is alive to the aesthetics of the movies will not make the mistake of assuming that the effect of a film can be conveyed by recounting its plot, or that the repetition of a theme is necessarily a measure of its importance, but he will still be concerned with those elements which he believes to be affecting or expressing "the audience" rather than with what he himself responds to. Sometimes, indeed, the sociological critic may try to resolve this difficulty—if he feels it as a difficulty—by a kind of forced identification with "the audience"; sociology and aesthetics then become one, "mass psychology" is likely to become "myth," and aesthetic value is likely to be identified with "mythic" intensity. The detached (if not necessarily objective) tone of social science is more typical, however, and if there are value judgments, they usually refer not to the films in themselves but to the social facts which the films are believed to reflect. Excellent examples of this type of criticism are Siegfried Kracauer's *From Caligari to Hitler* (1947), a study of German films during the period of the Weimar Republic, and Nathan Leites and Martha Wolfenstein's *Movies: A Psychological Study* (1950). David Riesman has also made use of the films in his more general studies of American life.

No student of the films can fail to acknowledge his debt to the brilliant work that has been done in these two broad fields of criticism; out of that work has emerged the general outline within which all future discussion must find its place. I think it may be said nevertheless that both these approaches, in their separate ways, have tended to slight the fundamental *fact* of the movies, a fact at once aesthetic and sociological but also something more. This is the actual, immediate experience of seeing and responding to the movies as most of us see them and respond to them. A critic may extend his frame of reference as far as it will bear extension, but it seems to me almost self-evident that he should start with the simple acknowledgment of his own relation to the object he criticizes; at the center of all truly successful criticism there is always a man reading a book, a man looking at a picture, a man watching a movie. Critics of the films, caught in the conflict between "high culture" and "popular culture," have too often sought to evade this confrontation.

The sociological critic is likely to be the more guilty, holding the experience of the movies entirely at arm's length. Indeed, it might be said that he pretends not to go to the movies at all; he merely investigates a social or psychological "phenomenon"—something, that is, which involves others. Even when he does try to acknowledge his own part in the experience, it is only by treating himself as one of the "others," just as a psychiatrist may observe the symptoms of neurosis in himself but by the very act of observation achieves a kind of momentary exemption. The aesthetic critic, on the other hand, may be perfectly willing to acknowledge his relation to the object—but only after he has transformed the object. For what he seeks in the films is almost always something that he can recognize as "legitimate" to the world of art—which is to say, analogous to the effects of other art forms on their highest levels. He goes to the movies, he would have us believe, as one goes to concerts or the ballet. No doubt his claim is often a truthful one; there is art in the movies, and there is an "art" cinema. Many of the products of the "art" cinema

xl

well deserve all the praise they have received. And yet, I think, one cannot long frequent the "art" cinema or read much of the criticism which upholds it without a sense of incompleteness and even of irrelevance. Really the movies are not quite that "legitimate"—they are still the bastard child of art, and if in the end they must be made legitimate, it will be a changed household of art that receives them. (Something of the sort has happened with the novel, I think.) The process cannot be rushed, and the critic whose chief concern is to advance the film's claim to legitimacy is evading the issue. The sociological critic says to us, in effect: It is not *I* who goes to see the movies; it is the audience. The aesthetic critic says: It is not the *movies* I go to see; it is art.

To state what seems to me the proper course for film criticism is not so easy as to express my sense of the shortcomings of the older approaches. I can do best, I think, by writing in personal terms.

I have gone to the movies constantly, and at times almost compulsively, for most of my life. I should be embarrassed to attempt an estimate of how many movies I have seen and how many hours they have consumed. At the same time, I have had enough serious interest in the products of the "higher" arts to be very sharply aware that the impulse which leads me to a Humphrey Bogart movie has little in common with the impulse which leads me to the novels of Henry James or the poetry of T. S. Eliot. That there is a connection between the two impulses I do not doubt, but the connection is not adequately summed up in the statement that the Bogart movie and the Eliot poem are both forms of art. To define that connection seems to me one of the tasks of film criticism, and the definition must be first of all a personal one. A man watches a movie, and the critic must acknowledge that he is that man.

I also know very well that I do not go to the movies in

order to discover what impulses are moving "the audience," though I am willing to make such discoveries when they happen to present themselves to me. Here again, it is I who goes to the movies (perhaps I should say: alas!) not the sociologist in me, if there is a sociologist in me. And it must be that I go to the movies for the same reason that the "others" go: because I am attracted to Humphrey Bogart or Shelley Winters or Greta Garbo; because I require the absorbing immediacy of the screen; because in some way I take all that nonsense seriously. For I must make one more confession: I have seen a great many very bad movies, and I know when a movie is bad, but I have rarely been bored at the movies; and when I have been bored, it has usually been at a "good" movie.

I have been writing about the movies, off and on, since 1947, and in the past few years it seems to me I have been able to recognize in my work a point of view—perhaps I mean only a vocabulary—that begins to be adequate to the complexities of the subject, doing some justice to the claims both of art and of "popular culture," and remaining also, I hope, in touch with the basic relation of spectator and object. I have felt my work to be most successful when it has seemed to display the movies as an important element in my own cultural life, an element with its own qualities and interesting in its own terms, and neither esoteric nor alien. The movies are part of my culture, and it seems to me that their special power has something to do with their being a kind of "pure" culture, a little like fishing or drinking or playing baseball—a cultural fact, that is, which has not yet fallen altogether under the discipline of art. I have not brought Henry James to the movies or the movies to Henry James, but I hope I have shown that the man who goes to the movies is the same as the man who reads James. In the long run, I hope that my work may even make some contribution to the "legitimization" of the movies; but I do not think one can make such a contribution by pretending that "legitimization" has already taken place.

I propose now to produce a book of essays on the movies, dealing with various key aspects of the subject, which will adequately express this point of view. While I believe that I have by now developed a kind of "theory" of the movies, and would expect this theory to emerge from my book, it will be in no sense a theoretical work. There are many theories of the movies—who would not wish to be the Aristotle of a new art form? My own ambition, in the present work, is only to produce a body of criticism dealing with specific films and types of films, with certain actors, certain themes, and with two or three of the general problems which may point towards a theory. If it is successful, the book should bring its readers pleasure and illumination in connection with one of the leading elements in modern culture, and perhaps go some way towards resolving the curious tension that surrounds the problem of "popular culture." At the best, I hope the volume may possibly be a contribution to literature. . . .

PART 1 AMERICAN POPULAR CULTURE

The Legacy
of the 30's

FOR MOST American intellectuals, the Communist movement of the 1930's was a crucial experience. In Europe, where
the movement was at once more serious and more popular,
it was still only one current in intellectual life; the Communists could never completely set the tone of thinking in Europe, and Communist intellectuals themselves were able to
draw a part of their nourishment from outside the movement.
But in this country there was a time when virtually all intellectual vitality was derived in one way or another from the
Communist party. If you were not somewhere within the
party's wide orbit, then you were likely to be in the opposition, which meant that much of your thought and energy had
to be devoted to maintaining yourself in opposition.

In either case, it was the Communist party that ultimately
determined what you were to think about and in what terms.

There resulted a disastrous vulgarization of intellectual
life, in which the character of American liberalism and radicalism was decisively—and perhaps permanently—corrupted.
As a measure of the damage, one need only compare the atmosphere that surrounded the Sacco and Vanzetti case in

3

1927 with the atmosphere during the period of the Moscow Trials and the Spanish Civil War ten years later. Indeed, the special poignancy with which we remember Sacco and Vanzetti is connected with a sense of regret for our own lost virtue; the excitement that grew up around their case was the last strong expression of uncorrupted radicalism: in 1927, nobody really wanted anything except that justice should win. But in the 30's radicalism entered upon an age of organized mass disingenuousness, when every act and every idea had behind it some "larger consideration" which destroyed its honesty and its meaning. Everyone became a *professional* politician, acting within a framework of "realism" that tended to make political activity an end in itself. The half-truth was elevated to the position of a principle, and in the end the half-truth, in itself, became more desirable than the whole-truth. It was fashionable at the time to speak of a "new maturity" in American intellectual life, and in a sense the phrase was accurate, but it was the kind of maturity that is really a willing acceptance of failure.

What had happened was more than the defection of one part of the intelligentsia. The whole level of thought and discussion, the level of culture itself, had been lowered. The soap-box speech merged with the Fourth of July oration. A poet became Librarian of Congress and denounced American intellectuals for weakening their country's spirit. Father Divine rode in the May Day parade. *The Grapes of Wrath* was a great novel. Eventually, *Confessions of a Nazi Spy* was a serious movie and "Ballad for Americans" was an inspired song. The mass culture of the educated classes—the culture of the "middle-brow," as it has sometimes been called—had come into existence. For the first time, popular culture was able to draw its ideological support from the most advanced sectors of society. If this represented a lowering of the level of serious culture, it also raised the level—or at least the tone—of popular culture. This is precisely what made it a "problem." It was not possible to ignore *The Grapes of Wrath* as it was possible to ignore Edna Ferber or Amos and Andy. *The Grapes of Wrath* had all the surface characteristics of serious literature and it made all the "advanced" assumptions. In order to see what was wrong with it, one had to examine those assumptions themselves—and there was no firm base from which to do this.

It is not necessary to claim that the Communist movement was in any real sense the *cause* of this development. In fact that movement, in the character it assumed in the 30's, was itself a part of the development; the real causes lay far back in the history of American culture and the social and psychological effects of industrial capitalism. Moreover, the cultural atmosphere of the 30's embraced a great many areas of American life that had no direct connection with the Communists at all; for most Americans, certainly, that atmosphere was expressed most clearly in the personality of President Roosevelt and the social-intellectual-political climate of the New Deal. For the intellectual, however, the Communist movement was the fact of central importance; the New Deal remained an external phenomenon, part of that "larger" world of American public life from which he had long separated himself—he might "support" the New Deal (as later on, perhaps, he "supported" the war), but he never identified himself with it. One way or another, he did identify himself with the Communist movement.

Thus the problem that confronts the American intellectual when he seeks to deal with the mass culture that surrounds him is, in its deeper meaning, the problem of his own past. For we are living still in the intellectual climate that was first established by the Communist-liberal-New Deal movement of the 30's (by this time there are many people who have

5

never known any other climate; that is what makes it so difficult to describe what has happened). The Communists themselves may be losing ground, but the terms of discussion are still fixed by the tradition of middle-class "popular front" culture which they did so much to create, and we are still without a vocabulary to break through the constriction it imposes on us.

On the practical level, the questions that center around the Communist movement may soon be out of our hands; indeed, they are out of our hands already—the *issue* of Stalinism is settled (though the danger is not). But if we are interested in understanding and evaluating the qualities of modern life, the *experience* of Stalinism remains a problem of peculiar complexity.* In its way, and for those who were affected by it, that experience is the most important of our time; it is for us what the First World War and the experience of expatriation were for an earlier generation. If our intellectual life is stunted and full of frustration, this is in large part because we have refused to assimilate that experience, but have dealt with it only politically—outlining again and again the terms of our opposition to Stalinism, but never trying to understand what it means as part of our lives.

For the serious intellectual, something more than an error of taste or judgment was involved when he accepted the pretensions of "proletarian literature," or when he assented to

* "Stalinism" is of course not a neutral term, but in many contexts the word "Communism" is too broad. We need a term to describe the Communist movement after its bureaucratic degeneration and its conversion, among other things, into a vehicle of mass culture. "Stalinism" is the only word that fills this need. The word will naturally appear entirely inadmissible to those who are not aware of the phenomenon to which it is applied.

the general opinion that *Bury the Dead* was a vital work of art, or when he rejected the work of Henry James because it was outside the "main stream" of American tradition. The very possibility of these errors, and of a thousand others like them, represented at bottom a fatal acquiescence, a kind of willing mortification of the self. It meant that judgment was no longer free, or at least that there were considerations more important than free judgment. In the last analysis, it meant that the intellectual had sold out—to the pressures that encompassed him, and to his sense of his own inadequacy. And he lived surrounded by the evidence of his betrayal: a culture solidifying in vulgarity and dishonesty, of which he was a part.

Even to stand out against this culture uncompromisingly —a thing very few were able to do; much more was required than just to be anti-Stalinist—was only a partial victory. One kept one's integrity, but this integrity became a purely personal satisfaction, without real weight—and the one assumption that everybody shared was that weight was important. The culture remained and spread and entrenched itself, and its mere existence—this climate in which one had to live—was a standing threat to one's personality, was in a sense a deep personal humiliation. (Is it not the final affront that these words themselves should sound too strong—too "personal"?) With each new *Bury the Dead*, with each new political debate, the humiliation grew deeper and more pervasive, and the problem of the American intellectual gradually emerged in the form in which it exists today.

The problem is nothing so simple as Stalinism; as I said before, that issue is settled: Stalinism today is not a point of view but a psychological and sociological phenomenon. Nor is it a problem of liberal ideology as such: the propositions of liberalism can still be examined and accepted or rejected. The intellectual's problem is to define his own position in the whole world of culture that came into being in the 30's—a world in which he must live and of which he is a full partaker. And the question to be asked is not: What is my opinion of all this? That question is easily answered, but those who ask only that have fallen into the trap, for it is precisely the greatest error of our intellectual life to assume that the most effective way of dealing with any phenomenon is to have an opinion about it. The real question is: What is my relation to all this?

This is a hard question for us because one's relation to experience is a matter of feeling, and our usable vocabulary is a vocabulary of opinion. The most important effect of the intellectual life of the 30's and the culture that grew out of it has been to distort and eventually to destroy the emotional and moral content of experience, putting in its place a system of conventionalized "responses." In fact, the chief function of mass culture is to relieve one of the necessity of experiencing one's life directly. Serious art, too, is separated from reality, for it permits one to contemplate experience without being personally involved; but it is not an evasion: by its very detachment, it opens up new possibilities of understanding and pleasure derivable from reality, and it thus becomes an enrichment of experience.

Mass culture, on the other hand, seeks only to make things easier. It can do this either by moving away from reality and thus offering an "escape," or by moving so close to reality as to destroy the detachment of art and make it possible for one to see one's own life as a form of art (this happens in such a novel as Sholem Asch's *East River*, for example). Even political discussion becomes a form of entertainment and a defense against experience: by providing a fixed system of moral and political attitudes, it protects us from the shock of experience and conceals our helplessness. The movies, the theater, the books and magazines and newspapers—the whole system of mass culture as creator and purveyor of ideas, sentiments, attitudes, and styles of behavior—all this is what gives our life its form and its meaning. Mass culture is the screen through which we see reality and the mirror in which we see ourselves. Its ultimate tendency is even to supersede reality. (In this sense, as Clement Greenberg remarks, art is more important in our civilization than it has ever been before.)

Now it is precisely this—the experience of an alienation from reality—which is the characteristic experience of our age. The modern intellectual, and especially the creative writer, thus faces the necessity of describing and clarifying an experience which has itself deprived him of the vocabulary he requires to deal with it. The writer who attempts a true re-creation of life is forced to invent the meanings of experience all over again, creating out of his own mind and sensibility not only the literary object but also its significance and its justification—in a sense, he must invent his own audience.

This is the source of the problem of communication in modern literature—which is a problem not only of communicating the quality of experience to a reader, but also, and more deeply, of making it possible for the writer himself to have a meaningful experience in the first place. There is no paradox in this, for it is only through an effective vocabulary —that is, through "valid" emotional, moral, and intellectual responses expressible in language—that we can truly know what we do and what happens to us. And the writer is *par excellence* the man of conscious experience; the problem of experience and the problem of a language for experience are for him one problem.

In modern poetry, the problem has been solved most frequently by a persistent use of irony. By employing the vocabulary of mass culture in a more serious context, the poet

9

expresses both his rejection of mass culture and the difficulty he faces in trying to transcend it, while at the same time this irony, by a kind of negative connotation, can also convey some of the quality of fresh and meaningful experience—or, more accurately, it can indicate what fresh and meaningful experience might be like if there existed a context and a vocabulary for it.

This is a possible solution as far as it goes, but its limitations are obvious: a whole literature cannot be built on irony. In addition, this ironic use of language is necessarily so indefinite that it easily slips over from the "negative" to the "affirmative," and the moment that happens it becomes a part of the mass culture from which it has tried to escape. The use of irony for purposes of "affirmation" is usually a device for stating banalities indirectly and tentatively and thus concealing their lack of real content; it is a technique of falsification. The clearest example of this is the style of "American" inarticulateness and diffidence affected by writers like Archibald MacLeish and Norman Corwin.

For the serious prose writer, at any rate, even this partial solution is not available: he must evolve some method of understanding and communicating experience directly—as it really is, as it really feels. And he finds at every turn that he is unable to realize and respond to his experience in any way that seems valid and fruitful to him. He lives within the mass culture, he meets experience through the mass culture, the words and ideas that come to him most easily, most "naturally," are the words and ideas of mass culture. The problem is inescapable; there is no corner of literature or experience where he does not face it. And it must be solved all over again every day.

To be sure, the problem is not confined to the United States. But it exists here in its most developed form; the Europeans are only beginning to face it, and for the Russians it would hardly be accurate to call it a problem at all: for them, the discussion is ended.

It is also true that the problem did not suddenly spring into being in the 30's; the poetry of T. S. Eliot is sufficient evidence to the contrary. But for American intellectuals of our time, as I have tried to show, the center of the problem is in the political-intellectual movement of the 30's. The problem developed over many years and through many historical factors, but it *happened* in the 30's. Thus it becomes our central intellectual task to evolve some method of assimilating the experience of those years, if only in order to perfect our understanding of our cultural failure.

Of the few serious efforts that have been made to deal with that experience, the most nearly successful is Edmund Wilson's *Memoirs of Hecate County,* an almost heroic attempt to create a valid emotional and moral response to modern life. Wilson states the problem of feeling directly: it is the point of his book that the modern world is suffering from a paralysis of feeling, and he communicates the quality of that paralysis with such success as to have called forth the most amusing of all the charges made against the book—that it is not "even" good pornography. But, having established a world that has lost the capacity to feel, he is still faced with the necessity of creating a valid response to that world. He solves this problem by obscuring the boundaries between fantasy and reality—strong and direct emotion is still "admissible" in dreams—but the nature of this solution is itself a kind of failure, emphasizing again the difficulty (perhaps the impossibility) of a straightforward solution. And in the end words fail him—quite literally, almost: he writes a kind of "key" to the book in French, as if the rhythms of a foreign language might conceal even from him that his resources have proved not quite sufficient. (Incidentally, the almost

11

universal rejection of Wilson's book, even among those who should have been most strongly aware of its significance, is one more sign of our intellectual impotence.)

Lionel Trilling's novel, *The Middle of the Journey*, is in some ways a more explicit attempt to deal with the problem of Stalinism: the hero, John Laskell, an intellectual fellow-traveler of the Communists, undergoes an experience that forces him to re-examine the ideological and cultural foundations of his life; in the end, after a series of personal encounters has made the choices clear to him, he rejects the Communist movement and the whole intellectual atmosphere that surrounds it, and seeks a new philosophy more adequate to the needs of experience.

Mr. Trilling's novel is less successful as literature than Wilson's, but—in part for that very reason—it constitutes a particularly clear example of how it is possible for a serious writer to find himself ultimately helpless in the face of mass culture.

Mr. Trilling has shown a profound awareness of the problem of the American intellectual; he has seen also that the center of that problem lies in the Communist-liberal tradition of the 30's. Moreover, his own position, if not unassailable, is at least more solid than most: he partakes of all the serious intellectual currents of our time, but he has not so alienated himself from the general life of American society as to be unable to understand it and sympathize with it. (This is of course an "adjustment," and it produces certain ambiguities of feeling and attitude. But nobody really escapes; in the long run, it is probably better that the ambiguities be near the surface.) Mr. Trilling has intelligence and honesty; more than honesty, he has a clear sense of all the possibilities of dishonesty—this is his greatest protection. Finally, he is a talented writer: there are parts of this novel that are written with beauty, imagination, and intensity.

As a number of critics have pointed out, Mr. Trilling is greatly indebted to E. M. Forster. His method, like Forster's, is to confront his characters with situations for which their moral preconceptions have left them unprepared; the tensions and readjustments that result from these confrontations make up the novel. And, again like Forster, Mr. Trilling is not embarrassed by the necessary artificiality of fiction: he accepts the novel form as a structure of contrivances consciously manipulated to a conscious end. He is thus willing to devote much of his book to the description of serious conversation and thinking, without suffering from the compulsion to be indirect. And he is willing to make use of melodramatic incidents as a convenient means of making his points and establishing the situations in which he is interested; he does not even attempt to disguise the close mechanical resemblance between the climactic incident of his novel and the climactic incident of Forster's *Howards End.* This common-sense approach gives the book a quality of bareness that amounts almost to poverty—a bareness not characteristic of Forster himself, who has a complex sense of character and a richness of wit that Mr. Trilling lacks. In a lesser novelist than Forster, the bareness is a virtue: it is honest poverty, so to speak, as if Mr. Trilling had resolved to make no appeal except to the intelligence, or to the emotions only in the degree that they remain subject to intelligence. But it is a virtue on the private level—or, at any rate, on the level of opinion. It permits Mr. Trilling to deal with experience without compromising himself intellectually; it endears him to the reader for the qualities of his mind—one feels that we should really be better off if more people were like him. But he is removed from experience *as* experience; the problem of feeling—and thus the problem of art—is not faced.

13

This evasion becomes particularly clear when one considers how much there was in the experience of Stalinism which Mr. Trilling has simply omitted. For a writer with a strong intellectual awareness of psychological complexities, he shows surprisingly little interest in the deeper layers of motivation: in his emphasis on the idea of responsibility, he makes it appear as if the surrender to Stalinism or its rejection was mainly a matter of philosophical decision. Even in his treatment of the character Gifford Maxim, whose guilt-ridden conversion from Stalinism to religion is plainly the result of deep psychological drives, Mr. Trilling prefers to leave the actual, experiential roots of his behavior unspecified: we never know whether Maxim's guilt is real or delusionary or metaphysical. Such vagueness is of course quite deliberate; it is part of Mr. Trilling's conception of Maxim's character that his motivations should remain unclear, and it is one of the underlying implications of the book's thesis that motivations do not really "count." But the point is that such a thesis and such an approach to character rest ultimately on the assumption that the most fruitful way of dealing with experience is to pass judgment on it—and this is not the assumption of a novelist.

For the same reason, Mr. Trilling does not deal adequately with the fact that Stalinism as he describes it was specifically an experience of the middle class: he is, indeed, constantly aware of the class origins of his characters, and of how their ways of living and thinking are determined by their class, but class, too, does not finally "count," and he does not show how Stalinism offered a way out of the particular psychological difficulties of the middle class as such. More than this, he ignores the fact that the middle class which experiences Stalinism was in large part a Jewish middle class, driven by the special insecurities of Jews in addition to the insecurities of the middle class in general. (This suppression is made all the more obvious by the inclusion of one minor Jewish character in a stock role.) Thus the characters exist in a kind of academic void of moral abstractions, without a history—but Stalinism was in the fullest sense a historical experience, a particular response to particular historical pressures; the people who involved themselves in it were not simply carrying on personal relations within a settled moral order. Here, again, Mr. Trilling is doubtless conscious of what he is doing: he seeks to universalize the Stalinist experience in order to make clear its "essential" significance. But the novel as an art form rests on particularity: the particular becomes universal without losing its particularity—that is the wonder. Mr. Trilling might have come closer to the "essence" of the experience he describes if he had been more willing to see it as the experience of particular human beings in a specific situation; perhaps this means: if he had been more willing to face his own relation to it.

When he does try to create an adequate emotional and moral correlative for his material, it is only to fail in another direction. In Forster's novels, melodrama is always a contrivance of plot or a device to emphasize the deeper content. But Mr. Trilling sometimes invests the deeper content itself with a melodramatic tone. This is especially noticeable in the opening pages, which are like the beginning of a sophisticated spy story, and in the presentation of the character Duck Caldwell, the irresponsible and vicious representative of the lower classes, who is burdened with a weight of moral significance that almost deprives him of all reality (though he is particularly well drawn on the realistic level). Indeed, the excitement that surrounds Duck Caldwell seems a little naive, as if Mr. Trilling were announcing the discovery of evil; if it was a sentimental error to credit the working class with a virtue and an innocence that it never possessed, it is

15

only another kind of sentimentality to make too much of correcting the error.

Yet this tendency to place upon the material a greater weight of meaning than it can bear is almost an unavoidable failing, one more sign of how the problem of creative writing is becoming too difficult for the ordinary talent. When the writer must invent all the meanings of experience, it is not surprising that he should sometimes fail to keep them in proportion.

Most of all, Mr. Trilling lacks Forster's detachment—that almost Olympian disinterestedness (not neutrality) which enables Forster to encompass all the complexities and impurities of experience without strain or shock. Forster is almost never taken in—as little by Margaret Schlegel as by Leonard Bast, not even by Mrs. Wilcox, and least of all by himself. But Mr. Trilling is taken in very often indeed. I have already mentioned Duck Caldwell and Gifford Maxim, whom Mr. Trilling takes at face value whenever, by doing so, he can make them more formidable. There is also Emily Caldwell, who is intended to constitute a kind of positive pole in the book, embodying the "real" world from which the mass culture of Stalinist liberalism has estranged us, but who turns out to be only another creation of that very culture. The brief sexual episode between Emily Caldwell and John Laskell is almost a paradigm of the liberal middle-class dream of sex; it is honest, straightforward, "adult"; it involves affection but no unmanageable passion; it creates no "complications"— which is to say, no responsibilities; it takes place in daylight in the open air, and—immediately after Emily has bathed.

Finally, there is John Laskell himself, the puzzled man of conscience and good will who comes to see the error of Stalinist liberalism and formulates the "conclusions" of the book. (It is worth noting that not even in the simplest of Forster's novels is it safe to take any character as the author's mouthpiece, but Mr. Trilling's identification with Laskell is unmistakable.) Precisely in this formulation one sees how completely Mr. Trilling has failed to detach himself from the cultural atmosphere he seeks to transcend, for he reduces the whole problem of modern experience to a question of right and wrong opinion. There are two opposing orthodoxies: the orthodoxy of Stalinist liberalism, which holds that man is the creature of his environment and thus free of moral responsibility, and the orthodoxy of religion, which holds that man is the child of God and bears an infinite responsibility—that is, an infinite guilt. Laskell rejects both: "An absolute freedom from responsibility—that much of a child none of us can be. An absolute responsibility—that much of a divine or metaphysical essence none of us is." Laskell stands for the free intelligence, for the "idea in modulation." That is what was lost and must be found again. Not to acquiesce is "the only thing that matters."

Mr. Trilling is here finally reduced to the level of his subject; like the Stalinists themselves, he can respond to the complexity of experience only with a revision of doctrine. His doctrine may be sound (though the *via media*, too, can be a form of cant), but the point is that it is irrelevant: the novelist's function is not to argue with his characters—or at least not to try too hard to win the argument.

One might think, perhaps, that the virtue of detachment belongs to the intelligence, and thus has nothing to do with the problem of feeling. But the detachment of a creative writer rests precisely on his ability to create what seems (at least to him) an adequate emotional and moral response to experience, a response that is "objectively" valid in the sense that it seems to inhere in the experience itself and to come into being automatically, so to speak, with the re-creation of the experience. Mr. Trilling, lacking an aesthetically effective relationship to experience, is forced to translate experience into ideas, embodying these ideas in his characters and giving his plot the form of an intellectual discussion reinforced by events. He thus becomes personally involved with his characters in a way that the true novelist never is, for some of the ideas are his own and some are ideas he disagrees with, and he must therefore convince his reader that some characters are "right" and others "wrong" (though "rightness" and "wrongness" are qualities not of human beings but only of ideas); whereas the true novelist tries only to make his characters and their behavior "convincing," which is something entirely different. There are a great many intellectual discussions in Forster's novels, and very often both Forster and his reader know who is "right"; but to have right or wrong ideas is part of experience—it is not an issue.

I have dwelt so much upon Forster because it is apparent that Mr. Trilling has tried to model himself most of all on Forster (though to some degree on James) and on the moral and intellectual quality that Forster embodies, and because the great gap that remains between the two writers is more than a disparity of talent. The point is not that Mr. Trilling is not a great novelist; a healthy culture has room for the minor talent. What is significant is that Mr. Trilling has not yet solved the problem of being a novelist at all. And this failure is not his alone: in his failure, he comes in a way to represent us all—as perhaps he would not represent us if he had succeeded. The problem remains: How shall we regain the use of our experience in the world of mass culture?

(1947)

Woofed with Dreams[*]

ON THE UNDERSIDE of our society, there are those who have no real stake at all in respectable culture. These are the open enemies of culture, despising indiscriminately a painting by Picasso and a painting by Maxfield Parrish, a novel by Kafka and a novel by A. J. Cronin, a poem by Yeats and a poem by Ella Wheeler Wilcox—these are readers of pulp magazines and comic books, potential book-burners, unhappy patrons of astrologers and communicants of lunatic sects, the hopelessly alienated and outclassed who can enjoy perhaps not even Andy Hardy but only Bela Lugosi, not even the *Reader's Digest* but only *True Detective*.

But their distance from the center gives them in the mass a degree of independence that the rest of us can approach only individually and by discipline. In the extremity of their alienation, they are ready to be assured and irresponsible, they are ready to say: Shoot the bankers, or Kill the Jews, or Let the Nazis come. They no longer care if the ship goes down, they go their own way. That is why an editorial in the *Daily News* is so much more interesting—and often so much

* Review of *Krazy Kat*, by George Herriman, Holt.

19

nearer the truth than an editorial in *PM*. *PM* has too many things to consider; only the *Daily News* can remain entirely reasonable and disinterested when it suggests that the human race is on the way to extinction.

When this *Lumpen* culture displays itself in mass art forms, it can occasionally take on a certain purity and freshness that would almost surely be smothered higher up on the cultural scale. The quality of a Marx Brothers movie, for example, comes from an uncompromising nihilism that is particularly characteristic of the submerged and dispossessed; the Marx Brothers are *Lumpen,* they spit on culture, and they are popular among middle-class intellectuals because they express a blind and destructive disgust with society that the responsible man is compelled to suppress in himself.

In "Krazy Kat," a very sweet-tempered fantasy, the gap between mass culture and respectable culture manifests itself not in an open rejection of society, but, more indirectly, in a complete disregard of the standards of respectable art. Working for an audience completely out of touch with the concerns of the serious-minded, George Herriman had the advantage that Lewis Carroll got by writing for children: so long as the internal patterns of his work—the personal and physical relationships of the characters—remained simple, he was fairly sure to please. Where no art is important, "Krazy Kat" is as real and important a work of art as any other—it is only supposed to divert its reader for two minutes at a time. (While the intellectuals had to "discover" "Krazy Kat," the comic-strip audience just read it.)

Thus Herriman's fantasy can be free and relaxed, it can go its own way. What came into his head went down on the paper. His language is built up of scraps of sound and meaning, all the echoes that his mind contained—Krazy talks an arbitrary dialect that has some connection with the speech of New York but is attributable in its finished form neither to foreignness nor to illiteracy but solely to the mind of its creator: "Et less my l'il korn butch yills a krop—now I will have korn bread, korn mill mutch, korn poems, korn plestas, korn kopias"; Offissa Pup tends to be highflown: "I mean none other than Ignatz Mouse—who makes evil the day by tossing bricks at that dear Kat." While the characters stand still, a potted tree behind them becomes a distant plateau and then a house and then a tree again. The continual flux is never mentioned and has no meaning; it is just that Herriman felt no obligation either to keep the background still or to explain its mobility. This absolute fantasy sometimes becomes mechanical, but it is never heavy and it frequently achieves the fresh quality of pure play, freed from the necessity to be dignified or "significant" and not obviously concerned even with entertaining its audience.

This is the plot: Krazy, inoffensive creature of uncertain sex, loves Ignatz Mouse. Ignatz despises Krazy—for his inoffensiveness, for his impenetrable silliness, and for his unshakable affection—and Ignatz (therefore?) devotes all his intelligence and energy to the single end of hitting Krazy on the head with bricks. He buys bricks from a brickmaker especially for this purpose; he conceals the bricks in innocent-looking packages or disguises them in innocent-looking shapes, he makes appointments hours in advance so that Krazy will be in the right place at the right time to be hit by a brick. Somewhere in this single-minded effort there must be passion, but it is not apparent, it is all channeled constructively into planning and action: Ignatz's *métier* is to hit Krazy on the head with a brick. The overt passion is all on Krazy's side; he can never get used to the routine, but waits every moment like a bride for the expected ecstasy, the blow always new and always the same and wonderful, the recurrent climax and reward of love. "L'il dahlink," Krazy murmurs as the brick comes—ZIP through the air and POW when

21

it hits—"Til dahlink, is there anybody in this woil more constint than him?" Offissa Pup, the guardian of law, loves Krazy, with the gentle and protecting love of the practical man for the poet and dreamer—"Dear K," he says of Krazy, "his life is warped with fancy, woofed with dreams." Offissa Pup's occupation is to keep Ignatz from throwing the brick and to put him in jail when he has thrown it.

Offissa Pup is the sole authority in the universe and Ignatz the sole evildoer. Evil always triumphs—Ignatz always throws the brick; but authority always triumphs, too—Ignatz is always put in jail. Krazy lives happily between the two. It is a very nice universe for Krazy; if there is an issue, Krazy does not understand it; he loves to be hit by the brick, but he respects Offissa Pup's motives.

One is tempted to read into this the meanings that one finds in the serious world of respectable culture. E. E. Cummings talks in his introduction about the opposition between the individual and society. But if Ignatz and Krazy are very good examples of individuals, Offissa Pup is not much of a society: his jail is always empty the next day. We do best, I think, to leave "Krazy Kat" alone. Good fantasy never has an easy and explicit relation to the real world. Even *Through the Looking-Glass* is weakest when Looking-Glass Land is *exactly* the opposite of the real world. The haphazard and irresponsible fancy of George Herriman was capable even of social comment, but it is not to be trusted with any systems. If Offissa Pup was society on Monday, that placed no restriction on his program for Tuesday. One thing remains the same: "Krazy Kat" is about a cat who gets hit on the head with bricks.

"Krazy Kat" is perhaps the best that the comic strip has produced. But it would be a mistake to think it a "higher" development of the comic strip. "Higher" development brings in the whole apparatus of respectable controls and produces

"Joe Palooka" helping to sell the country on conscription, or the hygienic, progressive-school fantasy of "Barnaby." "Higher" development makes "Krazy Kat" impossible. "Krazy Kat" is "pointless" and "silly," it comes from the peripheral world where the aims and pretensions of society are not regarded.

Something should be said also about the comic strip's dimension of time. "Krazy Kat" started before I was born, and it ended in 1944 only because Herriman died and the King Features Syndicate decided that there was no one who could continue his work. This was accidental; the usual practice is to appoint a successor to the dead artist—there is no internal reason why Orphan Annie, for instance, should not continue to face up to her troubles for ten million years. Thus the comic strip has no beginning and no end, only an eternal middle. It is an additional reality, running parallel with the *real* reality: for every day of one's own life, there is a day in the comic strip's life. This, too, is a characteristic of *Lumpen* culture: all gradations and distinctions are broken down, even the distinction between art and life. (The more realistic characters of the comic strips and the soap operas receive letters and gifts from their admirers.) A baseball game, an editorial, a comic strip, a kiss: all are *experiences*, varying in intensity but equally significant—for none is significant, and none has any meaningful connection with another. Almost every day for more than thirty years, Ignatz hit Krazy with a brick.

(1946)

Clifford Odets: Poet
of the Jewish Middle Class

Before migrating to America, all the ethnic groups of Yankee City possessed a family pattern of the patriarchal type in which the wife was subordinated to the husband and the children to the father. America has disrupted this pattern, increasing the wife's independence and making the children carriers of the new culture—a role that has brought them into open conflict with their parents. Among Jews these developments manifested themselves in their most extreme form.

"The Jews of Yankee City"
(*Commentary*, January 1946)

THE LITERARY TREATMENT of American Jewish life has always suffered from the psychological commitments of Jewish writers. Their motives are almost never pure: they must dignify the Jews, or plead for them, or take revenge upon them, and the picture they create is correspondingly distorted by romanticism or sentimentality or vulgarity. The romantic-sentimental picture, which endows the Jews with superior wisdom and an exaggerated spirituality, is typified in an earlier stage by the movie *The Jazz Singer*. It appears

25

in more dignified form in Elmer Rice's *Street Scene* and most recently in the Hollywood biography of George Gershwin. The vulgar exploitation of the Jews is more common; the work of Milt Gross is carried on for a later audience in the self-conscious burlesques of Arthur Kober and the banality of Leonard Q. Ross. A more serious and more savage type of satire, focusing on the economic and social behavior of Jews, has appeared recently in the work of such writers as Jerome Weidman and Budd Schulberg, but their picture, if more honest, is still limited and superficial.

By a considerable margin, the most important achievement in the literature of the American Jews is that of Clifford Odets. No one else has been able to maintain that degree of confidence in the value of the exact truth which made his best work possible. His social understanding is limited, but he has been able to keep his eyes on reality and to set down his observations with great imagination and remarkable detachment. Jews are never commonplace to him—they are never commonplace to any Jew—but neither are they prodigies, either of absurdity or of pathos or of evil. He has perceived that they are human beings living the life which happens to be possible to them.

The elements that make up for most American Jews the image of their group are to be found in the Jewish culture of New York City; more specifically, in the culture of the Jewish lower middle class, in the apartment houses and two-family houses of the Bronx and Brooklyn, among those who all these years have had to think mainly about getting along. Not all Jews actually participate in this culture—perhaps most do not—but almost all are intimately connected with it. The New York pattern is the master pattern, repeated in its main outlines wherever there is a large Jewish population. What is especially characteristic of other areas of Jewish life is often simply the extension of this; what appears most sharply opposed to it, or furthest away from it, is often the expression of a deliberate struggle against it.

The crucial fact is that there are few who cannot immediately recognize and understand its smallest forms of behavior, its accepted attitudes, its language. If it is not "Jewish life," strictly speaking, it is for most American Jews the area of greatest emotional importance. It is what a Jew remembers, it is what he has in his mind when he experiences his more private emotions about being a Jew—affection, pity, delight, shame. Just as the life of the small town can be said in some sense to embody the common experience of the older Americans, so the life of New York can be said at this particular stage in the process of acculturation to embody the common experience of the American Jews.

Clifford Odets is the poet of this life. In the body of his work so far, with its rather specious "development" and its persistent intellectual shallowness, the spectacular achievement which makes him a dramatist of importance is his truthful description of the New York Jews of the lower middle class.

Awake and Sing, his first full-length play, remains the most impressive. He has since become a more skillful dramatist, but his progress in theatrical terms has involved a loss in the simple observation of fact which is his greatest talent: he has become more superficial and more sentimental. His significant field of knowledge is among the Jews, and what he knows about the Jews is in *Awake and Sing*.

In reading *Awake and Sing*, one is likely to be struck by its crudity: there is an illegitimate pregnancy and a hasty marriage, a life insurance policy, a suicide; the final curtain is brought down on a puerile note of "affirmation" (Odets has said, "New art works should shoot bullets"). But in the last analysis these crudities are of no great importance. The special experience of reading or seeing the play has nothing to do with the dramatics used to make it progress through its three acts.

For the Jew in the audience, at least, the experience is recognition, a continuous series of familiar signposts, each suggesting with the immediate communication of poetry the whole complex of the life of the characters: what they are, what they want, how they stand with the world.

It is a matter of language more directly than anything else. The events of the play are of little consequence; what matters is the words of the characters—the way they talk as much as the things they say. Odets employs consistently and with particular skill what amounts to a special type of dramatic poetry. His characters do not speak in poetry—indeed, they usually become ridiculous when they are made to speak "poetically"—but the speeches put into their mouths have the effect of poetry, suggesting much more than is said and depending for the enrichment of the suggestion upon the sensibility and experience of the hearer. Many of the things said on the stage are startling for their irrelevance; they neither contribute to the progress of the plot nor offer any very specific light upon the character of the participants: the hearer supplies a meaning.

The peculiarity of this poetic process is that it operates exclusively between the writer and the audience; it is not *in* the play. The characters are in a state of ignorance, always saying something different from what they think they are saying. This differs from dramatic irony in the usual sense by the fact that the ignorance of the characters is essential instead of accidental: they *do* know what is happening in the play; what they do *not* know is what they are. In a sense they are continually engaged in giving themselves away.

The effect of the method is to increase the distance between the audience and the specific facts of the play, while bringing

28

before the audience more clearly than is usual the general facts about Jews and Jewish life which the play illustrates. The young son, Ralph, puts into one sentence the history of his frustration: "It's crazy—all my life I want a pair of black and white shoes and can't get them. It's crazy!" The mother, Bessie, responds, betraying the bitterness of her relations with her children, the difficulty of her life, the general picture of what it must be like to live with her: "In a minute I'll get up from the table. I can't take a bite in my mouth no more." Demolishing an argument for the abolition of private property, she presents her concept of man's fate: "Noo, go fight City Hall!" She offers a scrap of worldly wisdom to justify her tricking a young man into marrying her daughter, already pregnant by another man: "Maybe you never heard charity begins at home. You never heard it, Pop?" The old man, Jacob, shows what his daughter is to him: "All you know, I heard, and more yet. . . . This is a house? Marx said it— abolish such families." Bessie's husband, Myron, demonstrates his ineffectuality: "This morning the sink was full of ants. Where they come from I just don't know. I thought it was coffee grounds . . . and then they began moving." A sentence exhibits his tenuous grasp on American culture: "My scalp is impoverished," he says, out of nowhere. Sam Feinschreiber, the unfortunate object of Bessie's choice for her daughter ("In three years he put enough in the bank . . ."), reacts to the news that the baby is not his own: "I'm so nervous—look, two times I weighed myself on the subway station." Uncle Morty, the successful dress manufacturer, replies to the suggestion that he might send a little more money to take care of his father: "Tell me jokes. Business is so rotten I could just as soon lay all day in the Turkish bath." Uncle Morty prepares to leave the house: "Where's my fur gloves?"

To the experienced ear, every speech tells again the whole story, every character presents over and over the image of his

29

particular kind, the role of his kind in the culture which contains it. The characters are diminished as human beings in favor of their function as instruments of poetic evocation. Rich or poor, happy or not, they serve their purpose. The responses called forth by the play are responses to the life of the Jews, to the psychological roots of one's own life, never to the individual lives of the people on the stage.

In the end you really get something like a direct apprehension of sociological truth, the whole picture built up out of the words spoken on the stage, the tones of speech and thought, all is added to the knowledge already possessed by the audience.

It is not the whole picture of the Jews; there is no whole picture of the Jews. And even as a partial picture it calls for some reservations. Assuming all necessary reservations, the picture might be called: what happened to the Jews in New York.

The adult immigrant had some advantages. Whatever it was that drove him to come, he was able to carry with him a sense of his own dignity and importance. He had a kind of security, though it is a strange thing to say of a Jew. In Europe, with the club over his head, he had nevertheless lived in a community which was in important ways self-sufficient, and which permitted him to think of himself as a man of value: he was a scholar, or a revolutionist, at the very least he knew himself to be a more serious man than his Gentile persecutors. To be a Jew was a continual burden, even a misfortune, but it could not have seemed to him a joke or a disgrace.

He came off a boat, he had to find a job the very next day, and for the rest of his life he was likely to be taken up by the numberless techniques of getting by: how to make a dollar, how to pursue the infinitesimal advantages which made it possible for him to survive from day to day. The humilia-

30

tion of his poverty and impotence was tremendous, but he was already equipped with a mechanism for separating from it some of the needs of his personality. In his own mind, and in the semi-European atmosphere he created in the synagogues or the cafés and radical groups, he could contrive for his sad life the appearance of a meaning that went beyond the everlasting pettiness of which it actually consisted. He had a past.

For his children, helping after school with the family's piece-work or going themselves to work in the shops, and often suffering in addition under a savage moral discipline with no apparent relevance to the real world, the pretensions of the father could be nothing but nonsense. He could create in the minds of his children only an entirely generalized ideal of moral and intellectual superiority absolutely without content. (Bessie Berger: "I raise a family they should have respect.")

If the parents had a great deal of love and wisdom, or if the family made money soon enough, the children could sometimes arrive at a tolerable balance between dignity and economic pressure. But the familiar pattern was not often to be avoided: the children holding before them the image of a suffering and complaining mother and of a father whose life went on outside the home, who was somehow responsible—with his "ideas"—for the family's hardships. It was remembered with undying resentment that he had given money to the synagogue or the Party—to "make a show"—while his family went hungry, and the things he believed in came to represent a wilful refusal to understand the principle that charity begins at home. ("Go in your room, Papa. Every job he ever had he lost because he's got a big mouth. He opens his mouth and the whole Bronx could fall in. . . . A good barber not to hold a job a week.") If he made money at last, then his demonstrations of allegiance to the things he thought valuable might be received with more tolerance, even with pride, but they still remained for his children outside the area of practical life.

For his part, he was always disappointed in his children, and his sense of disappointment was often the only thing he could clearly communicate to them. He succeeded at least in becoming a reproach to them, and the bitterness of the personal conflict which ensued was aggravated by the fact that they could never quite see from what he derived his superiority or what it was he held against them.

The children took hold of what seemed to them the essential point—that they were living in a jungle. It would not be accurate to say that they failed to understand the rest; so far as they were concerned, the rest was not there to see, it had retired into the mind.

They tried to act reasonably. Every day they could see more clearly the basic truth: without a dollar you don't look the world in the eye. This truth was not for a moment welcome to them, they accepted it with all suitable reluctance, they doffed their hats continually in the direction of the "other things," but they really saw no alternative to following out the implications of what they knew. After all, their analysis of the situation was virtually a matter of life and death. ("Ralphie, I worked too hard all my years to be treated like dirt. . . . Summer shoes you didn't have, skates you never had, but I bought a new dress every week. A lover I kept— Mr. Gigolo! . . . If I didn't worry about the family who would? . . . Maybe you wanted me to give up twenty years ago. Where would you be now? You'll excuse my expression —a bum in the park!")

Between the facts as they saw them and the burden of undefined moral responsibility laid upon them by the father, no decision was possible. Money was at least effective, it

32

could really solve their worst problems. It was what they *had*
to have. What they wanted was not money, but it was nothing
very definite. The best basis they could find for their life was a
worldly compromise: money is filth, but money is all you'll
ever get.

In general terms, the kind of life they established for themselves is not different from the characteristic life of the rest
of their society: its primary concerns are economic security
and social prestige; its daydreams are of unlimited economic
security and unassailable social prestige. ("Ralph should
only be a success like you, Morty. I should only live to see the
day when he drives up to the door in a big car with a chauf-
feur and a radio. I could die happy, believe me.") Indeed,
they were especially quick to perceive the underlying pattern
of the society and to conform to it. Looking from the outside,
and suffering from the hostility of those around them, they
naturally understood the significant facts thoroughly; for
Jews, that had always been one of the necessities of life.

But it was not merely a matter of a generation moving from
one culture into another. As it happened, the newer culture
had already come to a point where it was unable to provide
much security or dignity even for those who indisputably belonged to it. Understanding was in this case a bar to adjustment, and the life of the Jews has been colored by their awareness of the terms of the compromise they have had to accept.
Their frustration is part of a universal frustration, but their
unhappiness is more acute because all along they have known
what they were doing.

Sometimes their special situation gave them a kind of edge,
as if they were a day older in history than everybody else.
They were capable of phenomenal success. Errand boys
made themselves into millionaires simply by shrewd and unremitting attention to the possibilities of capitalist enterprise.
Entertainers, exploiting the contrast between what they were

33

and what they wanted, found a huge audience suddenly ready to see the point. Hollywood became a gold mine, demonstrating that the Jews were not different from everybody else, only a little further along: they could feel the exact level to which culture had come.

Success made no essential difference. A million dollars was a great and wonderful thing—how can you refuse money if you don't know what would be better?—but they could never believe that it was really enough to make a man important. Uncle Morty says "Where's my fur gloves?" not to impress the others but to remind himself of how far he has come.

They wanted also to be good and wise men. Having no frame of reference by which to attach a meaning to "good" and "wise," even a false meaning, they were forced to seek what assurance they could find in the tangible evidences they knew to be valueless: money, prestige, the intellectual superiority of one man to another. Thus from the complex of their fears and desires they evolved the three imperatives that govern them: be secure, be respected, be intelligent. In their world a dentist is better than a machinist, a doctor is better than a businessman, a college professor is best of all. But an unsuccessful intellectual is worse than an unsuccessful businessman: he should have known better than to try.

Their economic strength comes from their ability to act as the situation demands even though the situation is abhorrent to them. But the gap between moral man and the requirements of reality has seemed to them so wide that they have been able to function successfully only by imposing cynicism on themselves as a kind of discipline. They have gone further than most in the acceptance of reality, and this is perhaps the strongest kind of subversion—to take capitalism without sugar.

What it costs them is their characteristic mental insecurity, a mixture of self-pity and self-contempt. Self-pity because

34

their way of life was forced upon them, self-contempt because they can accept no excuse.

Awake and Sing is a depression play, and its picture of Jewish life is sharper and more brutal than it would have been a few years earlier. The hidden framework of need and compulsion had come out. If it had ever been possible for the Jews to lull themselves completely in the material benefits of capitalism, that possibility was gone. With the depression, their painfully built structure of defenses shook and fell, respectability itself was threatened, and they looked again into the abyss of poverty, all the more frightening because it was so familiar, because they had given so much to get out of it.

The characters contemplate the meaninglessness of their lives. The image of their failure is constantly before them; they cannot contain themselves, they must burst out every minute in a fury of bitterness and impotence, justifying themselves, calling for pity, enveloping themselves and the world in indiscriminate scorn. They have ceased to communicate; each confronts his own unhappiness, using language primarily as an instrument of self-expression and a weapon of defense.

It is as if no one really listens to anyone else; each takes his own line, and the significant connections between one speech and another are not in logic but in the heavy emotional climate of the family.

> RALPH: *I don't know. . . . Every other day to sit around with the blues and mud in your mouth.*
> MYRON: *That's how it is—life is like that—a cake-walk.*
> RALPH: *What's it get you?*
> HENNIE: *A four-car funeral.*
> RALPH: *What's it for?*

35

JACOB: *What's it for? If this life leads to a revolution it's a good life. Otherwise it's for nothing.*

BESSIE: *Never mind, Pop! Pass me the salt.*

RALPH: *It's crazy—all my life I want a pair of black and white shoes and can't get them. It's crazy!*

BESSIE: *In a minute I'll get up from the table. I can't take a bite in my mouth no more.*

MYRON: *Now, Momma, just don't excite yourself—*

BESSIE: *I'm so nervous I can't hold a knife in my hand.*

MYRON: *Is that a way to talk, Ralphie? Don't Momma work hard enough all day?*

BESSIE: *On my feet twenty-four hours?*

MYRON: *On her feet—*

RALPH: *What do I do—go to night clubs with Greta Garbo? Then when I come home can't even have my own room? Sleep on a day-bed in the front room!*

BESSIE: *He's starting up that stuff again. When Hennie here marries you'll have her room—I should only live to see the day.*

HENNIE: *Me too.*

They live on top of one another, in that loveless intimacy which is the obverse of the Jewish virtue of family solidarity, and their discontentment is expressed in continual and undisguised personal hostility. The son, Ralph, is in love:

BESSIE: *A girl like that he wants to marry. A skinny consumptive . . . six months already she's not working—taking charity from an aunt. You should see her. In a year she's dead on his hands. . . . Miss Nobody should step in the picture and I'll stand by with my mouth shut.*

RALPH: *Miss Nobody! Who am I? Al Jolson?*

BESSIE: *Fix your tie!*

RALPH: *I'll take care of my own life.*

BESSIE: *You'll take care? Excuse my expression, you can't even wipe your nose yet! He'll take care!*

Someone is slow about coming to the dining-room: "Maybe we'll serve for you a special blue-plate supper in the garden?" Morty responds to one of Jacob's dissertations on the class struggle: "Like Boob McNutt you know! Don't go in the park, Pop—the squirrels'll get you."

In a brilliant climax, Bessie Berger reveals the whole pattern of psychological and moral conflict that dominates her and her family: when Ralph discovers that his sister's husband was trapped into marriage, Bessie, confronted inescapably with her own immorality, and trembling before her son's contempt, turns upon her *father*, who has said nothing, and smashes the phonograph records that are his most loved possessions and the symbol of his superiority. This act of fury is irrelevant only on the surface: one understands immediately that Bessie has gone to the root of the matter.

Purposeless, insecure, defeated, divided within themselves, the Bergers made a life like a desert. The process which produced them was not ironbound; one way or another, there were many who escaped. But the Bergers are important. The luckiest is not out of sight of them; no consideration of the Jews in America can leave them out; in the consciousness of most of us they do in some sense stand for "Jew."

(*1946*)

The "Idealism"
of Julius and Ethel Rosenberg

JULIUS AND ETHEL ROSENBERG were not put to death
for their opinions, but from their side, clearly, they died for
their opinions nevertheless. And not only did they choose to
give up their lives: each sacrificed the other, and both together sacrificed their two young children. Yet they must
have loved the children; it is true that they permitted them
to be exploited outrageously in the service of propaganda,
but from their side, again, this would not have appeared to be
exploitation. And obviously they loved each other; there is no
hint of disharmony between them, and only a gross want of
imagination could lead one to think they were not being spon-
taneous when, for instance, they stood holding hands to hear
their sentence. It would be hard to overstate the immensity
of their fortitude, which seems never to have come close to
failure, or the weight of their suffering.

For the two years in the death cells they lived within about
a hundred feet of each other but could be together only during brief weekly visits or when their lawyer came to confer
with them (apparently, if they had been brothers instead of
man and wife they might have had adjoining cells). They
therefore had to communicate frequently in letters. A selec-

tion of their letters to each other, together with some letters to their lawyer, Emanuel Bloch, has been brought out by the "Jero Publishing Company." The selection goes up to the middle of March of 1953, and the book itself went to press shortly before the Rosenbergs' execution, which took place on June 19. The volume includes also an outline of the chronology of the case and an appendix containing excerpts from the Rosenbergs' petition for clemency and statements from various people who either believed that the Rosenbergs were innocent or felt that their sentence was too severe. Proceeds from the sale of the book are supposed to go into a fund for the Rosenbergs' two children, Michael and Robert, who are ten years and six years old. In Europe these letters, like all the propaganda in the Rosenberg case, have been received with great excitement. Here, they appear to be making little impact, though there seems to be no inclination on the part of the Communists to let the propaganda campaign subside. (The weekend edition of the *Daily Worker* has been running a series of biographical articles about the Rosenbergs under the title "Two Immortals." Meetings and rallies continue to be held, and the National Committee to Secure Justice in the Rosenberg Case plans to distribute "throughout the world" the "Rosenberg Dedication Book," a slick-paper booklet offering an extremely skillful compendium of demagogy.)

The children came to visit, and the father and mother, like any anxious and intelligent parents, discuss in their letters how best to "approach" the situation, how to give "the impression that we are not unduly upset" and thus evoke a "proper reaction." In advance of the first visit, Ethel considers that she will say something like this: "Of course, it's not easy to know about the death penalty and not worry about it sometimes, but let's look at it this way. We know that a car could strike us and kill us, but that doesn't mean we spend every minute being fearful about cars. . . ." There is even a note of serene understanding about the "people who solved their own problems by lying about us," and she plans to assure the children that "it's all right to feel any way you like about those people, so long as your feelings don't give you pain and make you unhappy—" "Oh, yes," she adds in another letter, "if Michael neglects to question me as to the form of the death penalty, this job will fall to you. . . . Answer briefly that it is painless electrocution, which we believe will never come to pass, of course." After a second visit, Julius reports that Michael did indeed ask how the death penalty is carried out and whether there was an electric chair in the building; Julius answered straightforwardly. Michael said also, "Daddy, maybe I'll study to be a lawyer and help you in your case." "The fact is," Julius writes, "both children are disturbed."

Much of the correspondence deals with plans for the care of children. "I fully understand and share your anguish," Julius writes, "but we are very well qualified to organize the proper program of rehabilitation for our children. . . . The entire home, play and materials situation needs a radical change. . . . Mind you, I'm not alarmed, as I feel the necessary conditions exist to do a good job. . . . I'm counting on your analytical mind and sense of detail to help carry the ball for us." As Christmas approaches, he consults the *National Guardian* for a list of suitable books for the boys.

Ethel is often more rhetorical: "I . . . experience such a stab of longing for my boy that I could howl like a she-animal who has had its young forcibly torn from her! How dared they, how dared they, the low, vile creatures, lay unclean hands upon our sacred family? And tell me, oh my sister Americans, how long shall any of your own husbands and children be safe if by your silence you permit this deed to go unchallenged!"

41

The fact that Julius Rosenberg can speak of a lack of toys as the "materials situation" does not in the least permit us to assume he did not suffer for his children just as much as anyone else would have suffered. Nor does the impudence of Ethel's appeal to her "sister Americans"—whose lives she had been willing to put in danger—diminish in any way the reality of the "stab of longing for my boy." On the whole, the Rosenbergs in dealing with their children sound the authentic tone of parental love in the educated and conscientious middle class, facing each "problem" boldly and without displaying undue emotion, though "of course" not denying the existence of emotion either ("Of course it's not easy to know about the death penalty and not worry about it sometimes. . . ."). This is how we all deal with our children, and surely we are right to do so. If it happens that you must "prepare" the children for their parents' death in the electric chair instead of for having their tonsils out, then doubtless something better is required. But what, for God's sake? Some unique inspiration, perhaps, and the truth. But we cannot blame the Rosenbergs for their failure to achieve an inspiration, and the commitment for which they died—and by which, we must assume, they somehow fulfilled themselves—was precisely that the truth was not to be spoken.

Not spoken, not whispered, not approached in the merest hint. These letters were undoubtedly written, or revised, for publication; in any case, they were subject to examination by prison officials. Under the circumstances, they could not have been truthful. But there is something uncanny nevertheless in the way this husband and wife felt compelled to write to each other, never evading the issue but, on the contrary, coming back to it continually in order to repeat continually what was not true. "We are innocent"—again and again Julius tells this to Ethel and Ethel tells it back to Julius.

"What have we done to deserve such unhappiness? All our years we lived decent, constructive lives." "I firmly believe that we are better people because we stood up with courage through a very grueling trial and a most brutal sentence, all because we are innocent." "I'm certain we will beat this frame-up. . . ." The word "Communist" never appears except in quotation marks; when Julius seeks to define the faith for which he is prepared to die, he can say only that he is "a progressive individual"—this after a fragment of autobiography, addressed to his lawyer, which makes it especially clear that he was a Communist. He is even forced to speak of espionage—to him, surely, the very crown of the "decent, constructive" life of "a progressive individual"—as a "crime": "Can I deny the principles that are so much part of me? This I can never do. I cannot live a lie nor can I be like the Greenglasses and the Bentleys. My entire life and philosophy negates this and it is obvious that I could never commit the crime I stand convicted of."

No doubt there is a certain covert truth-telling in all this, with "we are innocent" standing for "my resolve is unshaken; I will not confess." But one is forced to wonder whether the literal truth had not in some way ceased to exist for these people. It is now about seventeen years since Communists told the truth about themselves—the "popular front" was inaugurated during Julius Rosenberg's student days at City College—and enough time has passed for the symbolic language of Communism to have taken on an independent existence. On July 4, 1951, Julius clipped a copy of the Declaration of Independence from the New York *Times* and taped it to the wall of his cell. "It is interesting," he writes to Ethel, "to read these words concerning free speech, freedom of the press and of religion in this setting. These rights our country's patriots died for can't be taken from the people even by Congress or the courts." Does it matter that the Declaration of Independence says nothing about free speech, freedom of the press, or freedom of religion, and that Julius therefore could not have found it "interesting" to read "these words" in that particular document? It does not matter. Julius knew that America is supposed to have freedom of expression and that the Declaration of Independence "stands for" America. Since, therefore, he already "knew" the Declaration, there was no need for him to actually read it in order to find it "interesting," and it could not have occurred to him that he was being untruthful in implying that he had just been reading it when he had not. He could "see himself" reading it, so to speak, and this dramatic image became reality: he *did not know* that he had not read it.

Similarly, when he says "it is obvious that I could never commit the crime I stand convicted of," we cannot assume that he is simply lying. More probably, what he means is something like this: If it were a crime, I could not have done it. Since in the language of the unenlightened what I did is called a crime, and I am forced to speak in that language, the only truthful thing to say is that I did not do it.

It is as if these two had no internal sense of their own being but could see themselves only from the outside, in whatever postures their "case" seemed to demand—as if, one might say, they were only the most devoted of their thousands of "sympathizers."

"We didn't ask for this; we only wanted to be left alone, but framed we were—and with every ounce of life in our bodies we will fight until we are free."

"Together we hunted down the answers to all the seemingly insoluble riddles which a complex and callous society presented. . . . For the sake of these answers, for the sake of American democracy, justice and brotherhood, for the sake of peace and bread and roses, and children's laughter, we shall continue to sit here in dignity and in pride. . . ."

"At stake here are the rights, security and very lives of all brave people of all shades of opinions."

"The world is watching our government's action in this case and the conscience of men of good will is outraged by the brutal sentence and the miscarriage of justice in the Rosenberg case."

"The Rosenbergs' calm prediction [it is Ethel Rosenberg who writes this!] that the people would refuse to acquiesce in legal murder has been borne out a thousand times over."

"Is it worth forfeiting two warm, young lives [this too is Ethel], about whose guilt the world says there is reasonable doubt, to save the face of the United States?"

"By our conduct in this case, when our lives are at stake, we are illustrating the fundamental tenets of our democracy."

The tone is no different, really, when they write of the more personal furniture of their lives:

"For about an hour beginning at about 9:00 P.M. I walk and sing songs, mostly folk music, workers' songs, peoples' songs, popular tunes and excerpts from operas and symphonies. I sing Peat Bog Soldiers, Kevin Barry, United Nations, Tennessee Waltz, Irene, Down in the Valley, Beethoven's Ninth Choral Symphony. . . . In all frankness, I feel good and strong while I sing."

"I am reading *Science and Politics in the Ancient World*, by Benjamin Farrington. He gives documentary proof that the enemy of scientific growth was superstition imposed on the people by the nobles of the state and heads of the church for the purpose of maintaining the status quo and their preferred class position."

". . . After a while, some of the pain gripping me eased. It needed only a radio program, and 'Ballad for Americans,' for the finishing touch. With Frank Sinatra's recording of 'House

45

I Live In,' I had a tremendous upsurge of 'courage, confidence and perspective'!"

"Did you ever notice the comfortable feeling one gets reading and listening to rain? I thought, what a wonderful world we live in, and how much man could do with full utilization of his creative ability."

". . . the Dodgers [have] made me bite off every last confounded nail; 10–0, what a trouncing! It's that indomitable spirit that has endeared them to so many. But it is chiefly in their outstanding contribution to the eradication of racial prejudice that they have covered themselves with glory."

"I have been reading again *Gentleman's Agreement,* and it made me realize how starved I was for intellectual exchange. . . ."

"I'm simply carried away, enthralled, enraptured! You can't guess. Well, I've been listening to 'Old Man Tosc' conducting the NBC summer symphony. What a magnificence of sound that guy can call forth; it's positively incredible."

It would be heartless to multiply these quotations merely in order to make a display of the awkwardness and falsity of the Rosenbergs' relations to culture, to sports, and to themselves. But it is important to observe the dimensions of their failure, how almost nothing really belonged to them, not even their own experience; they filled their lives with the secondhand, never so much as suspecting that anything else was possible. Communism itself—the vehicle of whatever self-realization they achieved—had disappeared for them, becoming only a word to be written in quotation marks as if it represented a hallucination, and they faced death armed not even with the clichés of the proletarian revolution but only with the spiritless echoes of a few fellow-traveling newspapers and the memory of City College in 1934.

We need not doubt that Julius was strengthened by singing "Kevin Barry" or "United Nations" and that Ethel was cheered by hearing "Ballad for Americans," or, making allowance for her language, that she was "enraptured" by the NBC summer symphony. It is even possible to believe that Ethel was actually excited at the "trouncing" administered by the Dodgers to the Giants (it was the second game of the 1951 pennant play-off), and that her excitement was related to her appreciation of the Dodgers' "outstanding contribution to the eradication of racial prejudice." We know how easily these responses could have been changed: if "Old Man Tosc" had slighted Paul Robeson, if the Dodgers had fired one of their Negro players, if *Gentleman's Agreement* had been unfavorably reviewed in the *National Guardian*. But the initial responses and their contradictories would have been equally real, and equally unreal.

There is something in this more profound than insincerity. The ideal Communist responds only to the universal—to Revolution, to Progress, or, in Julius Rosenberg's revealing phrase, to "the kind of people we are." *Gentleman's Agreement* or "Ballad for Americans" are merely particular objects in which the universal happens at the moment to embody itself, and it is all the same if these objects disappear so long as new ones take their place. Whether he cheers the Yankees or the Dodgers, whether he damns Franklin Roosevelt as a warmonger or adores him as the champion of human rights, the Communist is always celebrating the same thing: the great empty Idea which has taken on the outlines of his personality. Communists are still "idealists"—perhaps all the more so because their "idealism" is by now almost entirely without content—and the surprising degree of sympathy and even respect that they can command among liberals is partly to be explained by the liberal belief that "idealism" in itself is a virtue.

47

Consider the continual display of Judaism and Jewishness in these letters:

"Our upbringing, the full meaning of our lives, based on a true amalgamation of our American and Jewish heritage, which to us means freedom, culture and human decency, has made us the people we are."

"In a couple of days the Passover celebration of our people's search for freedom will be here. This cultural heritage has added meaning for us, who are imprisoned . . . by the modern Pharaohs."

". . . our fellow Jewish expression summarizes my feelings for [Emanuel Bloch]. *Ich shep nachuss und quell fun ihm.*"

"At Hebrew school . . . I absorbed quite naturally the culture of my people, their struggle for freedom from slavery in Egypt. I found the same great traditions in American history."

"The Jewish services were impressive. . . ."

"What solace to hear your voice during the Jewish services. . . ."

"It is amazing how intellectually stimulating Jewish services can be. . . ."

"I'd appreciate it if you would give the question of the Jewish holidays and their special significance for us, as part of a prison congregation, your serious consideration between now and our next talk."

"This holiday [Chanukah], signifying the victory of our forefathers in a struggle for freedom from oppression and tyranny, is a firm part of our heritage and buttresses our will to win our own freedom."

"The heritage of our Hebrew culture has served our people throughout the ages and we have learned its lesson well."

Except for the crudely calculated introduction of the word "Jewish" in places where it could not have been necessary in communication between a man and his wife, most of these sentences merely repeat the worn platitudes of a thousand sermons about the Jewish tradition. Since the propaganda built up around the case emphasized the fact that the Rosenbergs were Jewish, they simply adopted the role that was demanded of them.* If something else had been needed, they could as easily have taken up the pose of Protestantism or Catholicism or Gandhiism, and for any one of these roles they would have made use of the available platitudes (Communists are of course not alone in their predilection for the secondhand).

But is there any difference between the patently disingenuous passages about Judaism and the occasional passages where the Rosenbergs might be thought to be expressing sentiments closer to their hearts? Supposing even that they had been ready to confess their espionage and proclaim it defiantly as the service to humanity they must have believed it to be, can it be thought they would have expressed themselves any less falsely than they have done in their claims of innocence or their pious espousals of "our people's heritage"?

The point is that all beliefs, all ideas, all "heritages" were really the same to them, and they were equally incapable of truth and of falsehood. What they stood for was not Communism as a certain form of social organization, not progress as a belief in the possibility of human improvement, but only their own identity *as* Communists or "progressives," and they

* It is striking that the Rosenbergs' letters make no reference to the claim that they were "framed" because of anti-Semitism; this would seem to indicate that that particular line of propaganda has not paid off. Julius speaks in one of his letters of the possibility that the "frame-up" might stimulate anti-Semitism by encouraging the belief that all Jews are Communists. In another letter he refers to the "smear campaign" attributing anti-Semitism to the Soviet Union.

49

were perfectly "sincere" in making use of whatever catchwords seemed at any moment to assert that identity—just as one who seeks to establish his identity as a person of culture might try to do so either by praising abstract painting or by damning it. The Rosenbergs thought and felt whatever their political commitment required them to think and to feel. But if they had not had the political commitment could they have thought and felt at all?

Well, we cannot dispose of them quite so easily. They did suffer, for themselves and for their children, and though they seem never to have questioned the necessity of their "martyrdom" or the absolute rightness of all they had ever done (". . . when [the children] are older, they will know that all the way through, we . . . were right . . ."), they wept like anyone else at the approach of death; if it were not for that, one might wonder whether they had any real sense of what they were giving up when they chose to give up their lives.

For the final image is still their glassy serenity of conscience. It has been reported that when the United States Marshal came to tell Ethel Rosenberg that the final stay had been rescinded and the execution would take place in a few hours, she said simply, "Well, the Rosenbergs will be the first victims of American fascism." (The "Rosenberg Dedication Book" prints a brief note from Julius to Emanuel Bloch, dated on the day of execution, which also attributes these words to Ethel.) For her, this was a sufficient definition of what was about to happen to her. Perhaps the fact that she could say this, externalizing even her own death—not she was about to die, but a "victim of fascism"—should be for us a sufficient definition of what she had made of herself.

Inevitably it has been suggested that the Rosenbergs did not write these letters. Yet there is nothing in the quality of the letters to make one believe they could not have written them;

they were people of no eloquence and little imagination, and their letters display none. (The "Rosenberg Dedication Book" demonstrates that there were writers available who could have done better.) Unquestionably there has been heavy editing, but again there is no reason to suppose that the Rosenbergs themselves may not have done the editing, both after the letters were written and in the process of writing them. In any case, the question is of no importance. The letters, if they were not written by the Rosenbergs, are what the Rosenbergs would have written. In their crudity and emptiness, in their absolute and dedicated alienation from truth and experience, these letters adequately express the Communism of 1953.

(*1953*)

Paul, the Horror Comics, and Dr. Wertham

MY SON PAUL, who is eleven years old, belongs to the E.C. Fan-Addict Club, a synthetic organization set up as a promotional device by the Entertaining Comics Group, publishers of *Mad* ("Tales Calculated to Drive You MAD—Humor in a Jugular Vein"), *Panic* ("This Is No Comic Book, This Is a PANIC—Humor in a Varicose Vein"), *Tales from the Crypt, The Vault of Horror, Weird Science-Fantasy, Shock Suspen-Stories, Crime SuspenStories* ("Jolting Tales of Tension in the E.C. Tradition"), and, I imagine, various other such periodicals. For his twenty-five-cent membership fee (soon to be raised to fifty cents) the E.C. Fan-Addict receives a humorously phrased certificate of membership, a wallet-size "identification card," a pin and a shoulder-patch bearing the club emblem, and occasional mailings of the club bulletin, which publishes chitchat about the writers, artists, and editors, releases trial balloons on ideas for new comic books, lists members' requests for back numbers, and in general tries to foster in the membership a sense of identification with this particular publishing company and its staff. E.C. Fan-Addict Club Bulletin Number 2, March 1954, also suggests some practical activities for the members. "Everytime you pass your newsstand, fish out the E.C.'s from the bottom of the piles or racks and put 'em up on top. . . . BUT PLEASE, YOU MONSTERS, DO IT NEATLY!"

Paul, I think, does not quite take this "club" with full seriousness, but it is clear that he does in some way value his membership in it, at least for the present. He has had the club shoulder-patch put on one of his jackets, and when his membership pin broke recently he took the trouble to send for a new one. He has recruited a few of his schoolmates into the organization. If left free to do so, he will buy any comic book which bears the E.C. trademark, and is usually quite satisfied with the purchase. This is not a matter of "loyalty," but seems to reflect some real standard of discrimination; he has occasionally sampled other comic books which imitate the E.C. group and finds them inferior.

It should be said that the E.C. comics do in fact display a certain imaginative flair. *Mad* and *Panic* are devoted to a wild, undisciplined machine-gun attack on American popular culture, creating an atmosphere of nagging hilarity something like the clowning of Jerry Lewis. They have come out with covers parodying *The Saturday Evening Post* and *Life*, and once with a vaguely "serious" cover in imitation of magazines like *Harper's* or the *Atlantic*. ("Do you want to look like an idiot reading comic books all your life? Buy *Mad*, then you can look like an idiot reading high-class literature.") The current issue of *Mad* (dated August) has Leonardo's Mona Lisa on the cover, smiling as enigmatically as ever and cradling a copy of *Mad* in her arms. The tendency of the humor, in its insistent violence, is to reduce all culture to indiscriminate anarchy. These comic books are in a line of descent from the Marx Brothers, from the Three Stooges whose funniest business is to poke their fingers in each other's eyes, and from that comic orchestra which starts out playing "serious" music and ends up with all the instruments smashed. A very funny parody of the comic-strip "Little Orphan Annie," in *Mad* or *Panic*, shows Annie cut into small pieces by a train because Daddy Warbucks' watch is slow and he has arrived just too late for the last minute; Annie's detached head complains: "It hurts when I laugh." The parody ends with the most obvious and most vulgar explanation of why Annie calls Daddy Warbucks "Daddy"; I had some difficulty in explaining that joke to Paul. One of the funnier stories in *Panic* tells of a man who finds himself on the television program "This Is Your Life"; as his old friends and neighbors appear one by one to fill in the story of his life, it becomes clear that nobody has seen his wife since 11:30 P.M. on the ninth of October, 1943; shortly before that he had made some rather significant purchases: arsenic, a shovel, quicklime. Evidence piles up, including the actual bones of his wife (dug up by his old dog, Rover, who also appears on the program and will do nothing but growl at his former master). At the end of the program, of course, the man is arrested for murder; television's assault on privacy has reached its logical conclusion. I understand that *Mad* is rather popular among college students, and I have myself read it with a kind of irritated pleasure.

The straightforward crime and horror comics, such as *Shock SuspenStories, Crime SuspenStories,* or *The Vault of Horror,* exhibit the same undisciplined imaginativeness and violence without the leavening of humor. One of the more gruesome stories in *Crime SuspenStories* is simply a "serious" version of the story I have outlined from *Panic:* again a man murders his wife (this time with an ax) and buries her in the back yard, and again he is trapped on a television program. In another story, a girl some ten or eleven years old, unhappy in her home life, shoots her father, frames her mother and the mother's lover for the murder, and after their death in the electric chair ("Mommy went first. Then Steve.") is shown living happily with Aunt Kate, who can give her the emotional security she has lacked. The child winks at us from the last panel in appreciation of her own cleverness. Some of the stories, if one takes them simply in terms of their plots, are not unlike the stories of Poe or other writers of horror tales; the publishers of such comic books have not failed to point this out. But of course the bareness of the comic-book form makes an enormous difference. Both the humor and the horror in their utter lack of modulation yield too readily to the child's desire to receive his satisfactions immediately, thus tending to subvert one of the chief elements in the process of growing up, which is to learn to wait; a child's developing appreciation of the complexity of good literature is surely one of the things that contribute to his eventual acceptance of the complexity of life.

I do not suppose that Paul's enthusiasm for the products of this particular publisher will necessarily last very long. At various times in the past he has been a devotee of the Dell Publishing Company (*Gene Autry, Red Ryder, Tarzan, The Lone Ranger,* etc.), National Comics (*Superman, Action Comics, Batman,* etc.), *Captain Marvel, The Marvel Family, Zoo Funnies* (very briefly), *Sergeant Preston of the Yukon,* and, on a higher level, *Pogo Possum.* He has around a hundred and fifty comic books in his room, though he plans to weed out some of those which no longer interest him. He keeps closely aware of dates of publication and watches the newsstands from day to day and from corner to corner if possible; when a comic book he is concerned with is late in appearing, he is likely to get in touch with the publisher to find out what has caused the delay. During the *Pogo* period, indeed, he seemed to be in almost constant communication with Walt Kelly and the Post-Hall Syndicate, asking for original drawings (he has two of them), investigating delays in publication of the comic books (there are quarterly 15-cent comic books, published by Dell, in addition to the daily newspaper strip and the frequent paper-bound volumes published at one dollar by Simon and Schuster), or tracking down rumors that a Pogo shirt or some other such object was to be put on the market (the rumors were false; *Pogo* is being kept free of "commercialization"). During the 1952 presidential campaign, Pogo was put forward as a "candidate," and there were buttons saying "I Go Pogo"; Paul managed to acquire about a dozen of these, although, as he was told, they were intended primarily for distribution among college students. Even now he maintains a distant fondness for Pogo, but I am no longer required to buy the New York *Post* every day in order to save the daily strips for him. I think that Paul's desire to put himself directly in touch with the processes by which the comic books are produced may be the expression of a fundamental detachment which helps to protect him from them; the comic books are not a "universe" to him, but simply objects produced for his entertainment.

When Paul was home from school for his spring vacation this year, I took him and two of his classmates to visit the offices of the Entertaining Comics Group at 225 Lafayette Street. (I had been unable to find the company in the telephone book until I thought of looking it up as "Educational Comics"; I am told that this is one of five corporate names under which the firm operates.) As it turned out, there was nothing to be seen except a small anteroom containing a pretty receptionist and a rack of comic books; the editors were in conference and could not be disturbed. (Of course I knew there must be conferences, but this discovery that they actually occur at a particular time and place somehow struck me; I should have liked to know how the editors talked to each other.) In spite of our confinement to the anteroom, however, the children seemed to experience as great a sense of exaltation as if they had found themselves in the actual presence of, say, Gary Cooper.

One of Paul's two friends signed up there and then in the E.C. Fan-Addict Club (Paul had recruited the other one into the club earlier) and each boy bought seven or eight back numbers. When the receptionist obligingly went into the inner offices to see if she could collect a few autographs, the boys by crowding around the door as she opened it managed to catch a glimpse of one of the artists, Johnny Craig, whom Paul recognized from a drawing of him that had appeared in one of the comic books. In response to the boys' excitement, the door was finally opened wide so that for a few seconds they could look at Mr. Craig; he waved at them pleasantly from behind his drawing board and then the door was closed. Before we left, the publisher himself, William Gaines, passed through the anteroom, presumably on his way to the men's room. He too was recognized, shook hands with the boys, and gave them his autograph.

I am sure the children's enthusiasm contained some element of self-parody, or at any rate an effort to live up to the situation—after all, a child is often very uncertain about what is exciting, and how much. It is quite likely that the little sheets of paper bearing the precious autographs have all been misplaced by now. But there is no doubt that the excursion was a great success.

A few weeks later Mr. Gaines testified before a Congressional committee that is investigating the effects of comic books on children and their relation to juvenile delinquency. Mr. Gaines, as one would expect, was opposed to any suggestion that comic books be censored. In his opinion, he said, the only restrictions on the editors of comic books should be the ordinary restrictions of good taste. Senator Kefauver presented for his examination the cover of an issue of *Crime SuspenStories* (drawn by Johnny Craig) which shows a man holding by its long blond hair the severed head of a woman. In the man's other hand is the dripping ax with which he has just carried out the decapitation, and the lower part of the woman's body, with the skirt well up on the plump thighs, appears in the background. It was an illustration for the story I have described in which the murderer is finally trapped on a television program. Did Mr. Gaines think this cover in good taste? Yes, he did—for a horror comic. If the head had been held a little higher, so as to show blood dripping from the severed neck, that would have been bad taste. Mr. Gaines went on to say that he considers himself to be the originator of horror comics and is proud of it. He mentioned also that he is a graduate of the New York University School of Education, qualified to teach in the high schools.

I did not fail to clip the report of Mr. Gaines's testimony from the *Times* and send it to Paul, together with a note in which I said that while I was in some confusion about the comic-book question, at least I was sure I did not see what Mr. Gaines had to be so proud about. But Paul has learned a few things in the course of the running argument about comic books that has gone on between us. He thanked me for sending the clipping and declined to be drawn into a discussion. Such discussions have not proved very fruitful for him in the past.

They have not been very fruitful for me either. I know that I don't like the comics myself and that it makes me uncomfortable to see Paul reading them. But it's hard to explain to Paul why I feel this way, and somewhere along the line it seems to have been established that Paul is always entitled to an explanation: he is a child of our time.

I said once that the gross and continual violence of the comic books was objectionable.

He said: "What's so terrible about things being exciting?"

Well, nothing really; but there are books that are much more exciting, and the comics keep you from reading the books.

But I read books *too*. (He does, especially when there are no comics available.)

Why read the comics at all?

But you said yourself that *Mad* is pretty good. You gotta admit!

Yes, I know I did. But it's not that good. . . . Oh, the comics are just stupid, that's all, and I don't see why you should be wasting so much time with them.

Maybe they're stupid *sometimes*. But look at this one. This one is *really good*. Just read it! Why won't you just *read* it?

Usually I refuse to "just read it," but that puts me at once at a disadvantage. How can I condemn something without knowing what it is? And sometimes, when I do read it, I am forced to grant that maybe this particular story does have a certain minimal distinction, and then I'm lost. Didn't I say myself that *Mad* is pretty good?

I suppose this kind of discussion can be carried on better than I seem able to do, but it's a bad business getting into discussions anyway. If you're against comic books, then you say: no comic books. I understand there are parents who manage to do that. The best—or worst—that has happened to Paul was a limit on the number of comic books he was allowed to have in a week: I think it was three. But that was intolerable; there were special occasions, efforts to borrow against next week, negotiations for revision of the allotment; there was *always* a discussion.

The fundamental difficulty, in a way—the thing that leaves

both Paul and me uncertain of our ground—is that the comics obviously do not constitute a serious problem in his life. He is in that Fan-Addict Club, all right, and he likes to make a big show of being interested in E.C. comics above all else that the world has to offer, but he and I both know that while he may be a fan, he is not an addict. His life at school is pretty busy (this has been his first year at school away from home) and comics are not encouraged, though they certainly do find their way in. Paul subscribes to *Mad* and, I think, *Pogo* (also to *Zoo Funnies* and *Atomic Mouse*, but he doesn't read those any more), and he is still inclined to haunt the newsstands when he is in New York; indeed, the first thing he wants to do when he gets off the train is buy a comic. In spite of all obstacles, I suppose he manages to read a hundred in a year, at worst perhaps even a hundred and fifty—that would take maybe seventy-five to a hundred hours. On the other hand, he doesn't see much television or listen much to the radio, and he does read books, draw, paint, play with toads, look at things through a microscope, write stories and poems, imitate Jerry Lewis, and in general do everything that one could reasonably want him to do, plus a few extras like skiing and riding. He seems to me a more alert, skillful, and self-possessed child than I or any of my friends were at eleven, if that's any measure.

Moreover, I can't see that his hundred or hundred and fifty comic books are having any very specific effects on him. The bloodiest of ax murders apparently does not disturb his sleep or increase the violence of his own impulses. *Mad* and *Panic* have helped to develop in him a style of humor which may occasionally be wearing but is in general pretty successful; and anyway, Jerry Lewis has had as much to do with this as the comics. Paul's writing is highly melodramatic, but that's only to be expected, and he is more likely to model himself on Erle Stanley Gardner or Wilkie Collins than on *Crime*

SuspenStories. Sometimes the melodrama goes over the line into the gruesome, and in that the comic books no doubt play a role; but if there were no comic books, Paul would be reading things like "The Pit and the Pendulum" or *The Narrative of A. Gordon Pym*—which, to be sure, would be better. Now and then he has expressed a desire to be a comic-book artist when he grows up, or a television comedian. So far as I can judge, he has no inclination to accept as real the comic-book conception of human nature which sees everyone as a potential criminal and every criminal as an absolute criminal.*

* The assumption that human beings will always follow out the logic of their character to the limit is one of the worst elements in the comic books, and is pretty widespread in them. If a man is a burglar, he will not hesitate to commit murder; and if he is going to commit murder, he is often as likely to think of boiling his victim in oil as of shooting him. In the radio serial "Mark Trail," a program no longer in existence which was based on the comic strip "Mark Trail," men engaged in such illegal activities as hunting beaver out of season would unhesitatingly shoot any game warden who came upon them. (The theme of the program was supposed to be conservation.) This kind of "logic" may seem very proper to children. When Paul was about four or five, a baby-sitter read him the story of Bluebeard. I was a little disturbed when he mentioned this to me the next morning and I tried to probe his reactions.

I said something like: "An exciting story, eh?"

"Oh, yes," said Paul.

"That Bluebeard was quite a nasty character, wasn't he?" I said.

"Oh, I don't know," said Paul.

"What do you mean you don't know? Didn't he try to murder his wife?"

"Well," said Paul, "he *told* her not to look in that closet."

As you see, I really don't have much reason to complain; that's why Paul wins the arguments. But of course I complain anyway. I don't like the comic books—not even *Mad,* whatever I may have unguardedly allowed myself to say—and I would prefer it if Paul did not read them. Like most middle-class parents, I devote a good deal of over-anxious attention to his education, to the "influences" that play on him and the "problems" that arise for him. Almost anything in his life is likely to seem important to me, and I find it hard to accept the idea that there should be one area of his experience, apparently of considerable importance to him, which will have no important consequences. One comic book a week or ten, they *must* have an effect. How can I be expected to believe that it will be a good one?

Testifying in opposition to Mr. Gaines at the Congressional hearing was Dr. Frederic Wertham, a psychiatrist who has specialized in work with problem and delinquent children. Dr. Wertham has been studying and attacking the comic books for a number of years. His position on the question is now presented in full in his recently published book *Seduction of the Innocent.*

The most impressive part of the book is its illustrations: two dozen or so examples of comic-book art displaying the outer limits of that "good taste" which Mr. Gaines suggests might be a sufficient restraint upon the editors. There is a picture of a baseball game in which the ball is a man's head with one eye dangling from its socket, the bat is a severed leg, the catcher wears a dismembered human torso as chest protector, the baselines are marked with stretched-out intestines, the bases are marked with the lungs, liver, and heart, the resin-bag is the dead man's stomach, and the umpire dusts off home plate with the scalp. There is a close-up of a hanged man, tongue protruding, eyeballs turned back, the break in the neck clearly drawn. Another scene shows two men being dragged to death face down over a rocky road. "A couple more miles oughta do th' trick!" says the driver of the car. "It better," says his companion. "These ✱ ✱ ✱ ✱ ! ! GRAVEL ROADS are tough on tires!" "But you gotta admit," replies the driver, "there's nothing like 'em for ERASING FACES!" And so on. Dr. Wertham could surely have presented many more such examples if he had the space and could have obtained permission to reproduce them. From Paul's collection, I recall with special uneasiness a story in which a rotting corpse returns from the grave; in full color, the hues and contours of decay were something to see.

Among the recurrent motifs of the comic books, Dr. Wertham lists: hanging, flagellation, rape, torture of women, tying up of women, injury to the eye (one of the pictures he reproduces shows a horrifying close-up of a woman's eye about to be pierced by an ice pick). If a child reads ten comics of this sort a week (a not unusual figure), he may absorb in the course of a year from fifteen hundred to two thousand stories emphasizing these themes (a comic book contains three or four stories). If he takes them with any seriousness at all—and it is difficult to believe that he will not—they surely cannot fail to affect his developing attitudes towards violence, sex, and social restraint.

What the effects will be, and how deep-seated, is not so easy to determine. And here Dr. Wertham is not very helpful. When he tells us of children who have been found hanging, with a comic book nearby opened to a picture of a hanging, one can readily share his alarm. The fact that these children were probably seriously disturbed before they ever read a comic book, and the fact that fantasies of hanging are in any case common among children, does not relieve one of the feeling that comic books may have provided the immediate stimulus that led to these deaths. Even if there were no children who actually hanged themselves, is it conceivable that comic books which play so directly and so graphically on their deepest anxieties should be without evil consequences? On the other hand, when Dr. Wertham tells us of children who have injured themselves trying to fly because they have read *Superman* or *Captain Marvel,* one becomes skeptical. Children always want to fly and are always likely to try it. The elimination of *Superman* will not eliminate this sort of incident. Like many other children, I made my own attempt to fly after seeing *Peter Pan;* as I recall, I didn't really expect it to work, but I thought: who knows?

In general, Dr. Wertham pursues his argument with a humorless dedication that tends to put all phenomena and all evidence on the same level. Discussing *Superman,* he suggests that it wouldn't take much to change the "S" on that great chest to "S.S." With a straight face he tells us of a little boy who was asked what he wanted to be when he grew up and said, "I want to be a sex maniac!" He objects to advertisements for binoculars in comic books because a city child can have nothing to do with binoculars except to spy on the neighbors. He reports the case of a boy of twelve who had misbehaved with his sister and threatened to break her arm if she told anybody. "This is not the kind of thing that boys used to tell their little sisters," Dr. Wertham informs us. He quotes a sociologist who "analyzed" ten comic-book heroes of the *Superman* type and found that all of them "may well be designated as psychopathic deviates." As an indication that there are some children "who are influenced in the right direction by thoughtful parents," he tells us of the four-year-old son of one of his associates who was in the hospital with scarlet fever; when the nurses offered him some comic books, the worthy child refused them, "explaining . . . that his father had said they are not good for children." Dr. Wertham will take at face value anything a child tells him, either as

65

evidence of the harmful effects of the comic books ("I think sex all boils down to anxiety," one boy told him; where could he have got such an idea except from the comics?) or as direct support for his own views: he quotes approvingly a letter by a thirteen-year-old boy taking solemn exception to the display of nudity in comic books, and a fourteen-year-old boy's analysis of the economic motives which lead psychiatrists to give their endorsements to comic books. I suspect it would be a dull child indeed who could go to Dr. Wertham's clinic and not discover very quickly that most of his problematical behavior can be explained in terms of the comic books.

The publishers complain with justice that Dr. Wertham makes no distinction between bad comic books and "good" ones. The Dell Publishing Company, for instance, the largest of the publishers, claims to have no objectionable comics on its list, which runs to titles like *Donald Duck* and *The Lone Ranger*. National Comics Publications (*Superman*, etc.), which runs second to Dell, likewise claims to avoid objectionable material and has an "editorial code" which specifically forbids the grosser forms of violence or any undue emphasis on sex. (If anything, this "code" is too puritanical, but mechanically fabricated culture can only be held in check by mechanical restrictions.) Dr. Wertham is largely able to ignore the distinction between bad and "good" because most of us find it hard to conceive of what a "good" comic book might be.*

Yet in terms of their effect on children, there must be a

---

* I leave out of consideration a few comics like *Pogo Possum* and *Dennis the Menace* which I think could be called good without quotation marks, though it is possible Dr. Wertham might find grounds for objection to these also.

significant difference between *The Lone Ranger* or *Superman* or *Sergeant Preston of the Yukon* on the one hand and, say, the comic book from which Dr. Wertham took that picture of a baseball game played with the disconnected parts of a human body. If *The Lone Ranger* and *Superman* are bad, they are bad in a different way and on a different level. They are crude, unimaginative, banal, vulgar, ultimately corrupting. They are also, as Dr. Wertham claims, violent— but always within certain limits. Perhaps the worst thing they do is to meet the juvenile imagination on its crudest level and offer it an immediate and stereotyped satisfaction. That may be bad enough, but very much the same things could be said of much of our radio and television entertainment and many of our mass-circulation magazines. The objection to the more unrestrained horror and crime comics must be a different one. It is even possible that these outrageous productions may be in one sense "better" than *The Lone Ranger* or *Sergeant Preston,* for in their absolute lack of restraint they tend to be somewhat livelier and more imaginative; certainly they are often less boring. But that does not make them any less objectionable as reading matter for children. Quite the contrary, in fact: *Superman* and *Donald Duck* and *The Lone Ranger* are stultifying; *Crime SuspenStories* and *The Vault of Horror* are stimulating.

A few years ago I heard Dr. Wertham debate with Al Capp on the radio. Mr. Capp at that time had introduced into *Li'l Abner* the story of the shmoos, agreeable little animals of 100 per cent utility who would fall down dead in an ecstasy of joy if one merely looked at them hungrily. All the parts of a shmoo's body, except the eyes, were edible, tasting variously like porterhouse steak, butter, turkey, probably even chocolate cake; and the eyes were useful as suspender buttons. Mr. Capp's fantasy was in this—as, I think, in most of his work—mechanical and rather tasteless. But Dr. Wertham was not content to say anything like that. For him, the story of the shmoos was an incitement to sadistic violence comparable to anything else he had discovered in his reading of comics. He was especially disturbed by the use of the shmoo's eyes as suspender buttons, something he took to be merely another repetition of that motif of injury to the eye which is exemplified in his present book by the picture of a woman about to be blinded with an ice pick. In the violence of Dr. Wertham's discourse on this subject one got a glimpse of his limitations as an investigator of social phenomena.

For the fact is that Dr. Wertham's picture of society and human nature is one that a reader of comic books—at any rate, let us say, a reader of the "good" comic books—might not find entirely unfamiliar. Dr. Wertham's world, like the world of the comic books, is one where the logic of personal interest is inexorable, and *Seduction of the Innocent* is a kind of crime comic book for parents, as its lurid title alone would lead one to expect. There is the same simple conception of motives, the same sense of overhanging doom, the same melodramatic emphasis on pathology, the same direct and immediate relation between cause and effect. If a juvenile criminal is found in possession of comic books, the comic books produced the crime. If a publisher of comic books, alarmed by attacks on the industry, retains a psychiatrist to advise him on suitable content for his publications, it follows *necessarily* that the arrangement is a dishonest one. If a psychiatrist accepts a fee of perhaps $150 a month for carrying out such an assignment (to judge by what Dr. Wertham himself tells us, the fees are not particularly high), that psychiatrist has been "bought"; it is of no consequence to point out how easily a psychiatrist can make $150. It is therefore all right to appeal to the authority of a sociologist who has "analyzed" Superman "according to criteria worked out by the psychologist Gordon W. Allport" and has found him to be a "psychopathic deviate," but no authority whatever can be attached to the "bought" psychiatrist who has been professionally engaged in the problem of the comic books. If no comic-book publisher has been prosecuted under the laws against contributing to the delinquency of minors, it cannot be because those laws may not be applicable; it must be because "no district attorney, no judge, no complainant has ever had the courage to make a complaint."

Dr. Wertham also exhibits a moral confusion which, even if it does not correspond exactly to anything in the comic books, one can still hope will not gain a footing among children. Comic-book writers and artists working for the more irresponsible publishers have told Dr. Wertham of receiving instructions to put more violence, more blood, and more sex into their work, and of how reluctantly they have carried out these instructions. Dr. Wertham writes: "Crime-comic-book writers should not be blamed for comic books. They are not free men. They are told what to do and they do it—or else. They often are, I have found, very critical of comics. . . . But of course . . . they have to be afraid of the ruthless economic power of the comic-book industry. In every letter I have received from a writer, stress is laid on requests to keep his identity secret." What can Dr. Wertham mean by that ominous "or else" which explains everything and pardons everything? Will the recalcitrant writer be dragged face down over a rocky road? Surely not. What Dr. Wertham means is simply that the man might lose his job and be forced to find less lucrative employment. This economic motive is a sufficient excuse for the man who thought up that gruesome baseball game—I suppose because he is a "worker." But it is no excuse for a psychiatrist who advises the publishers of *Superman* and sees to it that no dismembered bodies are played with in that comic book. And of course it is no excuse for a publisher—he is "the industry." This monolithic concept of "the industry" is what makes it pointless to discover whether there is any difference between one publisher and another; it was not men who produced that baseball game— it was "the industry." Would Dr. Wertham suggest to the children who come to his clinic that they cannot be held responsible for anything they do so long as they are doing it to make a living? I am sure he would not. But he does quote with the greatest respect the words of that intelligent fourteen-year-old who was able to see so clearly that if a psychiatrist receives a fee, one can obviously not expect that he will continue to act honestly. And it is not too hard to surmise where this young student of society got the idea.

Apparently, also, when you are fighting a "ruthless industry" you are under no obligation to be invariably careful about what you say. Dr. Wertham very properly makes fun of the psychiatric defenders of comic books who consider it a sufficient justification of anything to say that it satisfies a "deep" need of a child. But on his side of the argument he is willing to put forward some equally questionable "deep" analysis of his own, most notably in his discussion of the supposedly equivocal relation between Batman and the young boy Robin; this particular analysis seems to me a piece of utter frivolity. He is also willing to create the impression that all comic books are on the level of the worst of them, and that psychiatrists have endorsed even such horrors as the piercing of women's eyes and the whimsical dismemberment of bodies. (In fact, the function performed by the reputable psychiatrists who have acted as advisers to the publishers has been to suggest what kind of comic books would be "healthy" reading for children. One can disagree with their idea of what is "healthy," as Dr. Wertham does, or one can be troubled, as

I am, at the addition of this new element of fabrication to cultural objects already so mechanical; but there is no justification for implying that these psychiatrists have been acting dishonestly or irresponsibly.)

None of this, however, can entirely destroy Dr. Wertham's case. It remains true that there is something questionable in the tendency of psychiatrists to place such stress on the supposed psychological needs of children as to encourage the spread of material which is at best subversive of the same children's literacy, sensitivity, and general cultivation. *Superman* and *The Three Musketeers* may serve the same psychological needs, but it still matters whether a child reads one or the other. We are left also with the underworld of publishing which produced that baseball game, which I don't suppose I shall easily forget, and with Mr. Gaines's notions of good taste, with the children who have hanged themselves, and with the advertisements for switch-blade knives, pellet guns, and breast developers which accompany the sadistic and erotic stimulations of the worst comic books.* We are left

---

* An advertisement on the back cover of recent issues of *Panic* and *Weird Science-Fantasy* strikes a loftier note:

BOYS, GIRLS, MEN, WOMEN!
The World Is On FIRE
Serve the LORD
and You Can Have These PRIZES!
We will send you the wonderful prizes pictured on this page . . . all WITHOUT ONE PENNY OF COST. *Crime, sin, graft, wars are the greatest they have ever been. Our leaders say a reawakening of Christianity is needed to save us. You can do your share by spreading the gospel into every house in your community. Merely show your friends*

71

above all with the fact that for many thousands of children comic books, whether bad or "good," represent virtually their only contact with culture. There are children in the schools of our large cities who carry knives and sometimes guns. There are children who reach the last year of high school without ever reading a single book. Even leaving aside the increase in juvenile crime, there seem to be larger numbers of children than ever before who, without going over the line into criminality, live almost entirely in a juvenile underground largely out of touch with the demands of social responsibility, culture, and personal refinement, and who grow up into an unhappy isolation where they are sustained by little else but the routine of the working day, the unceasing clamor of television and the juke boxes, and still, in their adult years, the comic books. This is a very fundamental problem; to blame the comic books, as Dr. Wertham does, is simple-minded. But to say that the comics do not contribute to the situation would be like denying the importance of the children's classics and the great English and European novels in the development of an educated man.

The problem of regulation or even suppression of the comic books, however, is a great deal more difficult than Dr. Wertham imagines. If the publication of comic books were forbidden, surely something on an equally low level would appear to take their place. Children do need some "sinful" world of their own to which they can retreat from the demands of the adult world; as we sweep away one juvenile dung heap, they will move on to another. The point is to see that the dung heap does not swallow them up, and to hope it may be

---

and neighbors inspiring, beautiful Religious Wall Motto plaques. Many buy six or more . . . only 35¢ . . . sell on sight. . . . Serve the LORD *and earn prizes you want.*

one that will bring forth blossoms. But our power is limited; it is the children who have the initiative: they will choose what they want. In any case, it is not likely that the level of literacy and culture would be significantly raised if the children simply turned their attention more exclusively to television and the love, crime, and movie magazines. Dr. Wertham, to be sure, seems quite ready to carry his fight into these areas as well; ultimately, one suspects, he would like to see our culture entirely hygienic. I cannot agree with this tendency. I myself would not like to live surrounded by the kind of culture Dr. Wertham could thoroughly approve of, and what I would not like for myself I would hardly desire for Paul. The children must take their chances like the rest of us. But when Dr. Wertham is dealing with the worst of the comic books he is on strong ground; some kind of regulation seems necessary—indeed, the more respectable publishers of comic books might reasonably welcome it—and I think one must accept Dr. Wertham's contention that no real problem of "freedom of expression" is involved, except that it may be difficult to frame a law that would not open the way to a wider censorship.

All this has taken me a long way from Paul, who doesn't carry a switch-blade knife and has so far been dissuaded even from subscribing to Charles Atlas's body-building course. Paul only clutches at his chest now and then, says something like "arrgh," and drops dead; and he no longer does that very often. Perhaps even Dr. Wertham would not be greatly alarmed about Paul. But I would not say that Paul is not involved in the problem at all. Even if he "needs" *Superman*, I would prefer that he didn't read it. And what he does read is not even *Superman*, which is too juvenile for him; he reads some of the liveliest, bloodiest, and worst material that the "ruthless" comic-book industry has to offer—he is an E.C. Fan-Addict.

I think my position is that I would be happy if Senator Kefauver and Dr. Wertham could find some way to make it impossible for Paul to get *any* comic books. But I'd rather Paul didn't get the idea that I had anything to do with it.

(*1954*)

E. B. White and the *New Yorker**

THE NEW YORKER at its best provides the intelligent and cultured college graduate with the most comfortable and least compromising attitude he can assume toward capitalist society without being forced into actual conflict. It rejects the vulgarity and inhumanity of the public world of politics and business and provincial morality, and it sets up in opposition to this a private and pseudo-aristocratic world of good humor, intelligence, and good taste. Its good taste has always been questionable, to be sure, but the vulgarity of the *New Yorker* is at least more subdued and less persistent than the ordinary vulgarity of journalism.

The *New Yorker* has always dealt with experience not by trying to understand it but by prescribing the attitude to be adopted toward it. This makes it possible to feel intelligent without thinking, and it is a way of making everything tolerable, for the assumption of a suitable attitude toward experience can give one the illusion of having dealt with it adequately. The gracelessness of capitalism becomes an entirely external phenomenon, a spectacle that one can observe with-

* A review of *The Wild Flag*, by E. B. White. Houghton Mifflin.

out being touched—above all, without feeling really threatened. Even one's own incompetence becomes pleasant: to be baffled by a machine or a domestic worker or an idea is the badge of membership in the civilized and humane minority. The maintenance of this posture demands a delicate balance of insecurity and security; the *New Yorker* can exploit its nervous distaste for modern society only so long as the distaste does not grow into fear. Any strong shock therefore requires a readjustment: this is why the Second World War and the atomic bomb have forced the *New Yorker* to become "serious." But the readjustment does not alter the magazine's function. On the one hand, the "seriousness" of the *New Yorker* is an expression of panic: they never dreamed that the world's inelegance could become so dangerous. On the other hand, it is a substitute for humor, a special technique for handling what is directly threatening, and its function is the same as the function of the humor: to reduce everything to the point where the assumption of a simple attitude will make it tolerable.

The publication of John Hersey's *Hiroshima* was the *New Yorker* equivalent of a desperate attempt to change the course of history, and it is the measure of the *New Yorker's* inadequacy that this effort should have turned out to be simply a journalistic *coup*. The real sensation was the fact that one article was permitted to take up a whole issue of the magazine —what could be more drastic? The article itself, as Mary McCarthy has pointed out, took Hiroshima out of history and politics and made it a familiar and somewhat reassuring picture of disaster. But the trouble is not that the *New Yorker* treated Hiroshima like any scene of death and suffering; the trouble is that the *New Yorker* has always treated death and suffering the way it treated Hiroshima.

The Wild Flag is a collection of E. B. White's *New Yorker* editorials about peace and world government. Mr. White has good will and intelligence, and he is trying to live up to his responsibilities as a citizen. Here is a selection of his thoughts:

"If the range of our planes continues to increase, the range of our thoughts will have to increase. . . ."

"We propose that *it shall be the policy of the United States to bring to an end the use of policy.*" (The italics are Mr. White's, indicating that this is an important point.)

"[Democracy] is the line that forms on the right. It is the don't in Don't Shove. . . . It is the feeling of privacy in the voting booths, the feeling of communion in the libraries, the feeling of vitality everywhere. Democracy is the score at the beginning of the ninth. It is an idea which hasn't been disproved yet, a song the words of which have not gone bad. It's the mustard on the hot dog and the cream in the rationed coffee. . . ."

"An arresting fact about warfare is that it is now unpopular with the men who are engaged in it and with the people who are supporting it. . . . And if a thing is unpopular, there is always the amusing possibility that it may not, then, be inevitable."

". . . we will continue to believe that although a man may have to compromise with Russia he can never compromise with truth."

"There's only one thing you can say for the German war—the men who fought and won it knew, in a general sort of way, what it was all about. . . . Allied soldiers had a hunch that they disliked the idea behind the word 'Heil.' They preferred the word 'Hi'—it was shorter and cleaner."

"Read the men with the short first names: Walt Whitman, John Donne, Manny Kant, Abe Lincoln, Tom Paine, Al Einstein."

The purpose of this writing is not to say anything about democracy or the nature of the war or the possibility of permanent peace, but only to arouse certain familiar responses in the liberal middle-class reader. Thus the word "amusing" appears in a context where it is totally without meaning, but it is a word associated with the *New Yorker* attitude and by this association it gives a certain modishness to a sentence that has nothing illuminating to say. In the same way, and for the same reason, a department-store advertisement might say: "Come and see our amusing nightgowns." Again, the sentence about the short first names is literal nonsense, but the liberal middle-class reader can recognize at once that the man who wrote it has the right feelings: anti-discrimination, pro-New Deal, anti-State Department, etc. And there is the facetiousness of the "Manny Kant" and "Al Einstein," to keep one from being taken in, even by one's own side. In this humane and yet knowing atmosphere, history and destruction and one's own helplessness become small and simple and somehow peaceful, like life back home on the farm: the *short* first names, the mustard on the hot dog, the *hunch* about the nature of fascism, the simple and clear relationships between the range of our planes and the range of our thoughts, between the little word "*Heil*" and the little word "Hi." History may kill you, it is true, but you have taken the right attitude, you will have been intelligent and humane and suitably melancholy to the end.

(*1947*)

An Old Man Gone

I must confess we come not to be kings:
That's not our fault.

The Jew of Malta

IN A WILL made some years before he died, my father directed that his body was to be cremated and that there was to be no religious ceremonial of any kind at his funeral. A later will, drawn up during his final illness, did not mention these points; I suppose the imminent possibility of death may have made him reluctant to go into details. (It was said later that he "must have known" he was dying; it is true that he made no direct reference to death during the fifteen months of his illness, except once at the very beginning and again a few hours before he died.) In any case, it was readily decided to carry out the instructions of the earlier will in this respect. Any other course would have been the grossest absurdity, and no other course was suggested or, I would guess, even thought of. He had expressed a point of view that we all shared.

It is interesting that the will made no provision about the disposition of his ashes, often the one point on which the free-thinker allows himself to betray something approaching a religious sentiment. Once or twice when my father had talked about his wish to be cremated—he talked about it rather often, indeed, with heavy and, to me, disturbing humor—I had asked him, in much the same tone, what was to be done with his ashes. He didn't care, he said—do anything, throw them into an ash can. When at last the problem really came up, I suggested that the ashes might be buried under a tree at the summer hotel he had built in the Catskills. This idea was greeted favorably (my mother recalled that she had "always told him," as he continued to invest money in that unprofitable enterprise, that he was building a mausoleum for himself), and I was secretly pleased when someone else in the family proposed that we might even put some kind of plaque on the tree. As it turned out, however, one of my sisters—of all his children, the one most disastrously unsuccessful in her relations with him—decided that she wanted the ashes, and they are buried now under a tree in her back yard on Long Island.

Since my father died in Florida—a final assertion of will had brought him to that health-giving climate, where he died within twelve hours—an uncompromising respect for common sense would have suggested that he be cremated there; and there was some sentiment for this plan, which would have avoided a great deal of trouble and expense. But various considerations, not all of them "pure," led to the decision that his body should be shipped to New York. I was very glad of this, because I found myself anxious to see the body: primarily, perhaps, to convince myself that he was really dead. As soon as the undertaker informed us that the body was "ready"—it was by then three days after his death—I went to see.

What could I have expected? So far as any evidence could go, it was convincing enough. He was dead as a doornail—

the crudity of this phrase served some purpose for me at the time, though it repels me now. The flesh of his face had shrunk, drawing the lips tight and thin in an upward curve only abstractly (which is to say, not at all) suggestive of a smile, as if he had had his face "lifted"; his nose, now bony and lean, revealed a sharp curve that had not been visible when he was alive; only the heavy gray hands were as they had been. Above all, there was that appearance of perfect grooming which is never to be found except on a corpse: the face shaved cruelly clean and carefully powdered, the few strands of gray hair motionlessly neat, the necktie (a surprisingly bright one) once and for all in place. I restrained a desire to touch the face, because I was not alone and even more because of an obscure fear that my hand might leave a mark on the dead flesh, which I thought of as being malleable.

It is a fact not surprising, perhaps, but worth remark, that no one looks out of place in a coffin; somehow the coffin itself, with its appearance of functional economy, its undisguisable appropriateness, is chiefly responsible for this. Barring the grosser accidents, and with the discreet support of the undertaker, we shall all make a good showing for a day or so after we are dead. I happened once to see a man dead whom I had never seen alive, and yet he filled his coffin completely; though he did not know it, he was still in the last stage of his existence, and if I was to see him at all, this was possibly as good a time as any. My father too, though he was my father, took his place among the dead with a kind of authority, as if, in a sense, it belonged to him—as surely in a sense it did. In the course of his long illness, I had often enough thought of him dead, but my fantasy, when it did not entirely skip over the event itself, had always placed it in a context of domestic disturbance and untidiness. I had forgotten the undertaker, who was to make him "ready."

81

Coming now upon his actual corpse in a bare room at the Riverside Memorial Chapel (a sign on the door said "Mr. Warshow," as though a man and not a corpse occupied the room), I had the feeling that I was watching him again in one of his public roles, fulfilling—and with a grace that should not, after all, have surprised me (and yet I was always surprised to discover he was graceful)—some peculiarly serious function of the "adult" world. It seemed that he was my father still, and this being dead was only a new form in which he expressed his importance. When I grow up, I too will have a funeral. . . .

I felt myself thus a participant in his dignity; but that was not what I had come for, and I tried also, in underhanded ways, to destroy it—he was not safe from me yet, nor I from him. There were flowers in the room, and I wondered with real uneasiness whether the odor of the flowers did not conceal an odor of decay: how long did it take for a corpse to begin to smell? what would it smell like? This led me to speculate also about the mysteries of embalming. What, exactly, does the embalmer do? What gross indignities, greater perhaps than the indignities of illness itself, might have gone to produce this final effect of ascetic withdrawal? Since the coffin was open only at the head, I was even frivolous enough, or unsettled enough, to wonder whether the corpse was wearing trousers: what a scandal if the Riverside Memorial Chapel were found to be trafficking in dead men's trousers! And one piece of private information seemed to assume enormous importance: the body in the coffin no longer contained a heart or lungs, these organs having been removed for laboratory examination.

The tendency of these thoughts—their "intimacy," so much like the forbidden speculations of a child (was it not, in a way, my last chance to "find out"?)—was distressing to me.

And yet, quite apart from the fact that they were unavoidable, such reflections were not really "inappropriate," even by the sensitive standards I was naturally inclined to apply to myself at the time. I took it that my father had said, in effect: no nonsense (probably he did not quite mean it, but I think that hardly matters), and it seemed to me there was somewhat more "nonsense" in the dignity surrounding his corpse—a dignity that even without my intervention could be maintained only so long as the embalmer's measures, whatever they might have been, held good—than in the one indestructible fact that it *was* a corpse. If it was a question of respect for the dead (and I suppose it was, or I should not have been troubled, or not quite in this way), I was willing enough to be "respectful"; the last thing I wished was to make any gesture of unconventionality. But I had my own rights in the matter, too; and besides, even in the simplest terms—in the terms, that is, which I should have used to defend myself if there had been anyone to accuse me—it was possible to claim that with the program the dead man had however sketchily laid down, too much "respect" might itself have been a form of "disrespect."

In practice, of course, it is a matter of some urgency to dispose of a dead body: a funeral is not supposed to raise questions, and though the particular form it finally assumes may be the result of numerous decisions, none of them is in itself fundamental; or, more accurately, it is never possible to know whether a decision is fundamental or not, but it is always easy to make it, since every decision must in any case lead to getting rid of the body. Can one properly ask, for instance, what was involved in such an element as the decision to spend two hundred and seventy-five dollars for a coffin when it would also have been possible to spend five hundred dollars or, I suppose, one hundred? The choice of a coffin was hardly important. Still, the coffin was to contain—and then be destroyed with—the body of someone who had proposed, no matter with what reservations, that his ashes should be thrown into an ash can. Was two hundred and seventy-five dollars "nonsense"? If it was, would one hundred dollars have been that much less "nonsense"? As you see, these questions are pointless; there had to be a coffin.

If nevertheless there was a problem involved somehow in all this, it is hardly to be stated so simply. Perhaps, even, "problem" is too formal a word. I mean only that every fact belonging to the process by which my father's body was disposed of seemed to require of me, not only that I should in the direct sense experience it, but also, and with a special force, that I should actively and conscientiously think about it, even "take a position," as if there were some definite "program" at stake that was every moment in danger of being misunderstood or compromised, though indeed this "danger" existed not quite on a public level but chiefly for me alone. I was anxious, in fact, that my father's death should not prove a disappointment, and I examined every detail for what it might have to offer. The "problem" was: what could I legitimately hope to find?

This question, at any rate, is not pointless; it is said so often, and with such obvious truth, that funerals are made to serve the living. And yet the issue always came back to the dead man himself; if the funeral was for us, it was still his funeral, all the more his for its appearance of having been created *ad hoc;* and the chief difficulty, for me, was to see some kind of "justice" done to an image of my father, part mine and part what I believed to be his own, that had not yet come clear and probably never would. I found myself offended, for instance, by the tendency of some of those around me to say that he had "passed away" when they meant he had died; this seemed not only an evasion on their part (though so accustomed a one that it could hardly have been effective), but also an injustice to my father, who, if he was often incapable of the right delicacies, was likewise incapable of the wrong. But I too, so militant (inwardly) to assert the corpse's absolute deadness, was to say later, with all suitable nodding of the head, that my father "would have been pleased" with his funeral—what an absurdity! My father himself, though he believed in the reality of death, put an extra clause in his will asking in effect that his children should think well of him and approve of his dispositions, and even suggesting that he loved them all equally, which was not true: the truth was only that he wanted them all to love him equally. And there were times during his illness when he became a child and allowed himself to be soothed like a child.

Indeed, I have already misrepresented him: he had not really said "no nonsense"—that was my invention to give his funeral "character." At most he had said that death changes a man into a corpse and there is no God; on the subject of death, this was as far as his commitment extended. I do not mean that it is necessarily possible to go further, but given the completeness of the statement, it was the tone that mattered: conceivably, he might actually have instructed us to throw his ashes into an ash can, and that, without altering the sense of his statement, would yet obviously have made an enormous difference. But he was not trying to be original, nor even, in fact, to make a "statement" at all; he had too much humor and was too sociable a man to place an exaggerated value on his "philosophy." The instructions contained in his will simply expressed his sense of what was fitting; after all, he was trying to fulfill certain conventions.

In its proper historical context, the complex of ideas on which these conventions rested had indeed constituted all that one could wish of a "philosophy," sufficient to engage fully those who embraced it and requiring of them some degree of honesty and even, at times, of courage. My father was born in 1876 in Russia, into that enlightenment which came so late but with such blinding clarity to the Jews of Eastern Europe; from the very little I ever heard him say about his early years, I suppose he was a materialist and a rationalist before he was sixteen, and apparently without the intense struggle which the adoption of this position involved for so many of his contemporaries. In America he was as a matter of course a Socialist and took some active part in the vicissitudes of that movement for about fifty years; shortly before his death he was involved in an abortive effort to reunite its remaining fragments. He belonged to the Socialist movement as one belongs to a certain city or a certain neighborhood: it gave him his friends and it embodied his culture—so fully, indeed, that he had little need for the more formal objects of culture, such as books, but was able to expend his considerable excess of intellectual energy in the public atmosphere of meetings and discussions, in the masculine (and indefinably "Jewish") rituals of card-playing, and in a peculiarly serious concern with the daily newspaper, which seemed always to yield more to his reading than it has ever done to mine. Even when he was young he could hardly have been anything like what we should call an "intellectual" (though in some sense he surely belonged to the "intelligentsia"), and he suffered from a sense of cultural inferiority that expressed itself sometimes as unnecessary humility and sometimes as gross philistinism; but it was always apparent that he had once lived receptively in a climate of ideas, and he continued to use his mind independently and to good effect in the areas that interested him, mainly business and politics.

In neither of these two fields of activity was he pre-eminently successful, but he enjoyed a relatively high status in both and had some of the expected rewards: an apartment on Central Park West (though in one of the less fashionable buildings), a small "country place," a month or so in Florida in the winter, posts of honor on various committees connected with the paper industry and the Socialist movement, a couple of testimonial dinners; before the end there was even a mink coat for my mother and made-to-order suits for him—this last, it seemed to me, a cultural accretion never quite assimilated. He was entitled to think of himself, if he chose, as a "success" rather than a "failure." (The New York *Times* printed his picture when he died: again a thing that "would have pleased" him, and also, as I found, important to me.) In business especially, he was conscious of having a personal weight disproportionate to the actual scale of his operations, and he took a particular though somewhat wry pride in the friendship of certain Gentile members of his industry, who for their part seemed to regard him with amused affection and a kind of astonishment, and were sometimes willing to grant him extraordinary favors in business merely because of the outrageous vehemence with which he demanded them. Indeed, to make demands was the largest part of his *modus operandi:* he affected to expose his needs with the directness and violence of a child, and insisted that they be satisfied. Since he was not a child, and since he was clever and had an acute though limited histrionic sense, this passed even with him as a form of wit; one hardly dared to imagine how much he might be in earnest. At his most outrageous, he was capable of jocularly accusing a paper-mill executive of anti-Semitism for refusing to grant him a special and entirely unwarranted reduction in price; by some trick of personality he could just save such jokes from complete vulgarity, and those schooled in a more conventional if perhaps no more polite tradition of humor often found it impossible to resist him—I sometimes thought they might even have been learning from him a quality of relaxation that he himself assuredly did not possess.

In the Socialist movement, where his rather heavy type of charm was more familiar, and the issues were after all more important, his personality necessarily took on a greater complexity. I was too young to know anything directly of his more active years; for me, "the movement" stretched back into a limitless past which, though it had in concrete ways continued into the present, was in its essence as remote from me as for instance my father's first marriage. In that past he had talked on the street corners to the unresponding masses, for whom he nevertheless retained a tender solicitude, and he had met "historical" figures like Emma Goldman and Trotsky and Debs. When I grew of an age to be a Socialist myself and asked him about these heroic progenitors, his answer expressed an easy detachment that eventually came to seem typical of his relation to the world of radicalism. He saw Emma Goldman as a "crazy" and "loose" Bohemian; Trotsky he remembered as a brilliant and egotistical man entirely incapable of respecting the opinions of others; and his great admiration of Debs was mingled with a familiar contempt because Debs had been a drunkard—in this there was surely some Jewish feeling about the "weaker" moral fiber of the *goyim*.

Toward himself also, in some contexts, he was capable of a similar detachment. My own image of politics was strongly affected by his refusal to take himself seriously as a candidate for public office; once, when he was running for Congress, he went so far as to deny his candidacy, explaining to a Republican business acquaintance that the name on the ballot belonged to "some crazy cousin of mine"—essentially, I think, this was an act not of cowardice but of mere good nature. Indeed, a certain tone of irony seems to have been characteristic of the Socialist movement as a whole; few of its adherents regarded it with absolute seriousness, and many of its peculiar virtues had their source in the expectation of failure.

When my father took me to shake hands with Norman Thomas (I imagine it was in 1928, when I was eleven), my excitement at the meeting was already tempered with an appreciation of the absurdity—though an "honorable" absurdity —of Thomas's endless running for office. Sometimes, falling naturally into the rhetoric of Socialism, my father found it possible to speak of himself as an "idealist" (it was a term of the highest praise: Debs had been an "idealist") who had devoted his life to the struggle for a better world and lived to taste the riper wisdom of disillusion. Here again, a saving element of irony partially retracted the statement, which was true only in its broadest outlines. But the note of pathos was real: like many energetic and willful men, he was extraordinarily conscious of the recalcitrance of the external world, which he was driven to be always nervously seeking to overcome, and he thought of life as a series of inevitable compromises and defeats. In his political thinking, this brought him perhaps too readily to the side of realism, but it largely protected him from that demoralizing pseudo-realism which consists of trying to play the game of power without the necessary strength, and which has been the special affliction of radical politics. On the private level, the mood of pessimism was the closest he ever came to passivity and contemplation, and it did more than anything else to soften the harsh outlines of his personality; it was perhaps the chief source of his personal dignity and charm, of his erratic and sometimes oppressive generosity, and also, ultimately, of his humor, which even at its most graceless seemed to express obscurely an acceptance of the human condition, as if his aggressions came out of some higher resignation that had taught him the uselessness of all ceremony. For me, when I felt myself laboring under the immeasurable weight of my father's presence, his pessimism became, oddly, a source of hope: perhaps, after all, my failure was only part of the general failure, and might be forgiven. For my own sake, I tried often to make pessimism the central fact of his character (as I have been doing here), and sometimes it became for me the very image of maturity; eventually, it was one of the elements that made him look "natural" in his coffin.

There is no doubt that he wanted more than he got. But how much more, and more of what? Nothing he might have said in answer could have been trusted, and perhaps nothing I can say either: the more I write, the more absurd seems this effort to be "truthful." He concealed himself behind a screen of restless, purposeful industry which did indeed bear fruit; but the sum of his activity in its very clarity never seemed to answer to the great unclear, unspoken demand which hung upon him like some faintly disturbing bodily effusion, always present but forcing itself upon one's attention only fitfully and indirectly, in brief explosions of rage and sudden acts of ruthlessness, or in the more prolonged tensions of silent emotional pressure, or even in the unpredictable impulses of his generosity. He asked everything and nothing; what he asked was never just what he wanted and he knew it, even if he did not know what he wanted. Money itself was almost too specific an object; though he was an imaginative businessman and apparently enjoyed the processes that brought him money, he made expensive mistakes and seemed to lack that final dedication which might have made him rich; money was not really interesting enough. Once he showed me some lines of poetry which he said—and doubtless believed—he had written when he was young; the lines were in fact very characteristic of him, expressing a generalized melancholy over the passage of time, but I came upon them later in the works of some nineteenth-century poet—Robert Southey, I think—and drew back in alarm at this glimpse of my father's inner confusion. What did he *not* want? Perhaps his demands were at bottom so enormous that he did not dare to define them. Or perhaps to the immigrant generation there seemed no real need of definition: simply to have come was their supreme act of definition: America was the land of opportunity-in-general. Doubtless I make too much of this; like everyone else, I suppose, my father wanted to be rich and powerful and wise and beloved, and was not lucky or talented enough. Must I re-create his fantasies? But I don't know what fantasies he might have permitted himself. He was most of the time a very reasonable man, quick to compromise.

In his personal life, too, it was impossible to know what he wanted—what, even, he would have been willing to receive —and yet quite clear that he had not got it. He had two wives and four children and two stepchildren, and we all belonged in varying degrees and each in his own way to that general disappointment which constituted, not perhaps the real content of my father's life but somehow its contrived form, the thing he was impelled to make of his experience. To my ear, at least, it seemed that he spoke of his children sometimes as if they were only elements of his fate, and his very affection had sometimes the tone of resignation; the rough gesture with which he tried to draw others to him was most often, in its deepest meaning, a gesture of attempted reconciliation: let us agree to forgive each other. The guilt of his own need meeting the guilt of the yielding unyielding world: this was his contact with those who stood near him. It was the closest possible contact and it was no contact at all. Like many Jews of his generation, he had an intense family feeling that operated with all the force of the particular and yet was fundamentally generalized and abstract; a family was necessary— I cannot imagine him not surrounded by dependents—but his relation to the family had little to do with the specific qualities of the individuals who belonged to it. He was happiest, I think, with the small children—his own first, and then

91

his grandchildren—whom he could treat as undifferentiated objects of feeling, and who had not yet failed him. In the end, the family was only one more area for the rigidly patterned operations of his personality; it satisfied his need to have others around him, but this compulsive sociability concealed a fundamental unwillingness to endure the tensions of real intimacy.

He had read the speeches of Robert Ingersoll, and perhaps heard some of them delivered, and he tried a number of times to make me see how important it was that Ingersoll had challenged God to strike him dead. (I think now that he was right: it was important.) In the course of time he changed his mind about many things, but it could never have occurred to him to question the truth of atheism: religion was the aberration of those who were unwilling to face the facts. (I owe it to my father that I myself have had little "meaningful" contact with religion.) Nor would he have been prepared to understand that quasi-religious "re-evaluation" of the liberal tradition which has occupied a number of intelligent men in recent years. He did not need to be told that life is difficult and men are imperfect; his error, if he was in error, was the opposite one: he lacked presumption.

I have said more than I intended and perhaps more than is necessary. Throw the ashes into an ash can: the idea was half brutality and half self-pity.

Several hundred people came to the funeral. I used them, as I had used the picture in the *Times*, to justify my own uncertain and somewhat shamefaced sense of my father's importance. I experienced, indeed, the warmest feelings toward all these people who had in one way or another participated in my father's existence, and I thought of them confusedly as possessing some special moral competence that after all could not fail to make the funeral a "success," whatever that might in the end turn out to mean; they became, for a short time, a kind of composite image of my father himself.

The corpse lay now at the front of a large hall, greatly diminished by its surroundings. Dignity still clung to it, but a dignity already a little questionable (was the necktie perhaps too bright?), no longer self-sufficient, like the dignity which surrounds those who submit quietly to humiliation; the corpse's existence was contained now in the eyes of those who had come to see it.

At the proper moment, instructed by one of the functionaries of the undertaking establishment, my brother and I escorted my mother past the open coffin, pausing for a few seconds to look at the corpse. When we reached our seats, the coffin had been closed. After it is closed, the coffin is no longer "appropriate" but obviously too small. It is even possible that the lid might press upon the nose of the corpse, but this does not matter.

Two friends of my father—one Socialist, one businessman —made short speeches of no particular distinction but also, it seemed to me, with a minimum of dishonesty. Then the crowd dispersed and we drove out past miles of cemeteries to the crematorium, where we sat in a shabby chapel while someone played vaguely religious music on a tiny organ; the music was offensive, but it did not seem worthwhile to make an issue of it: on the whole, the "program" had been carried out. After some papers had been signed, the coffin, with one wreath of flowers lying untidily on top of it, was pushed into an opening in a wall, and the door was closed on it. We all sat expectantly until someone came to tell us that was all.

(1951)

PART 2 AMERICAN MOVIES

The Gangster
as Tragic Hero

AMERICA, as a social and political organization, is committed to a cheerful view of life. It could not be otherwise. The sense of tragedy is a luxury of aristocratic societies, where the fate of the individual is not conceived of as having a direct and legitimate political importance, being determined by a fixed and supra-political—that is, non-controversial—moral order or fate. Modern equalitarian societies, however, whether democratic or authoritarian in their political forms, always base themselves on the claim that they are making life happier; the avowed function of the modern state, at least in its ultimate terms, is not only to regulate social relations, but also to determine the quality and the possibilities of human life in general. Happiness thus becomes the chief political issue—in a sense, the only political issue—and for that reason it can never be treated as an issue at all. If an American or a Russian is unhappy, it implies a certain reprobation of his society, and therefore, by a logic of which we can all recognize the necessity, it becomes an obligation of citizenship to be cheerful; if the authorities find it necessary, the citizen may even be compelled to make a public display of his cheerfulness on important occasions, just as he may be conscripted into the army in time of war.

Naturally, this civic responsibility rests most strongly upon the organs of mass culture. The individual citizen may still be permitted his private unhappiness so long as it does not take on political significance, the extent of this tolerance being determined by how large an area of private life the society can accommodate. But every production of mass culture is a public act and must conform with accepted notions of the public good. Nobody seriously questions the principle that it is the function of mass culture to maintain public morale, and certainly nobody in the mass audience objects to having his morale maintained.* At a time when the normal condition of the citizen is a state of anxiety, euphoria spreads over our culture like the broad smile of an idiot. In terms of attitudes towards life, there is very little difference between a "happy" movie like *Good News*, which ignores death and suffering, and a "sad" movie like *A Tree Grows in Brooklyn*, which uses death and suffering as incidents in the service of a higher optimism.

But, whatever its effectiveness as a source of consolation and a means of pressure for maintaining "positive" social attitudes, this optimism is fundamentally satisfying to no one, not even to those who would be most disoriented without its support. Even within the area of mass culture, there always exists a current of opposition, seeking to express by whatever

* In her testimony before the House Committee on Un-American Activities, Mrs. Leila Rogers said that the movie *None But the Lonely Heart* was un-American because it was gloomy. Like so much else that was said during the unhappy investigation of Hollywood, this statement was at once stupid and illuminating. One knew immediately what Mrs. Rogers was talking about; she had simply been insensitive enough to carry her philistinism to its conclusion.

means are available to it that sense of desperation and inevitable failure which optimism itself helps to create. Most often, this opposition is confined to rudimentary or semi-literate forms: in mob politics and journalism, for example, or in certain kinds of religious enthusiasm. When it does enter the field of art, it is likely to be disguised or attenuated: in an unspecific form of expression like jazz, in the basically harmless nihilism of the Marx Brothers, in the continually reasserted strain of hopelessness that often seems to be the real meaning of the soap opera. The gangster film is remarkable in that it fills the need for disguise (though not sufficiently to avoid arousing uneasiness) without requiring any serious distortion. From its beginnings, it has been a consistent and astonishingly complete presentation of the modern sense of tragedy.*

In its initial character, the gangster film is simply one example of the movies' constant tendency to create fixed dramatic patterns that can be repeated indefinitely with a reasonable expectation of profit. One gangster film follows another as one musical or one Western follows another. But this rigidity is not necessarily opposed to the requirements of art. There have been very successful types of art in the past which developed such specific and detailed conventions as almost to make individual examples of the type interchangeable. This is true, for example, of Elizabethan revenge tragedy and Restoration comedy.

For such a type to be successful means that its conventions

---

* Efforts have been made from time to time to bring the gangster film into line with the prevailing optimism and social constructiveness of our culture; *Kiss of Death* is a recent example. These efforts are usually unsuccessful; the reasons for their lack of success are interesting in themselves, but I shall not be able to discuss them here.

have imposed themselves upon the general consciousness and become the accepted vehicles of a particular set of attitudes and a particular aesthetic effect. One goes to any individual example of the type with very definite expectations, and originality is to be welcomed only in the degree that it intensifies the expected experience without fundamentally altering it. Moreover, the relationship between the conventions which go to make up such a type and the real experience of its audience or the real facts of whatever situation it pretends to describe is of only secondary importance and does not determine its aesthetic force. It is only in an ultimate sense that the type appeals to its audience's experience of reality; much more immediately, it appeals to previous experience of the type itself: it creates its own field of reference.

Thus the importance of the gangster film, and the nature and intensity of its emotional and aesthetic impact, cannot be measured in terms of the place of the gangster himself or the importance of the problem of crime in American life. Those European movie-goers who think there is a gangster on every corner in New York are certainly deceived, but defenders of the "positive" side of American culture are equally deceived if they think it relevant to point out that most Americans have never seen a gangster. What matters is that the experience of the gangster *as an experience of art* is universal to Americans. There is almost nothing we understand better or react to more readily or with quicker intelligence. The Western film, though it seems never to diminish in popularity, is for most of us no more than the folklore of the past, familiar and understandable only because it has been repeated so often. The gangster film comes much closer. In ways that we do not easily or willingly define, the gangster speaks for us, expressing that part of the American psyche which rejects the qualities and the demands of modern life, which rejects "Americanism" itself.

The gangster is the man of the city, with the city's language and knowledge, with its queer and dishonest skills and its terrible daring, carrying his life in his hands like a placard, like a club. For everyone else, there is at least the theoretical possibility of another world—in that happier American culture which the gangster denies, the city does not really exist; it is only a more crowded and more brightly lit country—but for the gangster there is only the city; he must inhabit it in order to personify it: not the real city, but that dangerous and sad city of the imagination which is so much more important, which is the modern world. And the gangster—though there are real gangsters—is also, and primarily, a creature of the imagination. The real city, one might say, produces only criminals; the imaginary city produces the gangster: he is what we want to be and what we are afraid we may become.

Thrown into the crowd without background or advantages, with only those ambiguous skills which the rest of us—the real people of the real city—can only pretend to have, the gangster is required to make his way, to make his life and impose it on others. Usually, when we come upon him, he has already made his choice or the choice has already been made for him, it doesn't matter which: we are not permitted to ask whether at some point he could have chosen to be something else than what he is.

The gangster's activity is actually a form of rational enterprise, involving fairly definite goals and various techniques for achieving them. But this rationality is usually no more than a vague background; we know, perhaps, that the gangster sells liquor or that he operates a numbers racket; often we are not given even that much information. So his activity becomes a kind of pure criminality: he hurts people. Certainly our response to the gangster film is most consistently and most universally a response to sadism; we gain the double satisfaction of participating vicariously in the gangster's

101

sadism and then seeing it turned against the gangster himself.

But on another level the quality of irrational brutality and the quality of rational enterprise become one. Since we do not see the rational and routine aspects of the gangster's behavior, the practice of brutality—the quality of unmixed criminality—becomes the totality of his career. At the same time, we are always conscious that the whole meaning of this career is a drive for success: the typical gangster film presents a steady upward progress followed by a very precipitate fall. Thus brutality itself becomes at once the means to success and the content of success—a success that is defined in its most general terms, not as accomplishment or specific gain, but simply as the unlimited possibility of aggression. (In the same way, film presentations of businessmen tend to make it appear that they achieve their success by talking on the telephone and holding conferences and that success *is* talking on the telephone and holding conferences.)

From this point of view, the initial contact between the film and its audience is an agreed conception of human life: that man is a being with the possibilities of success or failure. This principle, too, belongs to the city; one must emerge from the crowd or else one is nothing. On that basis the necessity of the action is established, and it progresses by inalterable paths to the point where the gangster lies dead and the principle has been modified: there is really only one possibility —failure. The final meaning of the city is anonymity and death.

In the opening scene of *Scarface*, we are shown a successful man; we know he is successful because he has just given a party of opulent proportions and because he is called Big Louie. Through some monstrous lack of caution, he permits himself to be alone for a few moments. We understand from this immediately that he is about to be killed. No conven-

102

tion of the gangster film is more strongly established than this: it is dangerous to be alone. And yet the very conditions of success make it impossible not to be alone, for success is always the establishment of an *individual* pre-eminence that must be imposed on others, in whom it automatically arouses hatred; the successful man is an outlaw. The gangster's whole life is an effort to assert himself as an individual, to draw himself out of the crowd, and he always dies *because* he is an individual; the final bullet thrusts him back, makes him, after all, a failure. "Mother of God," says the dying Little Caesar, "is this the end of Rico?"—speaking of himself thus in the third person because what has been brought low is not the undifferentiated *man*, but the individual with a name, the gangster, the success; even to himself he is a creature of the imagination. (T. S. Eliot has pointed out that a number of Shakespeare's tragic heroes have this trick of looking at themselves dramatically; their true identity, the thing that is destroyed when they die, is something outside themselves—not a man, but a style of life, a kind of meaning.)

At bottom, the gangster is doomed because he is under the obligation to succeed, not because the means he employs are unlawful. In the deeper layers of the modern consciousness, *all* means are unlawful, every attempt to succeed is an act of aggression, leaving one alone and guilty and defenseless among enemies: one is *punished* for success. This is our intolerable dilemma: that failure is a kind of death and success is evil and dangerous, is—ultimately—impossible. The effect of the gangster film is to embody this dilemma in the person of the gangster and resolve it by his death. The dilemma is resolved because it is *his* death, not ours. We are safe; for the moment, we can acquiesce in our failure, we can choose to fail.

(1948)

Movie Chronicle:
The Westerner

They that have power to hurt and will do none,
That do not do the thing they most do show,
Who, moving others, are themselves as stone,
Unmoved, cold, and to temptation slow;
They rightly do inherit heaven's graces,
And husband nature's riches from expense;
They are the lords and owners of their faces,
Others but stewards of their excellence.

THE TWO most successful creations of American movies are the gangster and the Westerner: men with guns. Guns as physical objects, and the postures associated with their use, form the visual and emotional center of both types of films. I suppose this reflects the importance of guns in the fantasy life of Americans; but that is a less illuminating point than it appears to be.

The gangster movie, which no longer exists in its "classical" form, is a story of enterprise and success ending in precipitate failure. Success is conceived as an increasing power to work injury, it belongs to the city, and it is of course a form of evil (though the gangster's death, presented usually as "pun-

105

ishment," is perceived simply as defeat). The peculiarity of the gangster is his unceasing, nervous activity. The exact nature of his enterprises may remain vague, but his commitment to enterprise is always clear, and all the more clear because he operates outside the field of utility. He is without culture, without manners, without leisure, or at any rate his leisure is likely to be spent in debauchery so compulsively aggressive as to seem only another aspect of his "work." But he is graceful, moving like a dancer among the crowded dangers of the city.

Like other tycoons, the gangster is crude in conceiving his ends but by no means inarticulate; on the contrary, he is usually expansive and noisy (the introspective gangster is a fairly recent development), and can state definitely what he wants: to take over the North Side, to own a hundred suits, to be Number One. But new "frontiers" will present themselves infinitely, and by a rigid convention it is understood that as soon as he wishes to rest on his gains, he is on the way to destruction.

The gangster is lonely and melancholy, and can give the impression of a profound worldly wisdom. He appeals most to adolescents with their impatience and their feeling of being outsiders, but more generally he appeals to that side of all of us which refuses to believe in the "normal" possibilities of happiness and achievement; the gangster is the "no" to that great American "yes" which is stamped so big over our official culture and yet has so little to do with the way we really feel about our lives. But the gangster's loneliness and melancholy are not "authentic"; like everything else that belongs to him, they are not honestly come by: he is lonely and melancholy not because life ultimately demands such feelings but because he has put himself in a position where everybody wants to kill him and eventually somebody will. He is wide open and defenseless, incomplete because unable to accept any limits or come to terms with his own nature, fearful, loveless. And the story of his career is a nightmare inversion of the values of ambition and opportunity. From the window of Scarface's bulletproof apartment can be seen an electric sign proclaiming: "The World Is Yours," and, if I remember, this sign is the last thing we see after Scarface lies dead in the street. In the end it is the gangster's weakness as much as his power and freedom that appeals to us; the world is not ours, but it is not his either, and in his death he "pays" for our fantasies, releasing us momentarily both from the concept of success, which he denies by caricaturing it, and from the need to succeed, which he shows to be dangerous.

The Western hero, by contrast, is a figure of repose. He resembles the gangster in being lonely and to some degree melancholy. But his melancholy comes from the "simple" recognition that life is unavoidably serious, not from the disproportions of his own temperament. And his loneliness is organic, not imposed on him by his situation but belonging to him intimately and testifying to his completeness. The gangster must reject others violently or draw them violently to him. The Westerner is not thus compelled to seek love; he is prepared to accept it, perhaps, but he never asks of it more than it can give, and we see him constantly in situations where love is at best an irrelevance. If there is a woman he loves, she is usually unable to understand his motives; she is against killing and being killed, and he finds it impossible to explain to her that there is no point in being "against" these things: they belong to his world.

Very often this woman is from the East and her failure to understand represents a clash of cultures. In the American mind, refinement, virtue, civilization, Christianity itself, are seen as feminine, and therefore women are often portrayed as possessing some kind of deeper wisdom, while the men, for all their apparent self-assurance, are fundamentally childish.

107

But the West, lacking the graces of civilization, is the place "where men are men"; in Western movies, men have the deeper wisdom and the women are children. Those women in the Western movies who share the hero's understanding of life are prostitutes (or, as they are usually presented, barroom entertainers)—women, that is, who have come to understand in the most practical way how love can be an irrelevance, and therefore "fallen" women. The gangster, too, associates with prostitutes, but for him the important things about a prostitute are her passive availability and her costliness: she is part of his winnings. In Western movies, the important thing about a prostitute is her quasi-masculine independence: nobody owns her, nothing has to be explained to her, and she is not, like a virtuous woman, a "value" that demands to be protected. When the Westerner leaves the prostitute for a virtuous woman—for love—he is in fact forsaking a way of life, though the point of the choice is often obscured by having the prostitute killed by getting into the line of fire.

The Westerner is *par excellence* a man of leisure. Even when he wears the badge of a marshal or, more rarely, owns a ranch, he appears to be unemployed. We see him standing at a bar, or playing poker—a game which expresses perfectly his talent for remaining relaxed in the midst of tension—or perhaps camping out on the plains on some extraordinary errand. If he does own a ranch, it is in the background; we are not actually aware that he owns anything except his horse, his guns, and the one worn suit of clothing which is likely to remain unchanged all through the movie. It comes as a surprise to see him take money from his pocket or an extra shirt from his saddlebags. As a rule we do not even know where he sleeps at night and don't think of asking. Yet it never occurs to us that he is a poor man; there is no poverty in Western movies, and really no wealth either: those great cattle domains and shipments of gold which figure so largely in the plots are moral and not material quantities, not the objects of contention but only its occasion. Possessions too are irrelevant.

Employment of some kind—usually unproductive—is always open to the Westerner, but when he accepts it, it is not because he needs to make a living, much less from any idea of "getting ahead." Where could he want to "get ahead" to? By the time we see him, he is already "there": he can ride a horse faultlessly, keep his countenance in the face of death, and draw his gun a little faster and shoot it a little straighter than anyone he is likely to meet. These are sharply defined acquirements, giving to the figure of the Westerner an apparent moral clarity which corresponds to the clarity of his physical image against his bare landscape; initially, at any rate, the Western movie presents itself as being without mystery, its whole universe comprehended in what we see on the screen.

Much of this apparent simplicity arises directly from those "cinematic" elements which have long been understood to give the Western theme its special appropriateness for the movies: the wide expanses of land, the free movement of men on horses. As guns constitute the visible moral center of the Western movie, suggesting continually the possibility of violence, so land and horses represent the movie's material basis, its sphere of action. But the land and the horses have also a moral significance: the physical freedom they represent belongs to the moral "openness" of the West—corresponding to the fact that guns are carried where they can be seen. (And, as we shall see, the character of land and horses changes as the Western film becomes more complex.)

The gangster's world is less open, and his arts not so easily identifiable as the Westerner's. Perhaps he too can keep his countenance, but the mask he wears is really no mask: its purpose is precisely to make evident the fact that he desperately wants to "get ahead" and will stop at nothing. Where the Westerner imposes himself by the appearance of unshakable control, the gangster's pre-eminence lies in the suggestion that he may at any moment lose control; his strength is not in being able to shoot faster or straighter than others, but in being more willing to shoot. "Do it first," says Scarface expounding his mode of operation, "and keep on doing it!" With the Westerner, it is a crucial point of honor *not* to "do it first"; his gun remains in its holster until the moment of combat.

There is no suggestion, however, that he draws the gun reluctantly. The Westerner could not fulfill himself if the moment did not finally come when he can shoot his enemy down. But because that moment is so thoroughly the expression of his being, it must be kept pure. He will not violate the accepted forms of combat though by doing so he could save a city. And he can wait. "When you call me that—smile!"—the villain smiles weakly, soon he is laughing with horrible joviality, and the crisis is past. But it is allowed to pass because it must come again: sooner or later Trampas will "make his play," and the Virginian will be ready for him.

What does the Westerner fight for? We know he is on the side of justice and order, and of course it can be said he fights for these things. But such broad aims never correspond exactly to his real motives; they only offer him his opportunity. The Westerner himself, when an explanation is asked of him (usually by a woman), is likely to say that he does what he "has to do." If justice and order did not continually demand his protection, he would be without a calling. Indeed, we come upon him often in just that situation, as the reign of law settles over the West and he is forced to see that his day is over; those are the pictures which end with his death or with his departure for some more remote frontier. What he defends, at bottom, is the purity of his own image—in fact his honor. This is what makes him invulnerable. When the gangster is killed, his whole life is shown to have been a mistake, but the image the Westerner seeks to maintain can be presented as clearly in defeat as in victory: he fights not for advantage and not for the right, but to state what he is, and he must live in a world which permits that statement. The Westerner is the last gentleman, and the movies which over and over again tell his story are probably the last art form in which the concept of honor retains its strength.

Of course I do not mean to say that ideas of virtue and justice and courage have gone out of culture. Honor is more than these things: it is a style, concerned with harmonious appearances as much as with desirable consequences, and tending therefore toward the denial of life in favor of art. "Who hath it? he that died o' Wednesday." On the whole, a world that leans to Falstaff's view is a more civilized and even, finally, a more graceful world. It is just the march of civilization that forces the Westerner to move on; and if we actually had to confront the question it might turn out that the woman who refuses to understand him is right as often as she is wrong. But we do not confront the question. Where the Westerner lives it is always about 1870—not the real 1870, either, or the real West—and he is killed or goes away when his position becomes problematical. The fact that he continues to hold our attention is evidence enough that, in his proper frame, he presents an image of personal nobility that is still real for us.

Clearly, this image easily becomes ridiculous: we need only look at William S. Hart or Tom Mix, who in the wooden absoluteness of their virtue represented little that an adult could take seriously; and doubtless such figures as Gene Autry or Roy Rogers are no better, though I confess I have seen none of their movies. Some film enthusiasts claim to find in the early, unsophisticated Westerns a "cinematic purity" that has since been lost; this idea is as valid, and finally as misleading,

111

as T. S. Eliot's statement that *Everyman* is the only play in English that stays within the limitations of art. The truth is that the Westerner comes into the field of serious art only when his moral code, without ceasing to be compelling, is seen also to be imperfect. The Westerner at his best exhibits a moral ambiguity which darkens his image and saves him from absurdity; this ambiguity arises from the fact that, whatever his justifications, he is a killer of men.

In *The Virginian*, which is an archetypal Western movie as *Scarface* or *Little Caesar* are archetypal gangster movies, there is a lynching in which the hero (Gary Cooper), as leader of a posse, must supervise the hanging of his best friend for stealing cattle. With the growth of American "social consciousness," it is no longer possible to present a lynching in the movies unless the point is the illegality and injustice of the lynching itself; *The Ox-Bow Incident*, made in 1943, explicitly puts forward the newer point of view and can be regarded as a kind of "anti-Western." But in 1929, when *The Virginian* was made, the present inhibition about lynching was not yet in force; the justice, and therefore the necessity, of the hanging is never questioned—except by the schoolteacher from the East, whose refusal to understand serves as usual to set forth more sharply the deeper seriousness of the West. The Virginian is thus in a tragic dilemma where one moral absolute conflicts with another and the choice of either must leave a moral stain. If he had chosen to save his friend, he would have violated the image of himself that he had made essential to his existence, and the movie would have had to end with his death, for only by his death could the image have been restored. Having chosen instead to sacrifice his friend to the higher demands of the "code"— the only choice worthy of him, as even the friend understands —he is none the less stained by the killing, but what is needed now to set accounts straight is not his death but the death of the villain Trampas, the leader of the cattle thieves, who had escaped the posse and abandoned the Virginian's friend to his fate. Again the woman intervenes: Why must there be *more* killing? If the hero really loved her, he would leave town, refusing Trampas's challenge. What good will it be if Trampas should kill him? But the Virginian does once more what he "has to do," and in avenging his friend's death wipes out the stain on his own honor. Yet his victory cannot be complete: no death can be paid for and no stain truly wiped out; the movie is still a tragedy, for though the hero escapes with his life, he has been forced to confront the ultimate limits of his moral ideas.

This mature sense of limitation and unavoidable guilt is what gives the Westerner a "right" to his melancholy. It is true that the gangster's story is also a tragedy—in certain formal ways more clearly a tragedy than the Westerner's— but it is a romantic tragedy, based on a hero whose defeat springs with almost mechanical inevitability from the outrageous presumption of his demands: the gangster is *bound* to go on until he is killed. The Westerner is a more classical figure, self-contained and limited to begin with, seeking not to extend his dominion but only to assert his personal value, and his tragedy lies in the fact that even this circumscribed demand cannot be fully realized. Since the Westerner is not a murderer but (most of the time) a man of virtue, and since he is always prepared for defeat, he retains his inner invulnerability and his story need not end with his death (and usually does not); but what we finally respond to is not his victory but his defeat.

Up to a point, it is plain that the deeper seriousness of the good Western films comes from the introduction of a realism, both physical and psychological, that was missing with Tom Mix and William S. Hart. As lines of age have come into Gary

113

Cooper's face since *The Virginian,* so the outlines of the Western movie in general have become less smooth, its background more drab. The sun still beats upon the town, but the camera is likely now to take advantage of this illumination to seek out more closely the shabbiness of buildings and furniture, the loose, worn hang of clothing, the wrinkles and dirt of the faces. Once it has been discovered that the true theme of the Western movie is not the freedom and expansiveness of frontier life, but its limitations, its material bareness, the pressures of obligation, then even the landscape itself ceases to be quite the arena of free movement it once was, but becomes instead a great empty waste, cutting down more often than it exaggerates the stature of the horseman who rides across it. We are more likely now to see the Westerner struggling against the obstacles of the physical world (as in the wonderful scenes on the desert and among the rocks in *The Last Posse*) than carelessly surmounting them. Even the horses, no longer the "friends" of man or the inspired chargers of knight-errantry, have lost much of the moral significance that once seemed to belong to them in their careering across the screen. It seems to me the horses grow tired and stumble more often than they did, and that we see them less frequently at the gallop.

In *The Gunfighter,* a remarkable film of a couple of years ago, the landscape has virtually disappeared. Most of the action takes place indoors, in a cheerless saloon where a tired "bad man" (Gregory Peck) contemplates the waste of his life, to be senselessly killed at the end by a vicious youngster setting off on the same futile path. The movie is done in cold, quiet tones of gray, and every object in it—faces, clothing, a table, the hero's heavy mustache—is given an air of uncompromising authenticity, suggesting those dim photographs of the nineteenth-century West in which Wyatt Earp, say, turns out to be a blank untidy figure posing awkwardly before some uninteresting building. This "authenticity," to be sure, is only aesthetic; the chief fact about nineteenth-century photographs, to my eyes at any rate, is how stonily they refuse to yield up the truth. But that limitation is just what is needed: by preserving some hint of the rigidity of archaic photography (only in tone and décor, never in composition), *The Gunfighter* can permit us to feel that we are looking at a more "real" West than the one the movies have accustomed us to—harder, duller, less "romantic"—and yet without forcing us outside the boundaries which give the Western movie its validity.

We come upon the hero of *The Gunfighter* at the end of a career in which he has never upheld justice and order, and has been at times, apparently, an actual criminal; in this case, it is clear that the hero has been wrong and the woman who has rejected his way of life has been right. He is thus without any of the larger justifications, and knows himself a ruined man. There can be no question of his "redeeming" himself in any socially constructive way. He is too much the victim of his own reputation to turn marshal as one of his old friends has done, and he is not offered the sentimental solution of a chance to give up his life for some good end; the whole point is that he exists outside the field of social value. Indeed, if we were once allowed to see him in the days of his "success," he might become a figure like the gangster, for his career has been aggressively "anti-social" and the practical problem he faces is the gangster's problem: there will always be somebody trying to kill him. Yet it is obviously absurd to speak of him as "anti-social," not only because we do not see him acting as a criminal, but more fundamentally because we do not see his milieu as a society. Of course it has its "social problems" and a kind of static history: civilization is always just at the point of driving out the old freedom; there are women and children to represent the possibility of a settled

115

life; and there is the marshal, a bad man turned good, determined to keep at least his area of jurisdiction at peace. But these elements are not, in fact, a part of the film's "realism," even though they come out of the real history of the West; they belong to the conventions of the form, to that accepted framework which makes the film possible in the first place, and they exist not to provide a standard by which the gunfighter can be judged, but only to set him off. The true "civilization" of the Western movie is always embodied in an individual, good or bad is more a matter of personal bearing than of social consequences, and the conflict of good and bad is a duel between two men. Deeply troubled and obviously doomed, the gunfighter is the Western hero still, perhaps all the more because his value must express itself entirely in his own being—in his presence, the way he holds our eyes—and in contradiction to the facts. No matter what he has done, he *looks* right, and he remains invulnerable because, without acknowledging anyone else's right to judge him, he has judged his own failure and has already assimilated it, understanding —as no one else understands except the marshal and the barroom girl—that he can do nothing but play out the drama of the gun fight again and again until the time comes when it will be he who gets killed. What "redeems" him is that he no longer believes in this drama and nevertheless will continue to play his role perfectly: the pattern is all.

The proper function of realism in the Western movie can only be to deepen the lines of that pattern. It is an art form for connoisseurs, where the spectator derives his pleasure from the appreciation of minor variations within the working out of a pre-established order. One does not want too much novelty: it comes as a shock, for instance, when the hero is made to operate without a gun, as has been done in several pictures (e.g., *Destry Rides Again*), and our uneasiness is allayed only when he is finally compelled to put his "pacifism"

116

aside. If the hero can be shown to be troubled, complex, fallible, even eccentric, or the villain given some psychological taint or, better, some evocative physical mannerism, to shade the colors of his villainy, that is all to the good. Indeed, that kind of variation is absolutely necessary to keep the type from becoming sterile; we do not want to see the same movie over and over again, only the same form. But when the impulse toward realism is extended into a "reinterpretation" of the West as a developed society, drawing our eyes away from the hero if only to the extent of showing him as the one dominant figure in a complex social order, then the pattern is broken and the West itself begins to be uninteresting. If the "social problems" of the frontier are to be the movie's chief concern, there is no longer any point in re-examining these problems twenty times a year; they have been solved, and the people for whom they once were real are dead. Moreover, the hero himself, still the film's central figure, now tends to become its one unassimilable element, since he is the most "unreal."

The Ox-Bow Incident, by denying the convention of the lynching, presents us with a modern "social drama" and evokes a corresponding response, but in doing so it almost makes the Western setting irrelevant, a mere backdrop of beautiful scenery. (It is significant that *The Ox-Bow Incident* has no hero; a hero would have to stop the lynching or be killed in trying to stop it, and then the "problem" of lynching would no longer be central.) Even in *The Gunfighter* the women and children are a little too much in evidence, threatening constantly to become a real focus of concern instead of simply part of the given framework; and the young tough who kills the hero has too much the air of juvenile criminality: the hero himself could never have been like that, and the idea of a cycle being repeated therefore loses its sharpness. But the most striking example of the con-

117

fusion created by a too conscientious "social" realism is in the celebrated *High Noon*.

In *High Noon* we find Gary Cooper still the upholder of order that he was in *The Virginian*, but twenty-four years older, stooped, slower moving, awkward, his face lined, the flesh sagging, a less beautiful and weaker figure, but with the suggestion of greater depth that belongs almost automatically to age. Like the hero of *The Gunfighter*, he no longer has to assert his character and is no longer interested in the drama of combat; it is hard to imagine that he might once have been so youthful as to say, "When you call me that— smile!" In fact, when we come upon him he is hanging up his guns and his marshal's badge in order to begin a new, peaceful life with his bride, who is a Quaker. But then the news comes that a man he had sent to prison has been pardoned and will get to town on the noon train; three friends of this man have come to wait for him at the station, and when the freed convict arrives the four of them will come to kill the marshal. He is thus trapped; the bride will object, the hero himself will waver much more than he would have done twenty-four years ago, but in the end he will play out the drama because it is what he "has to do." All this belongs to the established form (there is even the "fallen woman" who understands the marshal's position as his wife does not). Leaving aside the crudity of building up suspense by means of the clock, the actual Western drama of *High Noon* is well handled and forms a good companion piece to *The Virginian*, showing in both conception and technique the ways in which the Western movie has naturally developed.

But there is a second drama along with the first. As the marshal sets out to find deputies to help him deal with the four gunmen, we are taken through the various social strata of the town, each group in turn refusing its assistance out of cowardice, malice, irresponsibility, or venality. With this we are in the field of "social drama"—of a very low order, incidentally, altogether unconvincing and displaying a vulgar anti-populism that has marred some other movies of Stanley Kramer's. But the falsity of the "social drama" is less important than the fact that it does not belong in the movie to begin with. The technical problem was to make it necessary for the marshal to face his enemies alone; to explain *why* the other townspeople are not at his side is to raise a question which does not exist in the proper frame of the Western movie, where the hero is "naturally" alone and it is only necessary to contrive the physical absence of those who might be his allies, if any contrivance is needed at all. In addition, though the hero of *High Noon* proves himself a better man than all around him, the actual effect of this contrast is to lessen his stature: he becomes only a rejected man of virtue. In our final glimpse of him, as he rides away through the town where he has spent most of his life without really imposing himself on it, he is a pathetic rather than a tragic figure. And his departure has another meaning as well; the "social drama" has no place for him.

But there is also a different way of violating the Western form. This is to yield entirely to its static quality as legend and to the "cinematic" temptations of its landscape, the horses, the quiet men. John Ford's famous *Stagecoach* (1938) had much of this unhappy preoccupation with style, and the same director's *My Darling Clementine* (1946), a soft and beautiful movie about Wyatt Earp, goes further along the same path, offering indeed a superficial accuracy of historical reconstruction, but so loving in execution as to destroy the outlines of the Western legend, assimilating it to the more sentimental legend of rural America and making the hero a more dangerous Mr. Deeds. (*Powder River*, a recent "routine" Western shamelessly copied from *My Darling Clementine*, is in most ways a better film; lacking the benefit

119

of a serious director, it is necessarily more concerned with drama than with style.)

The highest expression of this aestheticizing tendency is in George Stevens' *Shane*, where the legend of the West is virtually reduced to its essentials and then fixed in the dreamy clarity of a fairy tale. There never was so broad and bare and lovely a landscape as Stevens puts before us, or so unimaginably comfortless a "town" as the little group of buildings on the prairie to which the settlers must come for their supplies and to buy a drink. The mere physical progress of the film, following the style of *A Place in the Sun*, is so deliberately graceful that everything seems to be happening at the bottom of a clear lake. The hero (Alan Ladd) is hardly a man at all, but something like the Spirit of the West, beautiful in fringed buckskins. He emerges mysteriously from the plains, breathing sweetness and a melancholy which is no longer simply the Westerner's natural response to experience but has taken on spirituality; and when he has accomplished his mission, meeting and destroying in the black figure of Jack Palance a Spirit of Evil just as metaphysical as his own embodiment of virtue, he fades away again into the more distant West, a man whose "day is over," leaving behind the wondering little boy who might have imagined the whole story. The choice of Alan Ladd to play the leading role is alone an indication of this film's tendency. Actors like Gary Cooper or Gregory Peck are in themselves, as material objects, "realistic," seeming to bear in their bodies and their faces mortality, limitation, the knowledge of good and evil. Ladd is a more "aesthetic" object, with some of the "universality" of a piece of sculpture; his special quality is in his physical smoothness and serenity, unworldly and yet not innocent, but suggesting that no experience can really touch him. Stevens has tried to freeze the Western myth once and for all in the immobility of Alan Ladd's countenance. If

Shane were "right," and fully successful, it might be possible to say there was no point in making any more Western movies; once the hero is apotheosized, variation and development are closed off.

Shane is not "right," but it is still true that the possibilities of fruitful variation in the Western movie are limited. The form can keep its freshness through endless repetitions only because of the special character of the film medium, where the physical difference between one object and another—above all, between one actor and another—is of such enormous importance, serving the function that is served by the variety of language in the perpetuation of literary types. In this sense, the "vocabulary" of films is much larger than that of literature and falls more readily into pleasing and significant arrangements. (That may explain why the middle levels of excellence are more easily reached in the movies than in literary forms, and perhaps also why the status of the movies as art is constantly being called into question.) But the advantage of this almost automatic particularity belongs to all films alike. Why does the Western movie especially have such a hold on our imagination?

Chiefly, I think, because it offers a serious orientation to the problem of violence such as can be found almost nowhere else in our culture. One of the well-known peculiarities of modern civilized opinion is its refusal to acknowledge the value of violence. This refusal is a virtue, but like many virtues it involves a certain willful blindness and it encourages hypocrisy. We train ourselves to be shocked or bored by cultural images of violence, and our very concept of heroism tends to be a passive one: we are less drawn to the brave young men who kill large numbers of our enemies than to the heroic prisoners who endure torture without capitulating. In art, though we may still be able to understand and

121

participate in the values of the Iliad, a modern writer like Ernest Hemingway we find somewhat embarrassing: there is no doubt that he stirs us, but we cannot help recognizing also that he is a little childish. And in the criticism of popular culture, where the educated observer is usually under the illusion that he has nothing at stake, the presence of images of violence is often assumed to be in itself a sufficient ground for condemnation.

These attitudes, however, have not reduced the element of violence in our culture but, if anything, have helped to free it from moral control by letting it take on the aura of "emancipation." The celebration of acts of violence is left more and more to the irresponsible: on the higher cultural levels to writers like Céline, and lower down to Mickey Spillane or Horace McCoy, or to the comic books, television, and the movies. The gangster movie, with its numerous variations, belongs to this cultural "underground" which sets forth the attractions of violence in the face of all our higher social attitudes. It is a more "modern" genre than the Western, perhaps even more profound, because it confronts industrial society on its own ground—the city—and because, like much of our advanced art, it gains its effects by a gross insistence on its own narrow logic. But it is anti-social, resting on fantasies of irresponsible freedom. If we are brought finally to acquiesce in the denial of these fantasies, it is only because they have been shown to be dangerous, not because they have given way to a better vision of behavior.*

* I am not concerned here with the actual social consequences of gangster movies, though I suspect they could not have been so pernicious as they were thought to be. Some of the compromises introduced to avoid the supposed bad effects of the old gangster movies may be, if anything, more dangerous, for the sadistic violence that once belonged only

In war movies, to be sure, it is possible to present the uses of violence within a framework of responsibility. But there is the disadvantage that modern war is a co-operative enterprise; its violence is largely impersonal, and heroism belongs to the group more than to the individual. The hero of a war movie is most often simply a leader, and his superiority is likely to be expressed in a denial of the heroic: you are not supposed to be brave, you are supposed to get the job done and stay alive (this too, of course, is a kind of heroic posture, but a new—and "practical"—one). At its best, the war movie may represent a more civilized point of view than the Western, and if it were not continually marred by ideological sentimentality we might hope to find it developing into a higher form of drama. But it cannot supply the values we seek in the Western.

Those values are in the image of a single man who wears a gun on his thigh. The gun tells us that he lives in a world of violence, and even that he "believes in violence." But the drama is one of self-restraint: the moment of violence must come in its own time and according to its special laws, or else it is valueless. There is little cruelty in Western movies, and little sentimentality; our eyes are not focused on the sufferings of the defeated but on the deportment of the hero. Really, it is not violence at all which is the "point" of the Western movie, but a certain image of man, a style, which expresses itself most clearly in violence. Watch a child with his toy guns and you will see: what most interests him is not (as we so much fear) the fantasy of hurting others, but to work out how a man might look when he shoots or is shot. A hero is one who looks like a hero.

---

to the gangster is now commonly enlisted on the side of the law and thus goes undefeated, allowing us (if we wish) to find in the movies a sort of "confirmation" of our fantasies.

Whatever the limitations of such an idea in experience, it has always been valid in art, and has a special validity in an art where appearances are everything. The Western hero is necessarily an archaic figure; we do not really believe in him and would not have him step out of his rigidly conventionalized background. But his archaicism does not take away from his power; on the contrary, it adds to it by keeping him just a little beyond the reach both of common sense and of absolutized emotion, the two usual impulses of our art. And he has, after all, his own kind of relevance. He is there to remind us of the possibility of style in an age which has put on itself the burden of pretending that style has no meaning, and, in the midst of our anxieties over the problem of violence, to suggest that even in killing or being killed we are not freed from the necessity of establishing satisfactory modes of behavior. Above all, the movies in which the Westerner plays out his role preserve for us the pleasures of a complete and self-contained drama—and one which still effortlessly crosses the boundaries which divide our culture—in a time when other, more consciously serious art forms are increasingly complex, uncertain, and ill-defined.

(*1954*)

The Anatomy
of Falsehood

THE BEST YEARS OF OUR LIVES presents an optimistic picture of American life, and of postwar America in particular, making suitable reference to such accepted symbols as democracy, the American character, the American way of life, etc., with the object of impressing the spectator with the dignity and meaningfulness of "typical" American experience (his own experience) and making him feel a certain confidence that the problems of modern life (his own problems) can be solved by the operation of "simple" and "American" virtues, while at the same time—though more indirectly—he is given a sufficient sense of the gravity of those problems to prepare him, if possible, to meet his "responsibilities"—which, so far as they are defined at all, seem to consist of the obligations to be patient and work hard (not to ask too much of life) and to face the future cheerfully.

The ideas on which such a movie rests are accepted readily enough as public symbols—that is, as accustomed stimuli calling for certain orthodox responses of no great intensity—but they will not bear serious examination and they cannot be made to emerge forcefully from any true presentation of reality. Since it is precisely the function of a "serious" movie to reaffirm and intensify these ideas by giving them concrete expression, the problem of technique is to embody them in a structure of character, plot, and background that is so real in detail as to be accepted, more or less continuously and unreservedly, as truthful, and so complete and self-contained as to engage the spectator's full attention and discourage any tendency to look beyond the fixed boundaries. The degree of artistry displayed in solving this problem seems to be what determines whether such a movie is successful with the educated and discriminating audience, for that audience (generally speaking) is distinguished not by any real unwillingness to accept the basic Hollywood myths—which are simply the basic American myths—but merely by a distaste for the cruder dramatic and ideological conventions ordinarily used to express them.

Thus, the success of *The Best Years of Our Lives* as a major document in Hollywood's picture of America is attributable to the unusual care that has been devoted to the reality of the surface. The camera, above all, catches the exact appearances of the metropolitan background: the orderly and impersonal comfort of an upper middle class apartment, the hard surfaces of a bank, the ugly and cheap profusion of a chain drugstore, the plain facts of a street—all photographed simply as what happens to be really there, without sympathy or revulsion, without "tricks"—almost, in a sense, without art, if one were not conscious all the time of how much arrangement has gone into this matter-of-fact detail. One recognizes everything and in the end this recognition is all the excitement, for what is on the screen becomes finally as accustomed and undramatic as the shabby décor of the theater itself. The actors, too, are so manipulated as to become embodiments of the physical reality of human beings. More clearly than the important events of the plot, one remembers how the actors hold their bodies: Teresa Wright slouched over a stove, so much like a real woman over a real stove that the scene can become almost unpleasant, as it was certainly not intended to be; or Fredric March and Dana Andrews quarreling across a table, with their muscles set, two stupid men acting as they think proper in what they conceive to be a moment of drama—this, too, was not intended, but the physical appearances have so strong a hold on the director that he is himself exactly on a level with his material: he sees how everything must look, but frequently he cannot see what it really means.

The dialogue follows the same pattern. Whatever is said is as close as possible to what people are likely to say; not *these* people, particularly (they have little individuality), but people in general, Hollywood's imagined American and everybody's possible neighbor, a little less infantile than Hollywood usually makes him (since this is a "serious" movie), but just as uncomplicated and predictable as he might appear to be (but probably would *not* be) if he were a real person on any real street. I do not recall that any character ever says anything that is particularly interesting in itself and that could not just as well be something else, but the talk is always quite real, except in two or three mawkish attempts at eloquence.

All this makes most of the movie flat and boring, unless one is ready to accept its pretensions or to delight in its mere virtuosity. What you see always has a certain interest because it is so recognizable, but what you see is all there is; each character announces himself immediately and in full, each situation is immediately and completely understood. This does not mean that everything is explicit, but the suggestions are kept strictly within limits: at any moment, whatever is meant but not stated is only one thing and is always clear. (I saw the movie a second time and found only occasional details of realism that I had missed, but no new meanings. This is significant, for one expects of a movie that exhibits so much talent and technical mastery that it should be almost infinitely suggestive, as *The Informer* was, for instance, or *Modern Times,* or even such unpretentious and disorganized entertainments as the movies of the Marx Brothers.) This disciplined clarity is used to control the explosive possibilities of the subject: where every statement is complete, clear, and limited, it can with less difficulty be made false. (The more Hollywood "matures" and tries to live up to its responsibilities as a major expression of our society, the more we shall see of this empty and extremely skillful precision. *Boomerang* is the most recent example, somewhat more acceptable than *The Best Years of Our Lives* because the actual limitations of its subject are more in accord with the limitations of the realistic technique.)

The falsehood has many aspects, but its chief and most general aspect is a denial of the reality of politics, if politics means the existence of real incompatibilities of interest and real *social* problems not susceptible of individual solution. The choice of subject is itself an evasion of politics, for the "veterans' problem" is not an issue, or at any rate it is a false issue, since nobody is against the veterans and since they do not constitute a social group, except temporarily and very vaguely. And even the rudimentary elements of politics that have in fact attached themselves to this problem are excluded from the movie: there is no mention of veterans' organizations, for instance, or of any general economic insecurity (one of the three main characters has to hunt for a job, but it is assumed that this is merely a matter of getting properly "located" somewhere at the bottom, working hard, and starting the automatic climb up the economic scale). Nor is there any hint of the veterans' harboring bitterness at what they have been forced to go through or resentment at

128

those who stayed home (a minor character is in fact set up as a target to encourage this kind of resentment in the audience: "With all these veterans coming back," he says in fussy and effeminate tones, *"nobody's* job is safe!").

A conscious effort is made to show that class differences do not matter. The infantry sergeant is a banker in civilian life ("Don't 'sir' me," he says to one nervous applicant for a GI loan, "I'm a sergeant"); the Air Force captain has been a soda-jerker, living with his workingman father in a miserable slum. The two men are presented as culturally equal: the soda-jerker can call the banker's wife by her first name and eventually marry the banker's daughter; this, too, is made possible by the technique of presenting everything as a surface, for the social equality of bankers and soda-jerkers *is* real—on the surface. (But both men are made culturally superior to the third veteran, the sailor from the lower middle class, who has been neither a banker nor an officer.)

In addition to these obvious evasions and distortions, the chief means of concealing the reality of politics is to present every problem as a problem of personal morality. (This device seems to be common to all forms of political obscurantism: when we are asked to feel guilty about the atomic bomb, for instance, or to take thought of "our" grave international responsibilities.) For every difficulty, there is conceived to be some simple moral imperative that will solve it, at least to the extent that it can be solved at all. Thus the problem of the monopoly of capital is reduced to a question of the morals of banks: if bankers are good men, then they will grant small loans (not large loans, apparently) to deserving veterans (those who are willing to work hard) without demanding collateral. (This is "gambling on the future of America"; the small loan is apparently conceived to be some kind of solution to the economic difficulties of capitalism—cf. *It's a Wonderful Life.*) And the veteran has a corresponding obliga-

129

tion to be grateful: "God bless you!" says the simple and reliable farmer whose application for a loan has been approved.

The makers of the movie are obviously happiest—and also most successful—in dealing with the sailor, who has lost both hands in the war and must go through life with a pair of hooks. His problem is at least quite clear, and the necessary moral patterns have already been established in a hundred movies: virtue for the sailor consists in assuming that his girl will marry him only out of pity and a sense of obligation; virtue for the girl consists in "really" loving him, so that the loss of his hands can make no difference. This moral deadlock can always be broken, and it is broken here, in an extremely affecting scene. (Everything about the sailor is especially affecting because the part is played by a man who really did lose his hands in the war. There was nothing else to be done, I suppose, but this is one of the elements that help to make the movie spill over into the real world, carrying its falsehood with it.) There is one very uncomfortable scene, when someone raises the real question: What did he lose his hands *for?* But the man who raises this question is made personally repulsive and, apparently, a fascist sympathizer, so one does not mind seeing him knocked down and the American flag plucked from his lapel (unless one is sufficiently at odds with the movie to realize that this is done not because he is a fascist but simply because he has put his finger on the really sore spot that no one is supposed to notice). Thus the political question of the sailor's hands is dealt with very easily, and the war comes safely back to the realm of simple morals: "We were pushed into it," says the unpleasant man. "Sure," the sailor replies, "the Germans and the Japs pushed us in!" And we in the audience, remembering all the time that this man has really lost his hands, can breathe easy: he does not begrudge his sacrifice.

A secondary element of some interest is the movie's sexual

130

pattern. Since the starting-point of the story is the veterans' need for "readjustment," the sexual relations of the characters form an unusually clear projection of the familiar Hollywood (and American) dream of male passivity. The men are inept, nervous, inarticulate, and childishly willful; the women are strong, dignified, wise, and forgiving. The women are to serve the men, care for them, and comfort them. (The captain's wife, who stands in the way of his marriage to the banker's daughter, is the one "bad" woman, and her badness consists essentially in being less instead of more mature than her husband; she is a problem and she should be a mother.) For each of the main characters, there is a scene in which the woman he loves undresses him (partly or completely, depending on whether the couple is married or not) and puts him to bed. And when it is the sailor who is put to bed, the dream becomes almost explicit. He is the man (the real man) who has lost his hands—and with them his power to be sexually aggressive (this fact is lightly emphasized a number of times). Every night, his wife will have to put him to bed, and then it will be her hands that must be used in making love. Beneath the pathos of the scene (certainly the most dramatic scene of the movie), one feels a current of excitement, in which the sailor's misfortune becomes a kind of wish-fulfillment, as one might actually dream it: he *must* be passive; therefore he can be passive without guilt.

(1947)

131

Father and Son—
and the FBI

MANY AMERICANS find themselves baffled and exasperated by that "anti-anti-Communism" which sees in overvigorous efforts to expose the Communist menace a growing threat to American freedom no less dangerous than Communism itself. Their bewilderment is understandable, for such an equation is clearly absurd and too often conceals a desire to remain "neutral" in the struggle against Soviet totalitarianism. But the fear of an irresponsible anti-Communism does not come entirely out of thin air; there *is* a wrong way, a dangerous way, to be anti-Communist. Those who do not believe this may find it illuminating to see Leo McCarey's new film, *My Son John*, an attack on Communism and an affirmation of "Americanism" that might legitimately alarm any thoughtful American, whether liberal or conservative.

The film opens on a "typical" American town of the kind that certain Hollywood directors could probably construct with their eyes shut: a still, tree-lined street, undistinguished frame houses surrounded by modest areas of grass, a few automobiles. For certain purposes it is assumed that all "real" Americans live in towns like this, and, so great is the power of myth, even the born city-dweller is likely to believe vaguely

133

that he too lives on this shady pleasant street, or comes from it, or is going to it. Church bells are ringing, and a "typical" American family—named Jefferson, in fact—is preparing to go to church. Two sons of the family, in army uniforms, stand before the house with their father, tossing a football back and forth; the mother is late in getting ready, and there is a good deal of "healthy" kidding about this. She comes out at last— a worn, tense woman, considerably out of key with her robust husband and sons, but playing up to their image of her—and the family drives off. It is the last day of the boys' leave, and they will soon be off to Korea; under the emotional weight of this fact, the Jeffersons behave as if they are carrying out some formal ritual of affirmation, trying to pack into every speech and gesture some complete statement of what they are and what they believe, very much like one of those advertisements in which some large corporation attempts with half a page of mawkish copy to set down "as a public service" the meaning of America. The mother in particular is treated as if she were the American flag or a familiar passage from the Declaration of Independence, ostentatiously *not* accorded any deference precisely because she is valued so profoundly and completely.

We learn soon that there hangs over this American family a shadow more menacing than the Korean War. The eldest son, John, a brilliant and rising young government official (already one's suspicions are aroused), has failed to get home to say good-bye to his brothers. When he does appear on the scene after they have left, he is a figure to fill any ordinary human being, let alone any red-blooded American, with loathing: pompous, supercilious, as sleek and unfeeling as a cat, coldly contemptuous of his father, patronizing to his mother; also, though nothing is said of this, one feels that he might be a homosexual. In fact, as will eventually be revealed, he is a Communist and a traitor, but at first there are only his father's truculent suspicions and his mother's half-acknowledged fears. Here, it may be said, the film does for a time present a "typical" American drama that is also something more than "typical"—it is real. Nothing is more characteristic of our fluid society than the process by which children so often become alienated from their parents, going beyond them in education and social status until the parents, who may have made great sacrifices to accomplish precisely this result, find themselves excluded from the triumph they have prepared, obliged to content themselves with taking a generalized pride in a child whose achievements they are perhaps not even equipped to understand.

This situation, agonizing for both parent and child, has the elements of tragedy, for it is full of guilt, and yet no one is to blame. But if this conflict of generations is to become the material of serious drama, the eye that sees it must retain a certain compassionate detachment and not itself be subject to the hallucinations that afflict the contending parties. In *My Son John*, the conflict is presented so naked and intense that it takes on the quality of a nightmare. Against the monstrous son—Robert Walker's characterization is essentially the same as in *Strangers on a Train*, where he played the role of a pathological murderer—there is set a father no less monstrous, a pillar of the American Legion presented as so outrageously bigoted, so hopelessly benighted, that one fails to understand why the Legion has not organized a boycott of the film, unless it be out of a truly selfless concern for freedom of expression. This father is principal of the local elementary school, where, as he informs us, he is engaged in teaching little children the "simple, down to earth" fundamentals of morality and Americanism. He has also been making a serious study of the problem of Communism, and he expresses his understanding of that problem in a song that is worth quoting in full:

If you don't like your Uncle Sammy
Then go back to your home o'er the sea,
To the land from where you came,
Whatever be its name,
But don't be ungrateful to me!
If you don't like the stars in old glory,
If you don't like the red, white, and blue,
Then don't act like the cur in the story,
Don't bite the hand that's feeding you!

The son responds to this piece of folk poetry with icy-delicate feline mockery—a beautiful bit of acting—creating an almost heroic tension and raising for a short time the hope that out of the unalleviated enmity between father and son, over-stylized though it may be, will come some serious dramatic examination of the way each blind intolerance feeds on its opposite and is mirrored in it. One suspects, even, that just such a counterpoint was for a while intended by the makers of the film.

But if they had such an intention, they found themselves unable to sustain it. For between the struggling titans of un-reason there is only the suffering mother, drawn out almost transparently thin by the pull of the contending forces—in most ways a psychologically true portrait, though presented by Helen Hayes with a mad jerky passion that affects one like a prolonged scratching on taut silk, but not at all the figure that is needed to make sense of the complex issues. For her there is no understanding, but only pain, and when the dreadful truth about her favorite son is no longer to be denied, she can do nothing but sink back definitively into the arms of her husband: since he was right about this, it follows that he has been right about everything. Farewell to the mistaken values that made her send her son to college, farewell to the risks of intellectual curiosity and broad humani-

136

tarianism and individual thinking: these things made her son a Communist spy, whereas her husband, who despised such things, is an anti-Communist; in her husband's stupidity will be her peace.

For in the end we are left in no doubt: what is being upheld is, precisely, stupidity. All through the film no effort is spared to emphasize the limitations of the father's thinking and his hatred and contempt for the mind; this image of him is built up deliberately and with considerable skill. I have already quoted the father's most sustained expression of political document. He also—this educator!—refers to Communists as "scummies." He makes a big show of being unable to remember the name of his son's beloved professor (something "foreign," no doubt), spits when he witnesses an affectionate greeting between the two, and worries about his son's falling into the company of "those intellectuals I've read about." In one of the climactic episodes, exasperated by the son's cool superiority, he hits him with a Bible and then goes out to get drunk, returning late at night to mouth some more of his "simple, down to earth" ideas while he can hardly stand up. And all this we are to regard, not as an excusable want of intelligence, but as a higher form of wisdom; we are to admire the father for his sincerity and his faith—qualities, it is implied, which are inseparable from muddleheadedness and incoherence, which indeed *equal* muddleheadedness and incoherence, just as in those "public service" advertisements about America the special virtues of our tradition turn out to reside less in the ideas the ads set forth than in the disjointed stammer which the copy writer conceives to be the natural accent of the man in the street. "You've got more wisdom than all of us," Lucille Jefferson says to her husband, "because you listen to your heart." It is clear that listening to your heart means not using your head. And John Jefferson, after he has repented of his crimes (for no apparent reason) and been

137

murdered by his former comrades, explains in a recorded posthumous confession that corruption first entered his soul when he began to respond to ideas and think for himself, forsaking "the only authorities I ever knew—my church and my father and mother." At the time of this confession, John is about thirty years old; we have seen what the "authority" of his parents amounts to. Besides, though this may be blasphemy, there are fathers—yes, and mothers too—who are Communists.

But John has spoken also of the authority of his church. This brings us to one of the most important and most disturbing elements of the movies. The Jeffersons are Roman Catholics, and Leo McCarey has before this been quite successful with what might be called "popularizations" of Catholicism, most notably in *Going My Way*. But if, as I have suggested, a thoughtful member of the American Legion might take little comfort in this film's "Americanism," a thoughtful Catholic might likewise find good reason to be disturbed at its Catholicism. Indeed, though some sections of the Catholic press welcomed the film, at least two leading Catholic periodicals, *America* and *Commonweal*, have criticized it severely.

The main thing to be said is that religion exists in this film only as a form of window-dressing, an essentially empty symbol to be counterposed occasionally to the symbols of Communism. Just as the elder Jefferson uses the family Bible to hit his son when he feels frustrated in argument, so the idea "religion" is used throughout the film as a kind of blunt instrument to settle every difficulty without resolving it. The film opens with the ringing of church bells, and it ends with John Jefferson's parents going into a chapel to pray for their dead son. But these elements are never realized in cinematic terms; they are presented so perfunctorily, so much as a matter of mere ideological decoration, that they have no strength

138

as screen images—and, of course, in a movie it is not the intrinsic worth of an idea that counts, but the power with which it is made into an image; in the movie theater, we think with our eyes.

There is also a priest, played by Frank McHugh, but he is presented as an ineffectual and slightly comic figure, bustling about occasionally in the background on parish affairs but never permitted to enter the action. This treatment of him may have been quite deliberate, designed to make him harmlessly appealing to non-Catholic audiences (like the foxy-grandpa priest played by Barry Fitzgerald in *Going My Way*, or the boys' counselor type played by Bing Crosby). But the result is that the moral authority of the church, to which the film finally appeals, simply does not show. One cannot imagine going to Frank McHugh for help with a serious problem, and in fact the elder Jeffersons never think of discussing their difficulties with him. He exists merely as one of the film's "properties," like the car or the house. At the same time, as Nathan Glick has remarked in a review of the film in *Commentary*, the function of the priest is taken over by an agent of the FBI. It is he who gently and lovingly brings Lucille Jefferson to an understanding of the situation and leads her to see her moral duty; it is he who urges upon John Jefferson the release of confession; it is he who pronounces what is in effect John's funeral oration. And where the priest is fussy, shallowly cheerful, a little shrill, the FBI man is dignified, serious, warm, full of understanding and wisdom—in short, a figure of profound moral authority, a priest, one might say, of the secular law. Perhaps I need not labor the significance of this transfer of the priestly function to a police agency, but it should be remarked that one of the signal virtues of the real FBI has been its refusal to assume such a role.

Finally, there is an element of falsity in the film's whole conception of Communism that deserves some mention. It is true, as we know, that the Communists are members of a conspiracy, and that this conspiracy is ready to employ almost any means to achieve its ends. But the conspiracy is a political one, its characteristic crimes are political, and its characteristic weapon, in the United States at this time, is much more often a mimeograph machine than a gun. When John Jefferson is killed by a burst of gunfire from a long black sedan, the event may not in itself be impossible, but as an image on the screen it falls too easily into a familiar pattern, the pattern of the gangster film. It is easy to see why a movie director would be tempted to follow that pattern, but it impedes understanding. Communists are not like gangsters; they are usually more complex and their lives are much duller. In their own way, they are often the epitome of stodgy respectability (think of Alger Hiss, for instance). The melodrama—it is true, there *is* a melodrama—is buried deep below the surface, perhaps too deep to be brought up where it can be photographed.

With the character of John Jefferson himself, perhaps, one does occasionally get a sense of that depth: in his monumental self-satisfaction, in his way of using certain opinions and attitudes like dead mechanical counters in his secret game of "history," testifying to the frozen rigidity of his mind and spirit. But one essential element is lacking: the subterranean fire of fanaticism. Without that, one cannot wholeheartedly believe in John Jefferson as an adequate representation of the Communist; it is as if he had picked up his Communism as another man might pick up a love of chamber music, simply as part of his cultural furniture (there are such Communists, of course, but they do not become spies). The fact is that Leo McCarey is not enough of an artist to imagine why anyone might become a Communist, what inner needs of the personality might be served. Of course he is not alone in this failure: even the explanations of ex-Communists are curiously inadequate. But the result is that he must fall back on easy clichés—for example, that Communism comes from "substituting faith in man for faith in God"—and thus, though he succeeds in making John Jefferson the most interesting figure in the movie, the character remains finally fragmentary and unrealized. Perhaps this may account in part for the unrelieved violence of the doctrine that this film expounds. The hidden logic seems to be: since we cannot understand Communism, it is likely that anything we cannot understand is Communism. The strongest and clearest image that one takes away from the film is that of the father, and his message is that we must fear and hate the best potentialities of the human mind.

(1952)

The Movie Camera
and the American

I AM NOT one of those who responded strongly to *Death
of a Salesman* when it was presented on the stage. Like many
"great" American plays, it seems to me gross and ungainly,
almost monstrous in its want of finesse, full of a self-conscious
energy masquerading as profundity and a mechanical realism
which hides a fundamental reluctance to give the real world
its due. Lee J. Cobb's performance in the leading role was
undoubtedly masterful, but in a sense it agreed too well with
the fixed intent of the play: one felt at times that the agonies
of the elephantine figure on the stage came not so much from
the ruin of his own life as from the merciless constrictions
of the playwright's vision, especially perhaps from that insanely "artistic" stagecraft which required him, like a great
rat in an invisible maze, to play at walking through imaginary
doors and around imaginary walls—no wonder that at last he
pounded the floor in his frustration.

And if Willy Loman is a grotesque, his sons, with their pat
"American" nicknames and their stilted confusions, are the
merest cardboard: Andy Hardy broken on the wheel of social criticism. Only the mother, Willy's wife, and the next-
door neighbor Charley have any honest reality; on the whole,

143

though not consistently, Arthur Miller does let these two speak for themselves. But their reality continually denies the reality of the play: Charley's final summation of Willy's tragedy (". . . for a salesman there is no rock bottom to the life") is his moment of greatest falsity, for he is no less a "salesman" than Willy, but a successful one; on the other hand, Mrs. Loman's failure at the end to understand what has happened expresses her essential solidity: it has not occurred to her that she was married to a symbol. (It is curious that the mother-figure, which is the focus of so much falsehood in American culture, seems also occasionally to represent its firmest grasp on the real.)

Taken point by point, the movie *Death of a Salesman* is inferior to the play. Fredric March, a more commonplace actor than Cobb, is also less imposing as a physical presence. Cobb's very bulk did much to disguise the pettiness of Willy Loman's failure; March's Willy, actually more believable than Cobb's, is to that extent more pathetic and more ridiculous, a crazy man talking to himself. The film suffers also from that exaggerated respect which Hollywood sometimes offers to a recognized work of art; where most films made from Broadway plays are automatically better than their originals merely by reduction of the amount of undistinguished dialogue, this one manages to include almost as much as the play. Another difficulty is in the constant presentations of Willy's memories and hallucinations, which were awkward enough on the stage but at least belonged to an accepted framework of theatrical convention; the film manages the transitions from the real to the hallucinatory more smoothly, but these sequences still wrench it out of shape: the very fluidity of the medium favors simpler and more direct exposition (even the accepted use of the "flashback"—Willy's hallucinations do not quite belong to that convention—is almost

144

never accomplished without a kind of purely technical senti-mentality).

Nor have the makers of the film taken much advantage of the greater mobility of the medium. It is true that Willy's house, which can now have solid walls and real doors, is more present than it was on the stage, though in fact the camera concentrates so obstinately on the figures of the actors that the house is never allowed the importance it ought to have. There is also a good opening sequence photographed from the back seat of Willy's car as he drives slowly over the George Washington Bridge, peering anxiously through the windshield and now and then fidgeting a little to bring himself closer to the steering wheel, just his shoulders and the back of his head, with the two big sample cases sticking up in the foreground, all conveying the impression of an aging and pitiable masculinity, a man who works hard with little success. This sequence represents the film's most intelligent use of March's body, which is best taken for granted (later there is constant overemphasis on bowed shoulders, worried eyes and forehead, middle-aged belly); it is also the closest sight we ever get of Willy Loman as a real salesman—a man who might actually drive into a town in New England and try to sell some specific line of goods. It tells much about the limitations of Mr. Miller's realism that he should have thought it a good idea not to mention just what it is that Willy sells, though in the play we are told the brand-names of his refrigerator and his various cars; the supposition that "universality" is achieved by suppression of the particular is a characteristic error of American writers.

Once the camera has brought Willy to his home—that is, to the point at which the play begins—it abdicates in favor of the playwright, and we never really get back to the figure in the car. Willy's Brooklyn—and his New England—remain as shadowy and unlocalized as ever; he dwells in an America not even of the imagination, but only of the idea. When one of the scenes of hallucination is placed in the subway, it is only to emphasize more strongly the refusal to fill in the concrete background of Willy's sufferings: everything is kept neat and blank, the other people no more than an orderly group of extras, the posters carefully out of focus in the background, and the camera never leaves Willy. Who would dream that a movie director could refuse the invitation of the subway? But of course it is in the nature of this picture to refuse every such invitation; the subway may be unpleasant, but we use it every day; if the subway or the streets or the real Brooklyn were permitted to exist, then it would be clear that Willy Loman had, if not a good life, at least a style of life, and the point of the film, as of the play, is that he had no life at all, he didn't "put a bolt to a nut or tell you the law or give you medicine," above all he did not work with his hands, which for Mr. Miller seems to represent the true meaning of failure—again, a characteristic American abstraction.

Yet the picture has a certain power which for me at least—apparently not for others—was lacking in the play. No film ever quite disappears into abstraction: what the camera reproduces has almost always on the most literal level the appearance of reality; that is one reason why the movies can afford to be so much more banal than the theater: when we complain of their "unreality" we do not mean exactly that they fail to carry conviction, but more probably that they carry conviction all too easily. In the blankest moments of *Death of a Salesman* one sees, if not Willy Loman, who is always more a concept than a human being, at least the actor Fredric March, brought so close and clear that his own material reality begins to assert itself outside the boundaries that are supposed to be set by his role. On the stage, this would be a fault, for it would mean that the actor was seeking to impose himself on the play; here there is no need for him to put himself forward: he need only be present, a passive object merely available to the camera's infinite appetite for the material. This is not to say that the actor's "real" personality replaces that of the character he portrays—though that may happen—but only that the actor as an object of perception is real and important irrespective of whether we believe in the character: the screen permits no vacancies, it will be filled one way or another. Thus as we lose interest in the aging salesman of the play, there emerges this other spectacle with its own quality and pathos, indeed its own drama, which is not at all foreign to the play though beyond its presumed limits: the spectacle of the aging movie star attempting to express what he believes is to be found in the play, exposing to inspection the bags under his eyes, the unpleasing sag of his thin mouth, as if to insist at whatever cost that he is engaged in a serious enterprise. There are moments when one becomes aware with almost too much clarity that March feels himself suddenly at the heart of the matter—for instance when he looks with his sick face at Bernard, the boy who stuck to his books and has become a "success," and asks, "Bernard . . . what's the secret?"—and at such moments he compels one's respect, not so much for what the playwright has written (though this line has some brilliance) as for the intensity of his own concern with it.

In the end, the quality of seriousness which is most visible in the presence of March becomes the dominant tone of the whole production—in the deliberate direction, in the solemn lighting, in the very rejection of cinematic opportunities which a "routine" film would take up as a matter of course— and though one need not finally acknowledge any personal involvement with the fate of Willy Loman, it is not so easy to deny an involvement with the film as such: not Willy Loman, but *Death of a Salesman* is the American phenomenon that

147

demands examination. Granted that the drama does not come to life in its own terms, what is the nature of the aura that undeniably surrounds it?

Some of the more illuminating recent sociological writing— I think especially of David Riesman's *The Lonely Crowd*— has described the typical American as abnormally concerned with personal attractiveness. We are all familiar with the advertising that plays upon our social anxieties, most often in a sexual context but also in the more general terms of status: if you don't use the right tooth paste or the right soap, if you have not read the right books and learned correct grammar, then you will not get a girl and you will miss that promotion you have been hoping for. These advertisements are only the most practical expression of a broad concept of American society which in fact we all assent to. The American stands outside any fixed social framework, and so he must create his own place, indeed he must create himself, out of the resources of his personality. If he believes still that the world lies open to him, he believes also, and with a greater clarity, that if he fails to measure up to his opportunity he will find himself an outcast. At one time this struggle for status was seen to have a certain logic: if you worked hard you would probably get along respectably, since it was more or less in your own power to find some useful area of activity; the danger of failure, though real enough, belonged to the accepted hazards. But now the individual must in most cases attach himself to some large bureaucracy over which he has no control and where his fate depends primarily on his pleasing his superiors, or if not his superiors, then simply "pleasing" in the most general sense; the roads to success have become vague and infinitely complex, the very content of success is no longer clear, and failure is a kind of insidious disease, like cancer: you may find out at any moment that you have had it all along. And our defenses become correspondingly vague, moving toward fantasy and propitiation; so long as our smiles are returned, we know that we are not yet cast away. In short, the American is a "salesman" with nothing to sell but his own personality. Mr. Miller's Charley sums it up in his speech at Willy Loman's grave: ". . . you get yourself a couple of spots on your hat, and you're finished. . . . A salesman has got to dream. . . . It comes with the territory."

No doubt this picture is true. We still teach our children that the world lies open to them and they must make their way—what else should we teach?—and we watch over them continually in fear that they may miss that exact balance of the physical, intellectual, and social graces without which their gifts will go to waste. It is true that we expend our energies in childish fantasies of success and power, and that on some level of our minds we go in expectation of the word of rejection that will leave us jobless, loveless, without a place. As admirers of *Death of a Salesman* have said, we are all Willy Lomans.

But this identification is taken more seriously than it deserves; on the upper levels of our culture it is assumed that literature is a form of explicit social criticism, and consequently all "negative" social images tend to be given undue weight as representing a "truer" reality, just as on lower cultural levels certain "positive" images—of home, religion, and the like— are still assured of an automatic response. If we look soberly at Willy Loman—this absolute "salesman" with his obsession about being "well liked" and his utter emptiness of values, behaving as if he himself had read *The Lonely Crowd* and been seized with a sociological delusion—it is obvious at once that we are not all Willy Lomans except in the sense that we are all sadists or homosexuals or "schizoids"; psychological and sociological types have their own reality, but only a luna-

149

tic runs true to type, perhaps not even a lunatic, and the dramatic uses of lunacy are limited. If Willy Loman were a valid creation, if we could believe thoroughly even in his lunacy, then the distortions of his personality would have to operate within a surrounding reality that might give them dramatic meaning; but the "purity" of the playwright's conception defeats all drama: one cannot quite believe that Willy ever sold anything, and even his death does not seem more a fact than the hallucinations that lead up to it.

Actually, the most illuminating analogy to Willy Loman is to be found not in life but in an earlier literature: he is a man possessed by a "humor." The fact that his particular humor is constructed out of a more advanced social science than that of the seventeenth century does not essentially alter its character; the more profound a scientific insight, the more it demands a kind of aesthetic appreciation: taken literally, its profundity becomes only a new shallows (we might be spared much boring amateur psychoanalysis if this truth were more widely accepted). The Jacobean comedy of humors was also in the most direct sense related to life—its characters were "recognizable" with the same excessive clarity as Willy Loman—and it had its special validity (which was not, however, the validity of social criticism). But there has never been a successful tragedy of humors: the protagonist of tragedy must walk whole upon the stage.

Death of a Salesman belongs to that culture of ideology which may eventually be all the culture we shall have. It is serious and in the most obvious ways honest, but if we take it as seriously as it asks to be taken, that is only one more evidence of our ability to refuse to recognize our own boredom (for another example, consider the reception of *The Cocktail Party*). As the mass audience escapes into easy sentiment, so the educated audience escapes into ideas, a tendency which does not necessarily reflect a real interest in ideas:

Death of a Salesman offers us not the fact but the atmosphere of thought.

Nor are these two audiences and their cultures so far apart as might appear. Thus, faced with the need to give his play some kind of dramatic movement, Mr. Miller confusedly allows himself to suggest that Willy Loman's having been unfaithful to his wife may be the only important factor in the collapse of his family—a possibility that threatens continually to make nonsense of the play's main point. And one is only momentarily surprised to learn that Stanley Kramer, the producer of the film, having refused to permit any sentimental alteration of the play's "negative" conclusion, has soothed the feelings of certain salesmen's associations by making a "positive" short film about the advantages of salesmanship as a career; I have not seen this short, but there is no reason why Mr. Kramer should not have brought to it all the honest conviction that can be seen in his handling of the longer film.

In the end, perhaps the most valid reaction to *Death of a Salesman* is the philistine one, which has at least the virtue of judging the play in terms of actuality. Perhaps as much to the point as anything I have written is the comment of that playgoer who is reported to have said as he left the theater, "That New England territory never *was* any good." The fact that this remark seems stupendously naive is testimony to the play's distance from reality.

As I have said, one of the basic appeals of *Death of a Salesman* lies in its pessimism. So much of "official" American culture has been cheaply optimistic that we are likely almost by reflex to take pessimism as a measure of seriousness. Besides, the element of pessimism is often for educated people an aid to identification: Willy Loman gains much of what reality he seems to have from the fact that we are all secretly inclined

151

to think ourselves "failures." But a pessimistic falsehood is no less false—and no less an escape—than an optimistic one.

A more "affirmative" picture of American life is offered in Samuel Goldwyn's production *I Want You*, which presents the vicissitudes of two generations of an American family at the time of the outbreak of the Korean War. Those concerned in the production of this movie doubtless believed in what they were doing, but none of the critics, so far as I know, has spoken of it as a significant work of art, and it has joined the endless ranks of "Hollywood" productions. On the whole, it deserves the reception it has got. Yet it is in many ways better and more serious than *Death of a Salesman*.

I Want You is apparently an effort to repeat the success of Mr. Goldwyn's earlier and greatly overrated *The Best Years of Our Lives* (1947), which attempted to give a generalized picture of American life soon after the end of the last war. *The Best Years of Our Lives* was a tissue of cheerful platitudes, using a notable technical virtuosity to present the surface of reality with such hard clarity as to discourage any looking beyond the film's narrow ideological boundaries; social tensions were presented only to be smoothly denied, political and economic problems were evaded (usually, in a characteristic American fashion, by reducing them to the plane of personal morality), and in the episodes concerning the veteran who had lost his hands a particularly dreadful example of personal suffering was used as one more occasion for a vulgar sentimental optimism. In *I Want You*, too, there is much falsity, but since the film does not pretend to be concerned with any broad social problems, only with the simpler fact of a threat of war, it does not have to make so many evasions. In addition, the external situation discourages any crude optimism: *The Best Years of Our Lives* was about the end of a war, this film is about the beginning of one, and its "affirmation" must be more subtle, residing not so much in the characters' larger actions or their occasional set speeches as in the unspoken assumption that they will prove equal to whatever may be demanded of them. This is an arrogant assumption, but it is presented with a kind of innocence; the chief falsification is in giving the characters a greater dignity than one would expect of them, and the result is something like an American version of those British films which do not so much extol the British character as quietly take its virtues for granted. Beneath their personal anxieties and emotional crudities, which are presented usually with external honesty and now and then with something more, the characters have an astonishing serenity, expressing not the absence of tensions but, more realistically, a confidence that the tensions will remain under control; even the very young characters, despite their deliberate gracelessness (and rather sickening graces) and even the weak and somewhat shiftless father, display at bottom the same self-containment. Actually this quality is far from new in American movies; it is the special quality of the most fully realized Western and soldier heroes, and in many other movies it has been offered, if unsuccessfully, as the essential component of the "American" character. But here for the first time one can sense a possibility of its being absorbed without violence into realistic pictures; it is still an untruth, but the precise area of its falsity seems no longer so easy to define: it may yet become an untruth organically assimilated, which is to say a myth. (It is hard to believe that such a development would be desirable, though it might produce good pictures, as it has done in the Westerns.)

Inseparable from this self-containment of the characters is a pervasive temperate melancholy which adds to the impression of a maturity not truly achieved but yet not easily to be called false. This melancholy has really nothing in common with the gross ideological pessimism of *Death of a Salesman*,

153

but belongs precisely to the "affirmation" of practical people who have accepted the burdens of their lives, however narrowly they may conceive them, and expecting no final victory or full satisfaction, are still unable to believe in the possibility of defeat, if only because a certain stupidity makes them incapable of imagining a threat to their inner selves. Again, it is a quality most clearly realized in film portraits of men of action—Western heroes and soldiers—but it is also one of the interesting elements in soap opera, sentimental popular fiction, or an occasional "serious" comic strip ("Mary Worth," for instance), and even in the novels of such writers as J. P. Marquand and James Gould Cozzens. And one finds again some difficulty in discerning the precise boundaries between the true and the false. When Dorothy McGuire hangs out her wash in the back yard, a contrived image of the conscientious young wife and mother, and expounds her "mature" view of life, certainly we are in the area of the false; but at other times, when the sharp, "refined" lines of her face and the controlled tension of her voice are allowed to make their effect without emphasis, one begins to believe even in the picture she was trying to create at the clothesline.

In general, what line of demarcation can be found between the true and the false is in the difference between what the actors with too much contrivance are made to represent and what in their mere physical appearance they seem "naturally" to be, a difference that remains even when the purpose of contrivance is only to "interpret" what is already there. The plot is of course ideologically determined: it concerns mainly the decision of a reserve officer (Dana Andrews) to go back into the army, and the initial rebellion and final reconciliation of his young brother (Farley Granger) at being drafted, these events set against a background designed to display the virtues of the American character and a general calm solidarity in the face of danger. The story is presented with unusual tact and in some ways a surprising honesty (it would have been unthinkable for a movie during the last war to show that a young man might regard a postcard from his draft board as a major calamity), and most of the action is in itself quite credible, but one is continually disturbed by the way everything agrees tidily with the initial purposes: honesty itself becomes only a part of the "effect," like the candor of a statesman. The film's real virtue is in the degree to which, despite its ideological commitment, it remains tied to physical appearances, and this not with the rigidity of intent that made *The Best Years of Our Lives* visually so shallow, but professionally, with that less purposive compulsion simply to make the most of visual opportunities which is the film camera's peculiar justification. Thus Dana Andrews's face of a thoughtful frog and his undistinguished competent body, which might easily with misguided artistry be built into an "American" symbol (as has been done with the more extreme lines of James Stewart, for instance), are wisely left to carry conviction in their own way; Andrews is an ideal film actor in the sense that his physical appearance never ceases to be interesting and "real," and almost never fails to carry suggestion, no matter what situation he may be placed in; here, he is completely believable even when he must sit with his little daughter on his lap telling her a bedtime story, and if any note of falsity does creep in, it is immediately redeemed by the clumsy line of his shoulders as he carries her to her crib.

In special contrast to *Death of a Salesman* is this picture's concentration on the material background. In *Death of a Salesman* the background is deliberately suppressed, apparently from a belief that the "essential" quality of American life is only obscured by its material basis—a curious assumption for a movie that might claim to be precisely a materialist

155

interpretation of our society, but, as I have remarked, a necessary one if it is to make its point. The more normal American view, though perhaps a less intellectual one, and certainly the natural view for anyone starting out to take pictures, is that the "essential," if it is to be found at all, will turn out to reside in the material. In *I Want You*, we are shown a good many details of the family business and are given opportunities to see Dana Andrews at work. When young Farley Granger goes for his appearance before the draft board, the waiting room is crowded with other young men, not empty extras as in the subway scene of *Death of a Salesman*, but actors adding their particular touches of fact (not very happily, it is true). And no opportunity is lost to fill in the appearance of the streets, the stores, a bar, the insides of homes.

The homes above all, of course: the dingy home of the older generation, with streaks of dust on the walls after Mildred Dunnock in her big scene has torn down her husband's collection of guns, bayonets, and helmets from the First World War, and the newer home of the younger couple with modern paneling and brighter upholstery, but just as cluttered and conventional, a ten-cent-store picture of a ship over the mantel and a big wing chair beside the fireplace; if the business does not do well, this house too will in its turn become dingy and characterless, not from any want of care but chiefly from a want of self-assertiveness: the home is so obviously important that it carries its meaning in its mere existence, like a business office—there is no need to make it a vehicle of self-expression. Presented with an unthinking conviction that makes the symbol something more than a cliché, the homes of this film do actually represent what these Americans are seeking to defend. They ask only to be left in undisturbed possession of their lives and their property: one could almost weep at the innocence which makes them think

156

this is a small thing to ask. But that innocence is in its own way a form of worldly wisdom; it belongs to that famous American materialism which, if it limits our understanding of other peoples and of ourselves, also offers some protection against the murderous "spiritualities" of ideology; perhaps one of the American virtues is that our slogans so often ring hollow. In the end, the "representative American" of this movie decides to go back into the army very much as he might decide that the time has finally come when he must fix the lawn mower, but this "materialist" decision is both wiser and more serious than the kind of "spiritual" impulse that might have sent his father into the army in 1917.

There is another illuminating point of comparison between *I Want You* and *Death of a Salesman* in their treatment of relations between the generations. Like Willy Loman, the father of *I Want You* is a liar and boaster, and the moment comes when his lies are exposed: the souvenirs of the First World War which clutter his living room were bought in the pawnshops of New York; he spent the time of the war in Paris as a general's orderly. But when the father on the night before his older son's return to the army feels it necessary to tell him the truth, the son surprisingly refuses this invitation to drama: he knew the truth all along, but "there are some lies a son doesn't call his father on." Willy Loman is of course a more extreme case, and I would not claim that his sons could have reacted similarly. On the other hand, there is no implication in this film that the father's lies were not important; what is significant is the refusal to go too far below the surface: we are left to feel the importance of the scene without having it interpreted to us. This refusal is a wise one, both in terms of the film medium itself, which is almost always embarrassed by a too conscious concern with profundities, and in terms of the particular characters of this film, whose common-sense relation to reality involves the assumption that their inner psychological conflicts are of no practical relevance so long as they can be kept under control. No doubt this assumption belongs to the film's superficiality; let me repeat that *I Want You* is not particularly good. But when we consider that no one in *Death of a Salesman* ever suggests that Willy Loman should be taken to a psychiatrist— again a philistine consideration—that superficiality begins to seem a kind of virtue.

It would be a mistake, however, to set up too sharp an opposition between these films. *Death of a Salesman* owes much of its success to the illusion of just such an opposition: it appeals to people who are dissatisfied with pictures like *I Want You*. And their dissatisfaction is justified; taken in the abstract, perhaps Arthur Miller's falsifications are in some sense better than Samuel Goldwyn's, since after all we are not entirely wrong in feeling that the more pessimistic view is usually the more serious one. But the point is that Mr. Miller's view forces him continually to slight the claims of the material world which constitutes all our experience, and Mr. Goldwyn's does not. This is not enough to make *I Want You* a successful work of art, or even, except in the remotest sense, a "hope" for art: those who hope for the improvement of American movies are usually hoping for more films like *Death of a Salesman*. But we are left with the fact that *I Want You* achieves almost as a matter of course that immediate contact with material reality which, in the world as we know it, is the only possible basis for serious drama or literature, but which seems to be conspicuously lacking in much that now passes for serious. This may help to explain why the "problem" of the movies continues to intrude itself, like some awkwardly literal questioner from the back row, into the criticism of American culture.

(1952)

The Liberal Conscience
in *The Crucible*

ONE OF THE THINGS that have been said of *The Crucible,*
Arthur Miller's new play about the Salem witchcraft trials,
is that we must not be misled by its obvious contemporary
relevance: it is a drama of universal significance. This statement, which has usually a somewhat apologetic tone, seems
to be made most often by those who do not fail to place great
stress on the play's "timeliness." I believe it means something
very different from what it appears to say, almost the contrary, in fact, and yet not quite the contrary either. It means:
do not be misled by the play's historical theme into forgetting
the main point, which is that "witch trials" are always with
us, and especially today; but on the other hand do not hold
Mr. Miller responsible either for the inadequacies of his presentation of the Salem trials or for the many undeniable and
important differences between those trials and the "witch
trials" that are going on now. It is quite true, nevertheless,
that the play is, at least in one sense, of "universal significance." Only we must ask what this phrase has come to mean,
and whether the quality it denotes is a virtue.

The Puritan tradition, the greatest and most persistent
formulator of American simplifications, has itself always con-

tained elements disturbingly resistant to ideological—or even simply rational—understanding. The great debate in American Calvinism over "good works" versus the total arbitrariness of the divine will was won, fortunately and no doubt inevitably, by those who held that an actively virtuous life must be at least the outward sign of "election." But this interpretation was entirely pragmatic; it was made only because it had to be made, because in the most literal sense one could not survive in a universe of absolute predestination. The central contradiction of Calvinism remained unresolved, and the awful confusions of the Puritan mind still embarrass our efforts to see the early history of New England as a clear stage in the progress of American enlightenment. Only Hawthorne among American writers has seriously tried to deal with these confusions as part of the "given" material of literature, taking the Puritans in their own terms as among the real possibilities of life, and the admiration we accord to his tense and brittle artistry is almost as distant as our admiration of the early New Englanders themselves; it is curious how rarely Hawthorne has been mentioned beside Melville and James even in recent explorations of the "anti-liberal" side of our literature.

The Salem witch trials represent how far the Puritans were ready to go in taking their doctrines seriously. Leaving aside the slavery question and what has flowed from it, those trials are perhaps the most disconcerting single episode in our history: the occurrence of the unthinkable on American soil, and in what our schools have rather successfully taught us to think of as the very "cradle of Americanism." Of Europe's witch trials, we have our opinion. But these witch trials are "ours"; where do they belong in the "tradition"?

For Americans, a problem of this sort demands to be resolved, and there have been two main ways of resolving it. The first is to regard the trials as a historical curiosity; a curiosity by definition requires no explanation. In this way the trials are placed among the "vagaries" of the Puritan mind and can even offer a kind of amusement, like the amusement we have surprisingly agreed to find in the so-called "rough justice" of the Western frontier in the last century. But the more usual and more deceptive way of dealing with the Salem trials has been to assimilate them to the history of progress in civil rights. This brings them into the world of politics, where, even if our minds are not always made up, at least we think we know what the issues are. Arthur Miller, I need hardly say, has adopted this latter view.

Inevitably, I suppose, we will find in history what we need to find. But in this particular "interpretation" of the facts there seems to be a special injustice. The Salem trials were not political and had nothing whatever to do with civil rights, unless it is a violation of civil rights to hang a murderer. Nor were the "witches" being "persecuted"—as the Puritans did persecute Quakers, for instance. The actual conduct of the trials, to be sure, was outrageous, but no more outrageous than the conduct of ordinary criminal trials in England at the time. In any case, it is a little absurd to make the whole matter rest on the question of fair trial: how can there be a "fair trial" for a crime which not only has not been committed, but is impossible? The Salem "witches" suffered something that may be worse than persecution: they were hanged because of a metaphysical error. And they chose to die—for all could have saved themselves by "confession"—not for a cause, not for "civil rights," not even to defeat the error that hanged them, but for their own credit on earth and in heaven: they would not say they were witches when they were not. They lived in a universe where each man was saved or damned by himself, and what happened to them was personal. Certainly their fate is not lacking in universal significance; it was a human fate. But its universality—if we must

161

have the word—is of that true kind which begins and ends in a time and a place. One need not believe in witches, or even in God, to understand the events in Salem, but it is mere provinciality to ignore the fact that both those ideas had a reality for the people of Salem that they do not have for us.

The "universality" of Mr. Miller's play belongs neither to literature nor to history, but to that journalism of limp erudition which assumes that events are to be understood by referring them to categories, and which is therefore never at a loss for a comment. Just as in *Death of a Salesman* Mr. Miller sought to present "the American" by eliminating so far as possible the "non-essential" facts which might have made his protagonist a particular American, so in *The Crucible* he reveals at every turn his almost contemptuous lack of interest in the particularities—which is to say, the reality—of the Salem trials. The character and motives of all the actors in this drama are for him both simple and clear. The girls who raised the accusation of witchcraft were merely trying to cover up their own misbehavior. The Reverend Samuel Parris found in the investigation of witchcraft a convenient means of consolidating his shaky position in a parish that was murmuring against his "undemocratic" conduct of the church. The Reverend John Hale, a conscientious and troubled minister who, given the premises, must have represented something like the best that Puritan New England had to offer, and whose agonies of doubt might have been expected to call forth the highest talents of a serious playwright, appears in *The Crucible* as a kind of idiotic "liberal" scoutmaster, at first cheerfully confident of his ability to cope with the Devil's wiles and in the last act babbling hysterically in an almost comic contrast to the assured dignity of the main characters. Deputy Governor Danforth, presented as the virtual embodiment of early New England, never becomes more than a pompous, unimaginative politician of the better sort.

As for the victims themselves, the most significant fact is Miller's choice of John Proctor for his leading character: Proctor can be seen as one of the more "modern" figures in the trials, hardheaded, skeptical, a voice of common sense (he thought the accusing girls could be cured of their "spells" by a sound whipping); also, according to Mr. Miller, no great churchgoer. It is all too easy to make Proctor into the "common man"—and then, of course, we know where we are: Proctor wavers a good deal, fails to understand what is happening, wants only to be left alone with his wife and his farm, considers making a false confession, but in the end goes to his death for reasons that he finds a little hard to define but that are clearly good reasons—mainly, it seems, he does not want to implicate others. You will never learn from this John Proctor that Salem was a religious community, quite as ready to hang a Quaker as a witch. The saintly Rebecca Nurse is also there, to be sure, sketched in rapidly in the background, a quiet figure whose mere presence—there is little more of her than that—reminds us how far the dramatist has fallen short.

Nor has Mr. Miller hesitated to alter the facts to fit his constricted field of vision. Abigail Williams, one of the chief accusers in the trials, was about eleven years old in 1692; Miller makes her a young woman of eighteen or nineteen and invents an adulterous relation between her and John Proctor in order to motivate her denunciation of John and his wife Elizabeth. The point is not that this falsifies the facts of Proctor's life (though one remembers uneasily that he himself was willing to be hanged rather than confess to what was not true), but that it destroys the play, offering an easy theatrical motive that even in theatrical terms explains nothing, and deliberately casting away the element of religious and psychological complexity which gives the Salem trials their dramatic interest in the first place. In a similar way, Miller risks the whole point of *Death of a Salesman* by making his plot turn on the irrelevant discovery of Willy Loman's adultery. And in both plays the fact of adultery itself is slighted: it is brought in not as a human problem, but as a mere theatrical device, like the dropping of a letter; one cannot take an interest in Willy Loman's philandering, or believe in Abigail Williams' passion despite the barnyard analogies with which the playwright tries to make it "elemental."

Mr. Miller's steadfast, one might almost say selfless, refusal of complexity, the assured simplicity of his view of human behavior, may be the chief source of his ability to captivate the educated audience. He is an oddly depersonalized writer; one tries in vain to define his special quality, only to discover that it is perhaps not a quality at all, but something like a method, and even as a method strangely bare: his plays are as neatly put together and essentially as empty as that skeleton of a house which made *Death of a Salesman* so impressively confusing. He is the playwright of an audience that believes the frightening complexities of history and experience are to be met with a few ideas, and yet does not even possess these ideas any longer but can only point significantly at the place where they were last seen and where it is hoped they might still be found to exist. What this audience demands of its artists above all is an intelligent narrowness of mind and vision and a generalized tone of affirmation, offering not any particular insights or any particular truths, but simply the assurance that insight and truth as qualities, the things in themselves, reside somehow in the various signals by which the artist and the audience have learned to recognize each other. For indeed very little remains except this recognition; the marriage of the liberal theater and the liberal audience has been for some time a marriage in name only, held together by habit and mutual interest, partly by sentimental memory, most of all by the fear of loneliness and the outside world; and yet the movements of love are still kept up—for the sake of the children, perhaps.

The hero of this audience is Clifford Odets. Among those who shouted "Bravo!" at the end of *The Crucible*—an exclamation, awkward on American lips, that is reserved for cultural achievements of the greatest importance—there must surely have been some who had stood up to shout "Strike!" at the end of *Waiting for Lefty*. But it is hard to believe that a second Odets, if that were possible, or the old Odets restored to youth, would be greeted with such enthusiasm as Arthur Miller calls forth. Odets's talent was too rich—in my opinion the richest ever to appear in the American theater—and his poetry and invention were constantly more important than what he conceived himself to be saying. In those days it didn't matter: the "message" at the end of the third act was so much taken for granted that there was room for Odets's exuberance, and he himself was never forced to learn how much his talent was superior to his "affirmations" (if he had learned, perhaps the talent might have survived the "affirmations"). Arthur Miller is the dramatist of a later time, when the "message" isn't there at all, but it has been agreed to pretend that it is. This pretense can be maintained only by the most rigid control, for there is no telling what small element of dramatic *élan* or simple reality may destroy the delicate rapport of a theater and an audience that have not yet acknowledged they have no more to say to each other. Arthur Miller is Odets without the poetry. Worst of all, one feels sometimes that he has suppressed the poetry deliberately, making himself by choice the anonymous dramatist of a fossilized audience. In *Death of a Salesman*, certainly, there were moments when reality seemed to force its way momentarily to the surface. And even at *The Crucible*—though here it was not Miller's suppressed talent that broke through, but the suppressed facts of the outside world—the thread that tied the audience to its dramatist must have been now and then under some strain: surely there were some in the audience to notice uneasily that these witch trials, with their quality of ritual and their insistent need for "confessions," were much more like the trial that had just ended in Prague than like any trial that has lately taken place in the United States. So much the better, perhaps, for the play's "universal significance"; I don't suppose Mr. Miller would defend the Prague trial. And yet I cannot believe it was for this particular implication that anyone shouted "Bravo!"

For let us indeed not be misled. Mr. Miller has nothing to say about the Salem trials and makes only the flimsiest pretense that he has. *The Crucible* was written to say something about Alger Hiss and Owen Lattimore, Julius and Ethel Rosenberg, Senator McCarthy, the actors who have lost their jobs on radio and television, in short the whole complex that is spoken of, with a certain lowering of the voice, as the "present atmosphere." And yet not to say anything about that either, but only to suggest that a great deal might be said, oh an infinitely great deal, if it were not that—what? Well, perhaps if it were not that the "present atmosphere" itself makes such plain speaking impossible. As it is, there is nothing for it but to write plays of "universal significance"—and, after all, that's what a serious dramatist is supposed to do anyway.

What, then, *is* Mr. Miller trying to say to us? It's hard to tell. In *The Crucible* innocent people are accused and convicted of witchcraft on the most absurd testimony—in fact, the testimony of those who themselves have meddled in witchcraft and are therefore doubly to be distrusted. Decent citizens who sign petitions attesting to the good character of their accused friends and neighbors are thrown into prison as suspects. Anyone who tries to introduce into court the voice of reason is likely to be held in contempt. One of the accused refuses to plead and is pressed to death. No one is acquitted; the only way out for the accused is to make false confessions and themselves join the accusers. Seeing all this on the stage, we are free to reflect that something very like these trials has been going on in recent years in the United States. How much like? Mr. Miller does not say. But *very* like, allowing of course for some superficial differences: no one has been pressed to death in recent years, for instance. Still, people have lost their jobs for refusing to say under oath whether or not they are Communists. The essential pattern is the same, isn't it? And when we speak of "universal significance," we mean sticking to the essential pattern, don't we? Mr. Miller is under no obligation to tell us whether he thinks the trial of Alger Hiss, let us say, was a "witch trial"; he is writing about the Salem trials.

Or, again, the play reaches its climax with John and Elizabeth Proctor facing the problem of whether John should save himself from execution by making a false confession; he elects finally to accept death, for his tormentors will not be satisfied with his mere admission of guilt: he would be required to implicate others, thus betraying his innocent friends, and his confession would of course be used to justify the hanging of the other convicted witches in the face of growing community unrest. Now it is very hard to watch this scene without thinking of Julius and Ethel Rosenberg, who might also save their lives by confessing. Does Mr. Miller believe that the only confession possible for them would be a false one, implicating innocent people? Naturally, there is no way for him to let us know; perhaps he was not even thinking of the Rosenbergs at all. How can he be held responsible for what comes into my head while I watch his play? And if I think of the Rosenbergs and somebody else thinks of Alger Hiss, and still another thinks of the Prague trial, doesn't that simply prove all over again that the play has universal significance?

One remembers also, as John Proctor wrestles with his conscience, that a former close associate of Mr. Miller's decided some time ago, no doubt after serious and painful consideration, to tell the truth about his past membership in the Communist party, that he mentioned some others who had been in the party with him, and that he then became known in certain theatrical circles as an "informer" and a "rat." Is it possible that this is what Mr. Miller was thinking about when he came to write his last scene? And is he trying to tell us that no one who has been a member of the Communist party should admit it? Or that if he does admit it he should not implicate anyone else? Or that all such "confessions" may be assumed to be false? If he were trying to tell us any of these things, perhaps we might have some arguments to raise. But of course he isn't; he's only writing about the Salem trials, and who wants to maintain that John Proctor was guilty of witchcraft?

But if Mr. Miller isn't saying anything about the Salem trials, and can't be caught saying anything about anything else, what did the audience think he was saying? That too is hard to tell. A couple of the newspaper critics wrote about how timely the play was, and then took it back in the Sunday editions, putting a little more weight on the "universal significance"; but perhaps they didn't quite take it back as much as they seemed to want to: the final verdict appeared to be merely that *The Crucible* is not so great a play as *Death of a Salesman*. As for the rest of the audience, it was clear that they felt themselves to be participating in an event of great meaning: that is what is meant by "Bravo!" Does "Bravo!" mean anything else? I think it means: we agree with Arthur Miller; he has set forth brilliantly and courageously what has

168

been weighing on all our minds; at last someone has had the courage to answer Senator McCarthy.

I don't believe this audience was likely to ask itself what it was agreeing to. Enough that someone had said something, anything, to dispel for a couple of hours that undefined but very real sense of frustration which oppresses these "liberals"—who believe in their innermost being that salvation comes from saying something, and who yet find themselves somehow without anything very relevant to say. They tell themselves, of course, that Senator McCarthy has made it "impossible" to speak; but one can hardly believe they are satisfied with this explanation. Where are the heroic voices that will refuse to be stilled?

Well, last season there was *The Male Animal,* a play written twelve or thirteen years ago about a college professor who gets in trouble for reading one of Vanzetti's letters to his English composition class. In the audience at that play one felt also the sense of communal excitement; it was a little like a secret meeting of early Christians—or even, one might say, witches—where everything had an extra dimension of meaning experienced only by the communicants. And this year there has been a revival of *The Children's Hour,* a play of even more universal significance than *The Crucible* since it doesn't have anything to do with any trials but just shows how people can be hurt by having lies told about them. But these were old plays, the voices of an older generation. It remained for Arthur Miller to write a new play that really speaks out.

What does he say when he speaks out?

Never mind. He speaks out.

One question remains to be asked. If Mr. Miller was unable to write directly about what he apparently (one can only guess) feels to be going on in American life today, why did he choose the particular evasion of the Salem trials? After all, violations of civil rights have been not infrequent in our history, and the Salem trials have the disadvantage that they must be distorted in order to be fitted into the framework of civil rights in the first place. Why is it just the image of a "witch trial" or a "witch hunt" that best expresses the sense of oppression which weighs on Mr. Miller and those who feel —I do not say think—as he does?

The answer, I would suppose, is precisely that those accused of witchcraft did *not* die for a cause or an idea, that they represented nothing; they were totally innocent, accused of a crime that does not even exist, the arbitrary victims of a fantastic error. Sacco and Vanzetti, for instance, were able to interpret what was happening to them in a way that the Salem victims could not; they knew that they actually stood for certain ideas that were abhorrent to those who were sending them to death. But the men and women hanged in Salem were not upholding witchcraft against the true church; they were upholding their own personal integrity against an insanely mistaken community.

This offers us a revealing glimpse of the way the Communists and their fellow-travelers have come to regard themselves. The picture has a certain pathos. As it becomes increasingly difficult for any sane man of conscience to reconcile an adherence to the Communist party with any conceivable political principles, the Communist—who is still, let us remember, very much a man of conscience—must gradually divest his political allegiance of all actual content, until he stands bare to the now incomprehensible anger of his neighbors. What can they possibly have against him?—he knows quite well that he believes in nothing, certainly that he is no revolutionist; he is only a dissenter-in-general, a type of personality, a man frozen into an attitude.

From this comes the astonishing phenomenon of Communist innocence. It cannot be assumed that the guiltiest of Communist conspirators protesting his entire innocence may not have a certain belief in his own protest. If you say to a Communist that he is a Communist, he is likely to feel himself in the position of a man who has been accused on no evidence of a crime that he has actually committed. He knows that he happens to be a Communist. But he knows also that his opinions and behavior are only the opinions and behavior of a "liberal," a "dissenter." You are therefore accusing him of being a Communist because he is a liberal, because he is for peace and civil rights and everything good. By some fantastic accident, your accusation happens to be true, but it is *essentially* false.

Consider, for example, how the controversy over the Hiss case reduced itself almost immediately to a question of personality, the "good" Hiss against the "bad" Chambers, with the disturbing evidence of handwriting and typewriters and automobiles somehow beside the point. Alger Hiss, for those who believe him innocent, wears his innocence on his face and his body, in his "essence," whereas Chambers by his own tortured behavior reveals himself as one of the damned. Hiss's innocence, in fact, exists on a plane entirely out of contact with whatever he may have done. Perhaps most of those who take Hiss's "side" believe that he actually did transmit secret documents to Chambers. But they believe also that this act was somehow transmuted into innocence by the inherent virtue of Alger Hiss's being.

In a similar way, there has grown up around figures like Whittaker Chambers, Elizabeth Bentley, and Louis Budenz the falsest of all false issues: the "question" of the ex-Communist. We are asked to consider, not whether these people are telling the truth, or whether their understanding of Communism is correct, but whether in their "essence" as

171

ex-Communists they are not irredeemably given over to false-hood and confusion. (It must be said that some ex-Commu-nists have themselves helped to raise this absurd "question" by depicting Communism as something beyond both error and immorality—a form of utter perdition.)

Or, finally, consider that most mystical element in the Communist propaganda about the Rosenberg case: the claim that Julius and Ethel Rosenberg are being "persecuted" be-cause they have "fought for peace." Since the Rosenbergs had abstained entirely from all political activity of any sort for a number of years before their arrest, it follows that the only thing they could have been doing which a Communist might interpret as "fighting for peace" must have been spy-ing for the Soviet Union; but their being "persecuted" rests precisely on the claim that they are innocent of spying. The main element here, of course, is deliberate falsification. But it must be understood that for most partisans of the Rosen-bergs such a falsification raises no problem; all lies and inconsistencies disappear in the enveloping cloud of the un-spoken "essential" truth: the Rosenbergs are innocent *be-cause* they are accused; they are innocent, one might say, by definition.

In however inchoate a fashion, those who sat thrilled in the dark theater watching *The Crucible* were celebrating a tra-dition and a community. No longer could they find any meaning in the cry of "Strike!" or "Revolt!" as they had done in their younger and more "primitive" age; let it be only "Bravo!"—a cry of celebration with no particular content. The important thing was that for a short time they could ex-perience together the sense of their own being, their close community of right-mindedness in the orthodoxy of "dis-sent." Outside, there waited all kinds of agonizing and con-crete problems: were the Rosenbergs actually guilty? was

172

Stalin actually going to persecute the Jews? But in the theater they could know, immediately and confidently, their own innate and inalienable rightness.

The Salem trials are in fact more relevant than Arthur Miller can have suspected. For this community of "dissent," inexorably stripped of all principle and all specific belief, has retreated at last into a kind of extreme Calvinism of its own where political truth ceases to have any real connection with politics but becomes a property of the soul. Apart from all belief and all action, these people are "right" in themselves, and no longer need to prove themselves in the world of experience; the Revolution—or "liberalism," or "dissent"—has entered into them as the grace of God was once conceived to have entered into the "elect," and, like the grace of God, it is given irrevocably. Just as Alger Hiss bears witness to virtue even in his refusal to admit the very act wherein his "virtue" must reside if it resides anywhere, so these bear witness to "dissent" and "progress" in their mere existence.

For the Puritans themselves, the doctrine of absolute election was finally intolerable, and it cannot be believed that this new community of the elect finds its position comfortable. But it has yet to discover that its discomfort, like its "election," comes from within.

(1953)

PART *3* CHARLES CHAPLIN

Monsieur Verdoux

CHAPLIN'S TRAMP, taken in his most direct significance, represented the good-hearted and personally cultivated individual in a heartless and vulgar society. The society was concerned only with the pursuit of profit, and often not even with that so much as with the mere preservation of the ugly and impersonal machinery by which the profit was gained; the Tramp was concerned with the practice of personal relations and the social graces. Most of all the Tramp was like an aristocrat fallen on hard times, for what he attempted in all his behavior was to maintain certain standards of refinement and humanity, to keep life dignified and make it emotionally and aesthetically satisfying.

The relationship between the Tramp and his society never solidified. Sometimes the Tramp was able to make use of the society for his own peculiar ends. Sometimes the society in its mysterious processes seized upon the Tramp and endowed him with wealth and honor. The constant difficulties between the two never developed to the point where the Tramp could begin to think of himself as opposed to the society; indeed, it was essential to his character that he should take the society as given and make his own life on its margin. And

177

the society, for its part, had nothing against the Tramp; even when it knocked him down, it did so not because he was a threat—the society was too impersonal even to conceive of such a possibility—but simply because his behavior was preposterous; the blow was always delivered in a fit of abstraction, so to speak, without serious intent. The satiric point of the relationship lay precisely in this element of fortuitousness and innocence: it *happened* that the Tramp and the society were in constant collision, but neither side was impelled to draw any conclusions from this. The absurdity of the Tramp's behavior consisted in its irrelevance to the preoccupations of the society; the viciousness of the society consisted in its failure to make any provision for the Tramp, in its complete indifference to his fate.

After 1933, it became increasingly more difficult to maintain such a picture of the relationship between the individual and his society. Now the two were compelled to become conscious of each other, openly and continuously, and the quality of innocence—even if it had been only an apparent innocence—could no longer be preserved between them; from this point on, there would always be on each side a clear *intent* in regard to the other. The society, seeing in the individual both an indispensable instrument and a constant danger, would find it necessary to take a more and more active and organized interest in all his concerns. And the individual would be forced thereby to assume a position: he would have to be for or against the society, and his decision in this regard would immediately become the determining factor in his life and the defining element of his character. The margin in which the Tramp had managed to survive and carry on his life, on however small a scale, was becoming narrower; at length it would disappear.

This had an immediate effect on Chaplin. The impact of his art, its comic point, has always come in large measure from his insistence on pushing everything to its extreme. He creates his movie world by a process of logical extension (this is of course true of most satire), and he has an unfailing instinct in the selection of precisely those leading elements that will bear extension. (In this he is helped rather than hindered by a certain simplicity in his conception of political and social problems.) From the moment that he could no longer define society (in its logical extreme) by its indifference to the individual, then, for his purposes, the position of the Tramp became questionable, for the Tramp and his society, despite the instability and tenuousness of their relations, were aesthetically inseparable.

The change begins to appear in *Modern Times*, made during the depression. In the factory's treatment of the Tramp there is neither accident nor innocence; the factory is a living, malevolent organism bent on putting the Tramp to certain specific uses. An atmosphere of personal and intended viciousness appears—in the inescapable, nagging voice of authority over the public-address system, or in the terrible experiment with the feeding machine—and this viciousness is a new thing in Chaplin's movies, residing as it does neither in individual human beings nor in the mechanical imperviousness of mere organization, but in a system that has acquired personality. The Tramp can still keep his innocence —he is put in jail because of a political demonstration that takes place *around* him, while he himself is not involved and does not understand what is happening—and in the end he can still escape from the system and disappear down the road. But he cannot circumvent the system or turn it to his own account, and there are ominous signs that the situation will soon be beyond his powers of adjustment. In this movie more than ever before, one is kept aware of his ultimate helplessness; certainly he never seems so *little* a man as when

179

he finds his arms still twitching after the hours of tightening an endless series of the same two bolts.

The end comes in *The Great Dictator,* where the whole mechanism of society is brought to bear against the Tramp in a deliberate effort to make him suffer and, ultimately, to kill him. This direct threat demands a direct response. Merely to escape is not enough, for the final meaning of such a society must be that there is no escape; what is required of the Tramp is that he should attempt to destroy the society. But the Tramp is simply not adequate to the attempt, and in the end Chaplin feels compelled to speak out in his own voice —what could the Tramp have to say about politics? (The quality of Chaplin's own politics is of course not in question here.) Thus the failure of *The Great Dictator* results primarily from Chaplin's reliance on an instrument that was no longer suitable. This becomes quite plain, I think, when one considers how successfully he handles the figures of Hitler and Mussolini; if it were simply a matter of his having chosen "the wrong theme," then one would expect this "wrongness" to be most apparent in just thoses scenes where the Tramp does not appear. The fact is that the theme was almost the only possible one for Chaplin; it was wrong only for the Tramp.

The Tramp has the proportions of a legendary figure. Though he is among the least "real" of artistic constructs, yet by the very disproportion of his personality, by his deep and un-shakable eccentricity, he can carry everything before him, like Falstaff or Micawber, achieving a kind of independent existence apart from the particular movies in which he has appeared. The Tramp creates his world, and everything else must take its color from his presence.

Verdoux is not so tremendous a creation. He exists for one

movie, and his whole meaning is contained in the movie. He has made his point, once and for all.

Verdoux does not create the world, he is only an element of the world. At bottom, it is his own consciousness of this limitation that drives him. He is a man with needs and responsibilities, he must make his way. What are the mechanisms of society? Where are the opportunities? These questions are vitally important to him; he is therefore a busy and enterprising man, full of plans. For the Tramp, it was enough simply to exist; Verdoux must analyze his situation and find ways to meet it. He is like the Tramp in many ways: he has the same social charm and physical gracefulness, above all the same civilized feeling for the possibilities of personal intercourse and good living; but he must put all these qualities to use—he becomes like a cultured jewelry salesman, or the manager of a high-class restaurant, making a profit out of his refinement.

He is only an element of the world, but he carries the world inside him. With Verdoux, the opposition between the individual and society has lost its old simplicity. The society has flowed into the individual, and the two have in a sense become co-extensive; the struggle is now an internal struggle, full of ambiguities and contradictions; it is man himself who is corrupt, both as individual and as society, and Verdoux's problem is to make some working order out of the conflicting needs of his own personality. When he makes his decision, it is as much a decision about his own nature as about the nature of society.

Indeed, we do not see the society at all, except in Verdoux and through Verdoux's eyes. There is no background. There is only Verdoux and his family and his victims, and a few supernumeraries—a friend, a girl in a flower shop, a detective, some reporters (the detective and the reporters are not society, they are only making a living in *their* way), a court of

181

justice, a priest (these are not society either, but only the necessary instruments for Verdoux's triumphal progress to the guillotine; he makes use of them). There is also, at one point, some political documentation—shots of Hitler and Mussolini, marching soldiers, newspaper headlines, ruined businessmen committing suicide, etc.—but this is really Verdoux's own documentation, the evidence in his defense. Verdoux remains an isolated figure without a context—or, rather, the context is a projection of his mind, and all we are told of it is what he tells us.

Thus there is no solid point of reference; everything is open to question. The meanings shift and turn and spread until the whole movie, and ultimately the whole world, is enveloped in ambiguity and irony, and it is no longer certain whom the joke is on. Not only is Verdoux caught in his own irony; sometimes it is we in the audience who are caught, and sometimes Chaplin himself—it is significant of the character of this movie, and to some extent, perhaps, of Chaplin's personal character, that one should feel that he does not always understand the implications of his work.

Complex and sustained irony is a rare thing in literature and rarer still in the movies, if indeed it has ever before appeared in the movies at all. Probably the closest analogy to *Monsieur Verdoux* is Swift's *Modest Proposal*, where, despite the simplicity of the basic idea, one can never quite get to the bottom of the irony. Just as there have been people who could see nothing funny about eating babies, so there are people who can see nothing funny about the mass murder of women. And there is in both cases a certain difficulty in critical discussion. I can do best here by paraphrasing what George Saintsbury wrote of the *Modest Proposal*: "That Chaplin does not really mean to recommend mass murder, though perfectly true, could hardly be urged by anybody capable of enjoying *Monsieur Verdoux*, and would

182

not be listened to by anyone whom it horrifies." But even this is too simple. While it *is* perfectly true that Chaplin does not mean to recommend mass murder, it is also true that he makes out the best possible case for it: the spectator is likely to find himself following Verdoux's activities with eagerness and sharing Verdoux's irritation when his plans are frustrated.

Verdoux's original point is clear enough: business is like murder and therefore murder is only a kind of business. Obviously this is not the strict truth; just as obviously, it is more valuable than the strict truth: no satirist could do much with the proposition that business is *sometimes* like murder. And, of course, the final product of the totality of the world's business usually does turn out to be murder. Verdoux is on firm ground, theoretically.

In practice, however, the matter immediately becomes more complicated, as Verdoux himself is to some extent forced to recognize. Crime does not pay, after all—not in a small way, that is. "Numbers sanctify," Verdoux says, trying to prove that his death on the guillotine is no more than a business failure. But he is wrong to minimize the guillotine. What could be worse than a business failure? Perhaps there is more justice in his death than he is prepared to admit.

The complications go further than this. Despite the clarity of his original perceptions, Verdoux becomes corrupt, and with the corruption not so much of a murderer as of a businessman. It is a hard struggle, he tells us; I go into the jungle only because I must fight for my wife and my child, all that I love in the world. When he says this he is not to be trusted. The jungle is everything to him and his home is only his convenient excuse—characterless blond child and colorless dull wife (how useful that she is crippled!), existing only so that he may have a symbol to justify his ambition. This is not my doing, he says; I found myself unwanted and I was forced to go into business for myself. But is it not best of all to be in business for oneself? He betrays himself as we watch: only in the jungle world of his calling does he display animation and charm, competence as a social being and a man of affairs, a sense of his own powers and his own position. At home he is only the suburbanite, momentarily relaxed and safe, indeed, but impatient to get back to the real world of business. Even a great domestic event—when Verdoux on his wedding anniversary brings his wife the deed to their home, a pledge of security and the happy fruit of his labors—is made flat and insignificant. "What is that?" the child asks, and the mother replies, "It is the deed to this beautiful house and garden"— the blessings of the bourgeois home must be counted to be seen.

Much later—after Verdoux has been ruined in a financial crash, and after the shots of newspaper headlines and marching men—there is one sentence to tell us what became of this home: "Soon after the crash, I lost my wife and child," Verdoux says, explaining why he has no more heart for business. And he adds, insisting on his point: "However, they are happier where they are." Thus with a word the crippled wife and the blond child are gone, and as their existence seemed not enough to account for his activity, so their disappearance seems not enough to account for his decline. One feels again that Verdoux is deceiving himself—is not self-deception the great bourgeois sin? Perhaps it was the crash itself that broke his spirit; perhaps it is simply that the aging and unsuccessful murderer, like the aging and unsuccessful businessman, comes to feel that his time has been wasted.

The peculiarly mechanical and almost unconcerned treatment of Verdoux's family is one of the elements that seem to get Chaplin himself involved in the movie's ambiguities. There has often been an obvious morbidity in Chaplin's sentiment: he has been really tender only with the maimed and

184

the helpless, as if he required some palpable sign of misfortune and innocence before he could feel sympathy. This sentimentality is in one aspect simply the reverse of his humor, for the helpless cripple is also a kind of logical extension. But where the satiric extension has the effect of broadening the satiric view of society, bringing more and more objects into the field of the ridiculous, the sentimental extension does not broaden sentiment. On the contrary, by concentrating all sympathy upon the obviously helpless, it becomes a means of narrowing the field of sentiment (if you are not crippled, then you are not innocent), and it thus reinforces the satire instead of counterbalancing it.

In *Monsieur Verdoux*, where Chaplin's view of society has taken on a new savagery, it would appear that he has correspondingly narrowed the field of his sympathies even further. The crippled wife and the helpless child are here, but they have become formal symbols without content, expressing only an abstract belief in the moral importance of helplessness. Chaplin still feels these figures to be necessary, but he seems unable to take a direct interest in them. The true object of his tenderness is another figure, the homeless girl on whom Verdoux plans to test his new poison. This girl personifies the gallant and lonely individual bearing up confidently against the cruelties of life. She is alone, but she is not helpless at all—except before Verdoux, and everyone is helpless before Verdoux: even when he is caught at last, it must be by his own choice. She is like Verdoux in many ways: she, too, is trying to make her way; she, too, has suffered the world's blows; he can feel that she understands the problem of life in his terms (she carries a volume of Schopenhauer), and if her conclusions are in opposition to his, this is all to the good, for it permits him to regard her as a child and to feel his own wisdom. (But in the end it will be she who "succeeds"—as the mistress of a munitions manufacturer—and she will sit weeping at Verdoux's trial.) Most important, she has loved an invalid—it is this that makes him decide to spare her life. Thus it is no longer the cripple who embodies virtue; it is only the person who loves the cripple. In short, it is Chaplin himself, and the projections of himself that he puts upon the screen.

The film's quality of ambiguity—its tendency to make its statements incompletely, or to take them back after they have been made, or to modify and complicate them—is perhaps most apparent in the talk. There is a great deal of talk, and a number of critics have found it objectionable, either because it bored them or because they saw it as a violation of the rather artificial principle that a movie must rely only on the camera. I do not wish to claim that Verdoux's expositions of his ideas are among the best things in the movie, but I found them full of interest in themselves and extremely important in developing the total effect of the movie's involved irony.

It may take some freshness of mind to reach the conclusion that business is like murder, but there is also a certain puerility in laboring the point. When Verdoux enunciates his ideas, they quickly become platitudes, so that in attacking capitalist society, however sharply, he simultaneously betrays the corruption of his own mind. But then the irony takes one more turn, for, as I have said, the corruption of Verdoux's mind is precisely the corruption of the bourgeois mind, and in exposing himself he again exposes his society. When he says, "This is a ruthless world," or "Violence begets violence," what is that but the self-satisfied voice of the practical man of business who takes a certain pride in his "philosophy"?

In the final scenes before Verdoux's execution, the irony of his speech and behavior reaches a climax of intensity and complication. "I go to meet my destiny," he says, half seriously, as he prepares to deliver himself to the police. And he

186

maintains this ironic grandeur to the end. He scores off everybody, for he has his clear-sighted "philosophy" and the others have only their miserable falsehoods. "As a mass killer, I am an amateur," he says in the court room, and then, his last little dig before he is sentenced: "I shall see you all very soon . . . very soon." In the death cell during his last minutes, he is still eloquent: good and evil—"too much of either will destroy us all"; sin—"who knows what ultimate purpose it serves?" Graciously, he dismisses a reporter: "I hope you will pardon me; my time is limited." He greets the priest, bowing: "Ah, Father! And what can I do for you?" He is, you might say, magnificent. Is this not how we should all wish to go to our executions—smiling, dignified, witty, waving aside the last cigarette, accepting the last drink ("Rum? I've never tasted rum . . ."), quietly laughing at the whole world? At the same time, this dream is after all a little childish (it is a curious fact that Chaplin actually looks like the elder Douglas Fairbanks in this last scene), and Verdoux's triumph is really not much: they *will* cut his head off, and the one thing he has failed to do with all his talk is to establish a single reason why they should not.

So everything goes down together, all caught in the same complex absurdity: the capitalist world; then, in a heap, Verdoux the murderer and man of business, Verdoux the cracker-barrel philosopher, Verdoux the lonely romantic; then Chaplin himself, who believes in Verdoux even if he also believes in the irony that denies him; then we in the audience, who sit watching Chaplin and somehow believing everything at once; finally, the capitalist world again, which produced Verdoux, murderer, philosopher, and all. The final word, canceling all others, is in the movie's last shot: Verdoux is a very small figure as he walks to the guillotine, limping, overshadowed by his guards.

The nearest approach to solidity and directness is in the

187

treatment of Verdoux's victims and intended victims. These women are not simple characters, but they are simpler than Verdoux, if only because he manipulates them, and the important facts about them are clear and unambiguous: they are stupid and unhappy, in varying degrees, and they want glamour and love. Since their dramatic function does not require them to be active, their qualities remain constant; they are not touched by the irony that envelops everything else —indeed, in the case of the Martha Raye character, Annabella, one cannot even conceive of the possibility of irony: she is too uncompromising a statement of the value of life. The women are stationary points, and the argument, so to speak, rages around them: they naturally have no idea that anything is at stake; it is only for Verdoux that the situation is complicated.

Chaplin does wonderful things with these women. Even Thelma, whom we never see except as a billow of black smoke pouring from an incinerator, is made clear to us: when we have seen her family, we know all we need to know. In the scenes with Lydia, the only woman actually murdered during the time covered by the movie, the menace of Verdoux's character, his immense coldness, is at its height. Lydia is an old and bitter woman, and we can see in her face and her posture the whole long unhappiness of her life, while Verdoux thinks only of her money, moving around like a cat as he makes his soft and gentlemanly speeches ("Life can so easily degenerate into something sordid and vulgar. Let us try to keep it beautiful and dignified") and glancing occasionally at the clock to see whether there is still time to win her over before the bank closes. Later, when it is time to go to bed, Verdoux flexes his fingers a little as he gets up to follow her, and they walk upstairs, Lydia nagging at him—did you lock the door? did you close the window?—and Verdoux answering softly, patiently: yes, dear, yes dear; then she goes

188

into the bedroom and he stops for a moment in the hall, looking out at the moon and quietly speaking some lines of poetry that occur to him; and then he follows her, to carry out his necessary and melancholy task.

With Madame Grosnay, the wealthy widow whom he pursues at various times throughout the movie, Verdoux is at his most charming—in this case, the question of murder is still in the future. And it is here that Verdoux is most like the Tramp —a man of taste and sensibility (how gracefully he handles the roses!), but awkward, impetuous, rather boyish. What finally wins Madame Grosnay's heart is most of all his delightful lack of sophistication, the seeming transparency of his intentions. In the midst of one speech, Verdoux suddenly falls out the window—how could she distrust him after that? And later, when Madame Grosnay has at last suggested that Verdoux need not hope in vain, there is one of Chaplin's great moments: overcome by this encouragement, the happy lover lunges at his lady on the sofa, overshoots the mark, recovers himself, and throws himself upon her again—all without spilling the cup of tea in his hand; it is the perfect symbol of the two sides of Verdoux's character.

But the most interesting of the women is Annabella. Any attempt to disentangle Chaplin's own values from the movie, or to identify him absolutely with Verdoux, must take her into account. Annabella is the full antithesis of Verdoux; she is loud and vulgar and stupid, and she is as far removed as possible from the world of practical business enterprise: her money has been won in a lottery, and she invests it in harebrained enterprises exclusively—for instance, a project for generating electric power by harnessing the rocking motion of the sea ("If it works, we'll just own the ocean, that's all!"). She is even in some degree resistant to Verdoux's charm, and she regards him with a moronic suspicion that is not to be overcome by the most disarming behavior. It is this creature who defeats Verdoux, and she defeats him not by opposing a superior reason or a superior morality to his, but simply by a kind of blind fatality, as if she were a force of nature. Not only does she defeat him: she overshadows him at every moment. With Annabella, Verdoux is a subdued man; intelligence is on his side, but in this case intelligence does not count—Annabella has the vitality. There is a kind of desperation in his painstaking and elaborate attempts to kill her: he is like a patient and conscientious man who tries to accomplish some perfectly reasonable and simple act and finds himself unaccountably blocked. In the end, when the lonely lake and the rope with a rock tied to it have failed, even he as he picks up the oars seems to sense that he is up against a force greater than his own.

Verdoux's society cannot completely destroy him, even on the guillotine, for he *is* the society, and his complete destruction would be the society's death. But the existence of Annabella means that a different answer is possible: the one thing that Verdoux cannot destroy, and thus the one thing that the society cannot destroy, is the simple and unrefined fact of mere vitality.

A great deal could be said of the many other elements that help to give the movie its moment-to-moment qualities of imagination and dramatic force: the peculiar involutions and profundities of Chaplin's feelings for women, the complete confidence of his technique (he always does whatever is needed in the most direct way possible), the variety of his invention, above all his unfailing awareness of *all* the emotional and dramatic possibilities of every situation. (This last quality is shown perhaps most brilliantly in the treatment of Annabella's maid. Few things in the movie are at once so completely funny and so completely terrible as the scene in which this miserable creature begins to lose her hair.) But

190

what I have primarily tried to demonstrate here is that the movie must be approached with a willingness to understand and enjoy it as a shifting pattern of ambiguity and irony, made up of all the complexities and contradictions not only of our society but of Chaplin's own mind and the mind of the spectator. Much of the hostility to the movie seems to come from reluctance to accept its shifting point of view, its remarkable quality of being at once uncompromising and uncommitted. We are used to flat and simple statements, especially in the movies; as a consequence, some who have seen *Monsieur Verdoux* have found it unpleasantly disturbing, and some have simply refused to recognize its complexity at all, condemning Chaplin because they disagree with *Verdoux* —though Verdoux certainly does not ask for agreement, and, if he did, it would still not be clear what he wanted us to agree to.

Chaplin is surely one of the few great comic geniuses who have appeared so far in history. It seems to me relatively unimportant to decide whether or not *Monsieur Verdoux* is his best movie; we do not have all his movies before us, and at any rate, as I have tried to show, *Monsieur Verdoux* is the product of a radical change in his vision of the world. Taken by itself, it is a great work of irony; and it is unique among movies, for it requires of the spectator that he should constantly reflect upon what he sees on the screen and what he discovers in his own mind.

(*1947*)

191

A Feeling
of Sad Dignity

BENEATH ALL the social meanings of Chaplin's art there
is one insistent personal message that he is conveying to us
all the time. It is the message of most entertainers, maybe,
but his especially because he is so great an entertainer.
"Love me"—he has asked this from the beginning, buttering
us up with his sweet ways and his calculated graceful mis-
adventures, with those exquisite manners so perfectly beside
the point, with that honeyed glance he casts at us so often,
lips pursed in an outrageous simper, eyebrows and mustache
moving in frantic invitation. Love me. And we have, apparently, loved him, though with such undercurrents of revulsion as might be expected in response to so naked a demand.

Does he love us? This is a strange question to ask of an
artist. But it is Chaplin himself who puts it in our mouths,
harping on love until we are forced almost in self-defense to
say: what about *you?* He does not love us; and maybe he
doesn't love anything. Even in his most genial moments we
get now and then a glimpse of how cold a heart has gone into
his great blaze. Consider the scene in *City Lights* when he
tactfully permits the Blind Girl to unravel his underwear in
the belief that she is rolling up her knitting wool; the deli-

193

cacy of feeling is wonderful, all right—who else could have conceived the need for this particular kindness?—but it is he, that contriving artist there, who has created the occasion for the delicacy in the first place. No, the warmth that comes from his image on the screen is only our happy opportunity to love him. He has no love to spare, he is too busy pushing his own demand: love *me*, love *me*, poor Charlie, sweet Charlie. Probably he even despises us because we have responded so readily to his blandishments, and also because we can never respond enough.

If there was any doubt before, surely *Monsieur Verdoux* made things clear. It gives us the Tramp no longer defeated by his graces but suddenly turning them to account, master of himself and all around him. And what is this mastery?— Verdoux is a murderer. I know very well that Verdoux is not the Tramp, but he rises from the ashes of the Tramp. In their separate ways they both represent the private life of cultivation and sensibility in its opposition to society with its crowds and wars and policemen. If the Tramp had an unconscious (which is not possible), it might make him dream of being Verdoux, for Verdoux's murders are committed so that he can carry on his own idyll with his own Blind Girl; it is true that the idyll is utterly overshadowed by the murders, but this may tell us as much about idylls as it does about murder. *Monsieur Verdoux* is a cold and brilliant movie, perhaps more brilliant than anything else ever done in the movies, but we must make a certain effort of will to like it, for it gives us no clear moral framework, no simple opportunities for sentiment, and not even, despite Verdoux's continual "philosophical" pronouncements, any discernible "message," but most of all an unremitting sensation of the absence of love. The effort should be made. It is no part of Chaplin's function as an artist to love us or anyone, and I do not offer these observations as a complaint.

194

But if *Monsieur Verdoux* was a disturbing experience for Chaplin's audience, it must have been a truly painful one for Chaplin himself. Sweet Charlie had changed his public personality, or at any rate had thrown off its more agreeable disguises, revealing what he must have thought a more serious and in that sense more "real" aspect of himself. And the experiment was apparently disastrous; nobody loved him any more: the "true" Chaplin was repulsive. There was even an organized campaign against the movie, which, though it ostensibly concentrated its fire on Chaplin's personal and political behavior, could be successful only because *Monsieur Verdoux* was so forbidding. When this campaign culminated some years later in the Attorney General's suggestion that Chaplin, then in Europe, might not be permitted to re-enter this country, there were surprisingly few Americans who cared. We can say easily enough that this is a national shame: once again America has rejected one of her great artists. And Chaplin, no doubt, is only too ready to say the same thing; he has said it, in fact, as crudely and stupidly as possible, by his recent acceptance of the "World Peace Prize." But for him, who has asked so insistently for our love, there must be more to it than that; there must be the possibility that he has given himself away.

Limelight, made during these years of the great comedian's disgrace and completed just before his departure for Europe, is his apology and, so far as he is capable of such a thing, his self-examination. "The story of a clown who has lost his funny-bone," he called it while it was being made, and he has tried to live up to the candor of this description, presenting himself to us from the "inside" so that we may understand what has happened to him and perhaps give him again the love he has forfeited. Of course it remains a question, with him as with any artist, whether there *is* an "inside"; candor

195

is one of the tools of art. Certainly he does not confess to anything, nor can one imagine what he might confess to if he did. But it is clear at any rate that he asks for clemency. He even brings his five children into court to sway the jury (the three youngest, though they appear for only a moment, would go far with any jury I was on). He makes little mocking references to his personal fortunes: "I've had five wives already; one more or less doesn't bother me." And he smiles at us sweetly as he has done so often in the past, but more gently now as fits his years; only once, in some "imitations" of flowers and trees, does he fully recall the archaic elfishness of the Tramp.

Now and then, it is true, he shows his teeth: as individuals, he tells us, we may possibly be lovable, but in the mass we are "a monster without a head"; Chaplin has the gift of stating such "insights" as if they have occurred to him for the first time, thus somehow redeeming them from banality. But most of the time he is rather humble, acknowledging at least the main point: that he cares for our applause. "What a sad business it is, being funny!" says the Blind Girl of this movie, and Calvero replies with a wry smile: "Yes, it is—when they don't laugh." Then he tries to explain more profoundly: "As a man gets on, he wants to live deeply. A feeling of sad dignity comes over him, and that's fatal for a comic." There is a moment when Calvero, in a dream of his past greatness, stands receiving the applause of an audience; then the smile fades, giving place to a fixed mask of the most extreme sorrow, the applause dies, the theater is empty. Again we are aware of a banality that somehow does not matter. The scene is false—how often we have been asked to believe that the sorrows of a clown are deeper than all other sorrows!—but Chaplin has lived with the falsehood and is committed to it. Besides, the statements of a clown are always false, his gestures excessive, his mask painted out of all credibility. *After*

196

all, we are supposed to say, there is something very real in all this—but only "after all."

Perhaps, then, if Chaplin is actually trying to tell the truth, he is trying what is not possible to him, and that is why we find ourselves uneasy in his altered presence. But I don't think he has made that mistake. He is only trying to tell a clown's truth, and the "inside" of a clown, if it exists, must be as distorted as the outside—at any rate if he is a thorough clown. Chaplin is among the subtlest of artists, but he is not corrupted by subtlety. His gestures remain broad, his statements marvelously simple and clear, his ideas self-confidently crude. When Calvero smells gas on entering his house, he looks first at the soles of his shoes to see whether he has stepped into dog's excrement. Even while he lectures on the Spirit of Life to the young girl he has saved from suicide, he remains primarily concerned with such distractions as the smell of kippered herring that has got onto his fingers—not exactly to underline what he is saying, though it has this effect, but simply because he knows a smell is always more arresting than an idea. And after all these past years of developing cinematic "art," Chaplin remains the most innocent of film technicians, using his camera only to seek the most direct means of exposition and his lighting only to illuminate; a clown's first task is to make his point unmistakably: if there is subtlety, it will come. What a world of sophistication has had to pass over Chaplin's head so that he may open this film with the epigraph, "The glamour of limelight, from which age must pass as youth enters. . . ."

Of course we would be wrong to take this epigraph entirely at face value. Chaplin often turns out to be more conscious of what he is doing than we suspect, and he has chosen to preserve the archaic tone. But with whatever reservations, he does certainly believe in what it expresses, in the "glamour of limelight"—which must mean the glamour of his own personality. It is true, perhaps, that he ought to be beyond that by now: we all know, don't we, that applause and "glamour" are not what really matter. But he is willing to admit he is not beyond it, just as he is willing to admit he can't keep his mind on the deeper questions of existence because of the smell of herring that clings to his hands. The joke is, of course, that we can't either: nobody ever gets "beyond" anything; that's probably the one joke there is in the world, and all the clowns have nothing to do but tell it to us over and over—no wonder they see no point in being anything but clear.

But though Calvero can never quite get away from the kippered herring, he keeps trying. Once awakened to the advantages of talking pictures, Chaplin in his last two movies has found it almost impossible to stop talking; it seems to have come upon him that he must bring forth all at once the stored-up wisdom of a lifetime. And like many who have thought to save their deepest statements for the last (Mark Twain is another example), Chaplin turns out to have nothing very illuminating to say; his true profundity is still in his silences. Verdoux, having discovered that men do not really live up to their moral ideas, not only drew the logical conclusion by becoming a murderer, but could not resist making little speeches about his discovery, continually poking us in the ribs for fear we might miss the point. In the end Verdoux turned out to be personally as vulnerable as his logic, and that saved the comedy, though one couldn't be sure how much of Chaplin had gone down with Verdoux. Calvero, quite as much a man of the world as Verdoux and sharing his slightly questionable elegance and half-baked independence of mind, is a more agreeable philosopher, preaching not murder but tolerance, vitality, and love. Yet his tone is not very different; like Verdoux, he is over-impressed with his ideas and must be always laboring the point. Now and then he strikes a real spark: "That's all any of us are—amateurs.

We don't live long enough to be anything else." More often he can only make a good try: "Life is a desire, not a meaning." Dying, Calvero can leave us only with this: "The heart and the mind—what an enigma!" Is it this kind of thing the Tramp might have been wanting to say during those years of his silence?

I suppose it is, and I suppose it might have been better if we had never found out. But now that Chaplin has broken the silence, I confess I do not find these platitudes of his quite so distressing or inappropriate as, perhaps, I ought to. To be a clown is not an art of detachment. With whatever deliberation he may contrive his effects, in the end the clown must submit *personally* to humiliation, receiving a custard pie in his own face, falling on his own behind. Even though the fall is not so painful as it looks, it is still a real fall. Every clown, no doubt, dreams that because he has practiced the fall in advance it will not truly touch him, his essential being will remain upright; this is the source of that "tragedy" of a clown's life that we have heard so much about. But if he is a true clown, then his essential being is precisely what consents to the fall, and we who refuse to separate him from his role are more right than he is.

In *Limelight*, as in *Monsieur Verdoux*, Chaplin has got caught in this paradox. He has grown reluctant to submit directly to humiliation and is anxious to be accepted as something "more" than a clown; this is the "feeling of sad dignity" that he speaks of. It is true he also takes great pride in being a clown, but pride itself he uses as a means to deny his identity: we become aware of him suddenly as belonging to a "tradition." Of course there *is* a "tradition" and Chaplin is its highest embodiment, but when he presents himself in that role he has to that extent violated it. He is never more dignified, never less a clown, than in the scenes where he appears as a street singer, dressed handsomely in motley, passing a

199

hat for pennies, thoroughly at ease because he has come back to his roots. "This is the only true theater," he says gesturing at the street and the world; the statement is true as it has always been, and he makes it with the authority that belongs to him, but there is something questionable in his making such a statement at all: it would come better from us who watch him.

Verdoux, despite his pretensions, was still basically a figure of absurdity, clearly unable to understand how one must get along; in his way he was just as "innocent" as the Tramp. Calvero, on the other hand, is not supposed to be in himself a clownish figure, he is just a clown by profession. In fact there must be such a division in Chaplin's personality; if there weren't, he would be insane. But his function as an artist is to demonstrate that in some fundamental sense the division is a false one; when he succeeds in obliterating it, as he was able to do entirely in the character of the Tramp and very largely even as Verdoux, he is closest to the kind of truth that most intimately belongs to him and most deeply implicates his audience. In *Limelight* he makes it very clear that he knows this. But, again, his knowledge is not what counts; a clown knows nothing, he only exists. Finding it necessary to make a direct examination of his problem as an artist, Chaplin is forced to repeat in the structure of the movie itself that division between reality and comedy, between dignity and drunkenness, which is the problem the movie deals with. The scenes of actual clowning are presented simply as stage performances, a kind of documentation of the case of the clown Calvero who has "lost his funny-bone," whereas the movie proper, so to speak, is only occasionally funny, and never very much.

The most disturbing thing about Verdoux was that one did not always know how much he was supposed to be accepted on his own terms, how much Chaplin himself was implicated in Verdoux's murders. With Calvero we are left in no such uncertainty: he is Charles Chaplin "in person" presiding at the telling of his own story and not for a moment relinquishing control. If Chaplin is willing in the role of Calvero to acknowledge his own sense of failure, it is only while making it plain that he will be the one to define what is meant by failure. If he has Calvero die breathing that lame little sentence about the enigma of the heart and the mind, it is not because he sees the sentence as dramatically appropriate, but because he thinks it expresses in itself a profound philosophical and poetic truth. The trouble is that it undeniably does, and there seems to be nothing in Chaplin's education or sensibility to tell him what the sentence lacks. And yet, whatever might be true of his education, has he not shown us over and over a sensibility a hundred times more delicate than our own?

Here we come back to that coldness of heart which seems to belong inextricably to Chaplin's genius. It must often have been said of him that he is an embodiment of childhood, and it is perfectly true. His perceptions have the eccentricity of viewpoint and the almost dazzling detailed clarity of a child's perceptions, and carry similar suggestions of unspecific and perhaps unintended depth. His feelings are as definite and as strong as a child's, and as irresistibly appealing. But like a child he is also imprisoned within the limits of his own needs and understanding, and can express no true relation with others. Precisely the lack of such a relation is what makes him a clown—the most childish kind of entertainer—and gives him his clown's subject matter. What is the Tramp but the greatest of all egotists?—an outcast by choice refusing to take the least trouble to understand his fellow men, and yet contriving by his unshakable detachment to put everyone else in the wrong, transforming his rejection of society into society's rejection of him. The Tramp can draw close only to those who are outsiders like him: children, animals, the Blind Girl—the maimed and the innocent. And in the end he is always walking away into the depths of the screen with his back turned. Verdoux, instead of protecting the lonely and innocent, preys on them, though the difference is not so absolute as it might seem: he is just as much a sentimentalist as the Tramp, as he demonstrates in sparing the life of one woman merely because he is touched by her history and because she has read Schopenhauer; and even for his victims he has a kind of icy kindness which might be one of the things that attract them.

Calvero, combining Verdoux's doubtful *savoir faire* with the Tramp's sweetness, is neither the victim of his world nor its victimizer, but a kind of benevolent observer with all the threads of life held loose in his hands. Though we come upon him when he is no longer successful as a performer, he has failed by becoming too good for his audience, too "dignified," not by falling below it. Besides, he is the only one who understands his failure, or if he doesn't exactly understand it, at least his tolerant acceptance of it takes the place of understanding. There has been a significant change in the role of the Blind Girl—this time not blind, of course, but lonely, defeated, and suffering from a functional paralysis of the legs. Having saved her from suicide and reluctantly taken her into his lodgings, Calvero in a few minutes of psychoanalysis discovers the cause of her paralysis and proceeds to cure it. Soon she becomes a ballet star. This moment of her success is when the Tramp would have found himself rejected. But now the girl makes a declaration of love—that declaration which the Tramp never had the courage to make for himself—and though Calvero lets himself be persuaded for a time, it is he who eventually refuses; he must be the one to decide who loves whom, and he has settled it that she belongs to the young composer (a part played by Chaplin's son). This is no very great renunciation, nor indeed is it presented as one. Calvero has simply avoided an entanglement as the Tramp always did, and he has bettered the Tramp by accomplishing this in such a way as to emphasize his own attractiveness. When he has gone away and the girl after many months finds him again to say she still loves him, he replies with magnificent candor: "Of course you do. You always will."

It is easy to believe him, too, for no one else in the movie is allowed to rival his charm and the mature strength of his presence, or even to become real. The girl herself, though she takes her place readily enough in the gallery of Chaplin's heroines, has less independent power than any who have preceded her. Chiefly, her function is to listen attentively, to offer herself as a passive object for his benevolence, and, since she is not actually blind, to look at him with adoration as once the Tramp would have looked at her; the looks Calvero casts back at her are looks of kindness. As for the young man, his function is to be young and nothing more. Calvero will give way to him because age must give way to youth, fathers must give way to sons, the "glamour of limelight" cannot last forever; that is the theme of the movie. But again Chaplin sets his own terms, and if he yields, it is only in principle: between the young man's stiff, undifferentiated "youth" and Calvero's lively and self-assured "age," there can be no real contest. It is Calvero whom the girl will always love—"of course."

Only among the minor characters is the color of reality allowed to emerge: in the frowzy, small-minded landlady, and in her dreadful friend who appears for just a few seconds and says nothing; in an armless music-hall performer encountered in a bar (later cut out of the film); and most of all in the self-contained, almost grotesquely prosaic street musicians who keep reappearing through the movie as representatives

203

both of the hard everyday world where one must make a living as one can and of the "universal" world of art. In his treatment of these marginal figures Chaplin comes closest to a free and disinterested feeling for others; he could not have made such honest and simple use of them without a certain kind of love, even if this love is expressed sometimes only in the pitilessness of his observation.

The peculiarly stilted quality that troubles one in *Limelight* comes, then, not from any failure of sensibility but from a further narrowing of the field of associations and sympathies in which Chaplin's sensibility can operate, and from a consequent suppression of drama. The Tramp, despite his ultimate frigidity, at least maintained an active flirtation with the world, always escaping in the end but keeping up the excitement of the chase and even hinting strongly that he might like to be caught if only he did not like more to get away. Verdoux, having turned his frigidity into a means of making a living, is necessarily involved with the world from the start, though he tries hard to claim he is not; and he does get caught, to have his head cut off—which is possibly the kind of thing the Tramp was afraid might happen. Calvero is too self-contained either to commit murder like Verdoux or to run away like the Tramp; it would be undignified. He simply does not let anyone approach him. Certainly the five wives have left no traces; the pictures on Calvero's walls are pictures of himself. When the girl is practically forced on him, he hastens to proclaim his detachment (". . . one more or less doesn't bother me") and to lay down the terms of their relation, which is to be "platonic." It does not appear that this prescription is ever violated.

Thus Calvero stands alone on the stage—in the fading "limelight"—and does not so much play out his personal drama as expound it. In the very tones of his voice one can feel his refusal to communicate dramatically. The girl, to whom he does most of his talking, is often little more than a point in space toward which he may orient himself; his words pass over and beyond her—they are not really intended for her at all. At bottom they are probably not even intended for us in the audience—the "monster without a head"—though, like the girl, we are allowed to listen and expected to admire. It is as if the whole movie were one of those dreams in which Calvero, trying to reassert his identity, dreams not of *being* on the stage but of *seeing* himself on the stage. He is his own audience, and his "inside," even to him, is only a mirror image of the outside. When he speaks, it is to hear his voice re-echoing within the isolation of his own being. How could he possibly have learned to sense when his words and postures begin to be false?—he has never watched the faces of those he has pretended to be talking to.

But I am not willing to leave it at that. It is not at all necessary that a clown should be in a true relation with others, or even that he should always be funny; the only necessity is that he should fail and that there should be moments when we are able to imagine that his failure is, "after all," a kind of success. Calvero's failure is clear enough: he cannot get us to take him seriously in the way he wants to be taken. We believe as much as he does in "Life" and the "miracle of consciousness"; it is an impertinence for him to lecture us about these things unless he can be eloquent, and eloquence is beyond him: all he can do is suggest the need for eloquence without ever really attaining it. Even his jokes are too often labored and stuffy. "What can the stars do?" he asks in his discourse on consciousness. "Nothing!—sit around on their axes." To hear this from the greatest comedian in the world!

But is his failure also a kind of success? I can only say it is possible to see it that way. I have no convincing argument to advance against those who see *Limelight* as no more than a crude structure of self-pity and banal "philosophy" interspersed here and there with glimpses of a past greatness. But the crudities of a great artist always have an extra dimension; Chaplin cannot so easily divest himself of his talent no matter how he may blunder. Nor can we divest ourselves of the sense of his presence, perhaps one might say his "tradition": the face and body that move before us on the screen have belonged also for all these years to the Tramp, and then to Verdoux; even the voice and the words come somehow not unexpected. This is an extra-aesthetic element, maybe, but there it is. One way or another, the movies are always forcing us outside the boundaries of art; this is one source of their special power. And of Chaplin perhaps it could even be said that in some sense he has never been an artist at all—though he is full of arts—but always and only a presence.

Calvero's failure has at least this in common with the Tramp's failure and Verdoux's: he fails in dead earnest and with a straight face, intelligently prepared for failure, it is true, but not for the particular kind of failure that comes to him, and never dreaming that his essential worth can be called into doubt. He is an honest bankrupt, so to speak, doing his best to the very end and concealing no assets; it just happens that the money in his vault is in some way devalued —not exactly counterfeit, but not altogether sound either. And yet there is something in the confidence with which he hands it over that makes one hesitate to examine it closely, at least in his presence. Suppose he should demand to see what money *we* are paying our debts with? "We're all grubbing for a living, the best of us," Calvero says once, and he is right as usual, though uninspired. For he does manage in spite of everything to implicate us in his failure. He does it not by detachment and true insight—as he might do if he were the projection of a "real" artist instead of a clown—but, on the contrary, by the hopeless depth of his own involvement; by his suspicious eagerness to have us look into his messy, unilluminating, and amateurishly doctored account books; and above all by the irresistible, brilliant purity of his egotism.

Nothing escapes the deflecting force of this uncompromising self-absorption. When Calvero philosophizes, he puts all philosophy under a cloud. Falling miles short of the kind of profundity he wants, he achieves instead a clown's profundity: we are moved not by what he says, but by his desire to speak. If he ends up with nothing but a worn-out "enigma" —well, so do the real philosophers. Supposing he were to ask us how one enigma can be better than another, could we give him a clear answer? The gap between Calvero and the philosophers is enormous, but in such gaps a clown has his victories: as Calvero gropes confidently in his darkness, it occurs to one finally that this gap between him and the philosophers is nothing compared to the gap between the philosophers and the truth. Again, when Calvero rhapsodizes on the "miracle of consciousness," he manages to suggest not only that we are all responding to life inadequately, but at the same time, by his aggressive "sincerity," that consciousness may be some kind of fake—and also that the possibility of its being a fake does not matter. And when he speaks with his most genuine emotion about love while demonstrating his own impenetrable isolation, and in his "secondary" role as a performer deflates his own sentiment with a savage little song consisting only of a meaningless repetition of the word "love," then he is striking at us very deeply, for at bottom we all fear we are incapable of love, and that what we call love is only something we wish to receive from others. That Chaplin himself is as much a "victim" in all this as we who watch him is only the completion of the irony. A clown's function is to be ridiculous and to make the world ridiculous with him. In this, Calvero has his success.

It remains to be said, nevertheless, that the famous scene near the end of the movie when Calvero performs on the stage as a comic violinist, with Buster Keaton as his accompanist, represents a kind of success far beyond the complex and unsteady ironies of the earlier parts. In this there is no longer any problem of interpretation and choice, no "victims" and no victories, no shifting of involvements back and forth between the performer and his role and his audience, no society, no egotism, no love or not-love, no ideas—only a perfect unity of the absolutely ridiculous. Perhaps the Tramp's adventure with the automatic feeding machine in *Modern Times* is as funny, but there it is still possible to say that something is being satirized and something else, therefore, upheld. The difficulties that confront Calvero and Keaton in their gentle attempt to give a concert are beyond satire. The universe stands in their way, and not because the universe is imperfect, either, but just because it exists; God himself could not conceive a universe in which these two could accomplish the simplest thing without mishap. It is not enough that the music will not stay on its rack, that the violin cannot be tuned, that the piano develops a kind of malignant disease—the violinist cannot even depend on a minimal consistency in the behavior of his own body. When, on top of all the other misfortunes that can possibly come upon a performer humbly anxious to make an impression, it can happen also that one or both of his legs may capriciously grow shorter while he is on the stage, then he is at the last extreme: nothing is left. Nothing except the deep, sweet patience with which the two unhappy musicians accept these difficulties, somehow confident —out of God knows what reservoir of awful experience—that the moment will come at last when they will be able to play their piece. When that moment does come, it is as happy a moment as one can hope for in the theater. And it comes to us out of that profundity where art, having become perfect, seems no longer to have any implications. The scene is un-endurably funny, but the analogies that occur to me are tragic: Lear's "Never, never, never, never, never!" or Kafka's "It is enough that the arrows fit exactly in the wounds they have made."

(*1954*)

PART 4 THE ART FILM

The Flight
from Europe

PROBABLY NO EVIDENCE will ever be sufficient to make us fully understand the experience of Europe's Jews in the past fifteen years; but all evidence is immensely important. We owe a debt to Meyer Levin for *The Illegals,* a film record of the flight of one group of Jews along the path of illegal emigration, from Poland to Haifa (and thence to Cyprus), during the fall of 1947. I wish *The Illegals* were a better film; but a camera automatically records what is before it, and in this case it is the record that counts most—the faces and bodies of the Jews who survived: it is impossible to watch them in even their most commonplace actions without feeling the presence of the events to which they can testify. (I think it tells something of our state of mind that there were perhaps twenty people in the theater when I saw the film. I should not have been there myself if I had not been asked to go.)

The Illegals is like a travelogue made in a tunnel: no scenery, no incidents, only a destination. Most often the Jews are seen walking in a tight procession through some forest across some border—it might be anywhere—or packed into closed trucks, or in a cramped and characterless room in some camp or reception center, once or twice in a freight car. Poland to Czechoslovakia to Austria to Germany to France to Italy—these places are only names; the Jews move across Europe in a trance, noticing nothing, offering no comment, speaking only to those who can tell them what step must be taken next: tear up your papers; go to the Judengasse and ask for Shlomo; go to this or that village and from there across the Alps.

The camera wanders sometimes, but usually within very narrow conceptual limits, diminishing the characters against a monotonous background of destruction, picking out ruined buildings, wrecked tanks, and once, with hesitant and ambiguous opportunism, a crucifix. But for the Jews, once they have seen the absolute emptiness of the ruined ghetto of Warsaw, even ruins have no meaning. They stay inside their windowless vehicles and constricted dormitories, their private world, touching bodies in an intimacy that seems all the stronger because it is usually sexless and practical; they stand always in a circle, looking inward, at each other. The main characters, Sara and Mika, have one possession, a camera: they use it only to photograph each other in stiff poses standing on a heap of rubble; it is a way of saying all they have to say: we have survived. This is not even a statement of triumph; it is simply, for this moment and these people, the one fact of their experience that they are ready to absorb and make use of. Some day they may be willing to say more, but not in Europe and not *for* Europe; for the moment, like the featureless mass of the ruined ghetto itself, they have been drained of content.

Indeed, Europe does not exist for them; it is only meaningless boundaries and anonymous officials—a whole system, no doubt, but no longer any concern of theirs except to circumvent it and get away. And for this, there is a countersystem, equally vague and impersonal: committees, offices, card indexes, the Shlomos and Reubens of Haganah with their dis-

214

creet conspiratorial skills. Within this countersystem, there is a password, the greeting "Shalom," which runs through the film like a slogan, bearing an intolerable weight—this word and the word "Palestine" must serve these people almost as the whole of culture and belief: the only world that really exists is the one they have heard of but not seen—Palestine, an idea at the end of the tunnel.

Shut off from experience, they use their names as proof of their existence, and when the necessities of escape require that names be changed to match whatever papers are available, they will not quite give in. "Rachel Benyamin," Sara says to the man checking off names on a list, "but my *real* name is Sara Wilner." And they write their names on Europe's walls—*my* flesh touched *this* spot; how else can one know one is alive in a world without landmarks? One man searches on the wall of a freight car: "I wrote my name in a car like this on the way to Auschwitz." But Auschwitz was more than a word, and no one says anything.

There is also a kind of plot, in which Sara and Mika are separated and meet again finally on the ship that takes them from Europe. But the plot counts for little: one does not care that this particular couple has been separated and reunited; indeed, one hardly cares about the particulars of anyone's suffering: if there are to be survivors, then for the spectator—and for the "system"—one survivor is the same as another: it matters only to Sara Wilner that she is not Rachel Benyamin. They are a mass of statistics, differentiated only enough to show that the statistics do refer to real human beings. But for the Jew in the audience, it is the very bareness of their personalities that brings these people inescapably close. In the theater, one's own name matters as little as Sara Wilner's: Jews, as Jews, are interchangeable; if even one man has been killed because he was a Jew, then we are all survivors.

215

From the beginning, one is conscious of a certain amateurishness in the film: situations are sketched crudely and hastily; the main characters move stiffly and speak their lines like children in a high-school play, hardly ever achieving just the right tone and emphasis; the very use of the camera sometimes suggests those films of family excursions that are made to be shown to friends, and the voice of the commentator, especially in the early parts, is too often like the voice that accompanies such films: there's John swimming; there's Mika in the ruins of the ghetto.

Some of this crudity reflects a lack of imagination and taste. One example is the unspecific journalistic "effect" of the crucifix shot I have already mentioned; in a film that permits so few "intrusions" of the non-Jewish world, this particular symbol is almost the worst possible choice, since the meaning of the crucifix, under the circumstances, can only be ironical, but the irony itself belongs to the Christians (for a Jew, there must be more relevant comments on the treatment of Jews than to say it is un-Christian) and is in any case too general. Another example is the introduction of "voices" rising from the ruined ghetto, as if it were necessary to establish that the murdered Jews had a claim to live. Much of the crudity, also, must be the result of the conditions under which the film was made: in the movement from place to place, it was most important to record as much as possible and as quickly as possible; many sequences had to be filmed at night and necessarily without adequate lighting; and the characters speak English, a language they have not assimilated.

But before the film is over, one comes to feel its crudity—and even, in some sense, its lapses of taste—as something essential, a quality of the life it portrays. In flight from their past, these Jews are forced to reconstitute themselves out of nothing—at best, out of the merest scraps, a hasty and rough amalgam of the anti-culture of the camps and the (to them) mythical culture of Palestine. This is their awkward age; one cannot watch even their gaiety, though it is genuine enough, without feeling that it lacks true cohesion. Like adolescents, they have not yet developed a style—or, rather, the style is a hastily assembled surface, and they remain frozen in formlessness underneath: what is their constant singing but an *attempt* to achieve form?

But the spectacle of normal adolescence is made tolerable by its character as part of a social whole, one stage in a more or less determined life-history; we think we know what the adolescent is likely to become. These people are not adolescents; their "awkwardness" springs precisely from the fact that they have been wrenched from the normal social and historical context and have become a world to themselves. And therefore their personalities take on a certain fixity and abstraction, just as their own image of the world, contained as it is in a number of symbols and ceremonials referring to a mythical future, is necessarily fixed and abstract. They are like figures in some pageant expressing a meaning that must remain ultimately unclear simply because this particular spectacle is the only means of expressing it; and the crudity of the figures who enact this spectacle—their archaicism, so to speak—is a part of the meaning: they exist, one might say, for this occasion only, this moment of history, deprived of the past and therefore deprived also of the future, which can have meaning for us only as a development out of the past. It is almost impossible to think of them as moving back into what we regard as the normal stream of life without at the same time denying the significance of what has happened to them: this is what makes it so difficult to confront them clearly, and why so much that has been said about them seems mere rhetoric, whether the rhetoric of optimism or that of despair.

It is possible to ask whether these figures can ever really become anything else than what they are. The film has no answer to give and it makes a bad mistake in trying. Mr. Levin identifies himself very closely with the people in his film (he himself plays one of the few "acted" roles), and much of the film's documentary value comes, no doubt, from its having been made so completely from the inside. But this necessarily leaves it with no perspective beyond those scattered elements of life and culture which the fleeing Jews themselves have hastily collected, and which they employ less as definitive ways toward any clearly defined state of "health" than as temporary psychological expedients to protect them from an intolerable past. Perhaps one cannot expect that they themselves should at once face and assimilate their experience—though if there is any way to health for them, it must require this sooner or later. But if we are to understand what they represent (I assume it is important to try), then we should not too readily accept their own version of the meaning of their behavior—more especially because in their desperation they have seized upon certain cultural elements that are likely to be accepted as automatically meaningful.

These elements consist, on the one hand, of the more or less official symbols of a Zionist future—Hebrew songs and dances, the Jewish flag, the word "Shalom," the word "Palestine"—and, on the other, of certain "fundamental" concerns (also connected with Zionism): the conception of Palestine as a "soil" in which to strike "roots"; above all, a fierce concentration on children—the expected baby who *must* be born in Palestine, the child of the new "generation," who is to represent victory, happiness, life, everything that Europe is not. There is a profusion of children in the film, but the camera rarely lingers on them for their own sake—as if they were not interesting because they are not survivors. And the Jews carry them across Europe like so much necessary furniture to be used in setting up their homes in the new land. As the ship

218

sails into Haifa harbor, escorted by a British warship, a child is born. In another shot, the camera moves in for a close-up of a child at its mother's breast. And as the film ends, Sara looks hopefully to the future, expecting her own child.

For these Jews, it is the mere fact of survival that counts most. Perhaps Palestine itself is sometimes no more to them than a symbolical embodiment of their survival, a name to be written on the earth as they write their own names on the walls of their stopping-places, to prove that they have lived. How much more than this Palestine can be will be determined only in the future—the real future, not the future they create as a protection against the past—and for each of them separately. (Even the obvious analogy between the modern exodus from Europe and the biblical exodus from Egypt, which is immediately suggested by this film and has become almost a standard formula in journalism, requires examination: the Jewish awareness of a *long* history often masks a refusal to be aware of history at all.) And those children, too, born to be a new generation in the new land, must be recognized for what they are: a psychological expedient, one more *evidence* of survival and thus, perhaps, a way out of the real problem, which is not survival but the re-establishment of humanity. The fact that the children are also real children only makes the problem sharper. In the context of the events that stand behind this film, is a picture of a baby at its mother's breast *necessarily* a symbol of hope?

(*1948*)

219

Paisan

THE FORCE of *Paisan* is in certain images of danger, suffering, and death that remain in one's consciousness with the particularity of real experience. Like the stacked dry corpses of Buchenwald or the clownish figure of Mussolini hanging by the heels, these images have an autonomy that makes them stronger and more important than any ideas one can attach to them.

In the Sicilian episode, a few American soldiers pick their way in the dark along some vague path beneath a wall, crouching slightly, talking in whispers; one of them chews gum rapidly. Various qualities belong to the men: they are young; they have a certain motor efficiency that makes them appear in general well trained, courageous, and intelligent; they exhibit a solidarity that is practical rather than emotional, resting on a common-sense acceptance of their situation; they are in innumerable ways "soldierly," masculine, and American.

In an American film, these men would be "GI's"—the rough and serviceable vessels of democracy; their personal qualities would be expressed through contrived and carefully differentiated patterns of symbols and ideas (one of the group might

221

be a little comical, and another "spiritual" or "cultured"; one might be named Rosenbloom, and—at the very best—one might be a Negro); and their presence on the coast of Sicily would be given some specifically "universal" relevance (probably the episode would begin with shots indicating the scale of the invasion, and then move in to pick up this "representative" group). But here the qualities of the men and the nature of their situation are inseparably contained in the particulars of their physical presence—for example, the way the large and ungraceful helmets diminish the faces beneath them, forcing one to see each man as a whole body, with his "personality" expressed in movement and in the details of his clothing and equipment; or the astonishingly flat and metallic voice of the leader, at once childish and self-assured, suggesting a lack of sensitivity that may be appropriate to his function; even the chewing gum is for once not a symbol of value but simply a fact of nature. And the situation of the men—removed from the elaborate political, moral, and military framework that an American director would use to give it "meaning"—becomes also a part of the screen image, a visible fact of experience: these moments of tension are among the possibilities in a man's life.

This quality of "existential" truth is vitiated later in the episode, when an attempt at communication between one of the soldiers and an Italian girl is used (in a typically "American" manner) to draw vague populist sentiment out of a purely accidental limitation, as if there were some great truth still to be discovered in the fact that one person speaks English and another Italian, and yet both are human beings. But the earlier quality is regained in the treatment of a group of German soldiers and in the image of the Italian girl herself, whose large and somehow undefined body—to an American eye almost repellent in its lack of physical charm, and at the same time disturbing in its persistent suggestion that charm is irrelevant—becomes the leading visual element of the episode. At the end, when this body is seen for a moment dead and sprawling on the rocks, hardly more ungraceful than when it was alive, it contains in its visible presence the dramatic meaning and conclusion of the episode (the product of war is always a corpse, but always a *new* corpse)—though Rossellini's fundamental lack of taste permits him to spoil this effect with a final scene of cheap irony.

In the Florentine episode, there is a moment when a group of partisans captures two Fascist snipers. A confused knot of men bursts around a corner into the sunny street and moves rapidly toward the camera, growing larger and clearer. One man is dragged along by the shoulders, kicking and struggling; another, erect, is propelled by blows that force him to move ahead as if he were part of the group, rather than its object, and shared the general desire to bring matters to a quick conclusion. Just in front of the camera, the men are thrown to the ground and left for a moment inside a small circle, the camera pointing downward at their backs. One of them cries, "I don't want to die!" There is a burst of machine-gun fire, and the scene is over.

This scene moves so rapidly that the action is always one moment ahead of the spectator's understanding. And the camera itself remains neutral waiting passively for the action to come toward it and simply recording as much of the action as possible, with no opportunity for the variation of tempo and the active selection of detail that might be used to "interpret" the scene; visually, the scene remains on the same level of intensity from beginning to end, except for the increasing size and clarity of the objects as they approach the camera—and this has the effect of a "natural" rather than an interpretive variation. The speed of the action combined with the neutrality of the camera tends to exclude the possibility of reflection and thus to divorce the events from all questions of opinion. The political and moral distinctions between the snipers and their captors do not appear (even the visual distinction is never very sharp), and the spectator is given no opportunity to assent to the killing. Thus the scene derives its power precisely from the fact that it is not cushioned in ideas: events seem to develop according to their own laws and to take no account of how one might—or "should"—feel about them.

The final episode, which describes the defeat and capture of a group of Italian partisans and American OSS men on the Po River, is full of these strong images: a corpse floats down the river, held up by a life preserver, with a crude sign —"partigiano"—stuck behind its shoulders; a baby walks among the unresponding corpses of its family, crying as if it will never stop—only the baby and a dog remain alive; a hanged man sways and turns quietly in the wind, while the other prisoners, lying on the ground below him, talk in whispers ("What will they do to us?" "I have wet myself like a baby."), and the legs of a German guard move back and forth in the foreground; a row of prisoners stands at the edge of a boat, and the Germans push them off one by one to drown (but in this there is perhaps too much contrivance; Rossellini slows up the tempo a little, and one is allowed to become aware of the beauty of the shot).

Again there is no room for ideas. All questions have been decided long before the episode begins, and to reaffirm the decisions would be as irrelevant as to reconsider them. All that matters is the events themselves in their character as recorded experience: not why these things happen, but the fact that they happen, and above all the particular forms of their happening.

I began by suggesting what might have happened to some of Rossellini's material in the hands of an American director.

Since the film is concerned throughout with relations between Italians and Americans, this contrast is particularly relevant, and I should like now to carry it further.

American culture demands victory; every situation must somehow be made an occasion for constructive activity. The characters and events in serious American films are given a specifically "universal" or "representative" meaning in order to conceal the fact that there are situations in which victory is not possible. The idea survives—that is a victory; the man dies —that is a defeat; the "GI" is created to conceal the man's death.*

But *Paisan* is the product of a country that has known itself compromised and defeated for (at least) twenty-five years. In the presence of Mussolini, Victor Emmanuel, and the Pope, no public myth could survive; all action and all ideas of action become contemptible, and the sensitive Italian was forced into idealist philosophy or into the cultivation of personal experience—that is, into a passive and aesthetic attitude to life. (See Guido Piovene's remarkable article in

* A typical figure in our culture is the "commentator," whose accepted function is to make some "appropriate" statement about whatever is presented to his attention. "Grim evidence of man's inhumanity to man," he remarks of the corpses of Buchenwald. "The end of the road," he says as we stare at dead Mussolini on the newsreel screen. (And what can one do but agree?) Even in its most solemn and pessimistic statements, this voice is still a form of "affirmation" (its healthy tone betrays it); at bottom, it is always saying the same thing: that one need never be entirely passive, that for every experience there is some adequate response; at the very least, there is always—there must be— something to say.

the March *Horizon.**) Even an active political figure like Silone reveals in his novels a distinctly masochistic relationship to the very political realities he opposes; in the United States, only Southern and Negro writers (for obvious reasons) ever approach the utter self-abasement represented by Silone's portraits of the peasants with whom he identifies himself.

Rossellini neither requires nor dreams of victory; indeed, it is only defeat that has meaning for him—defeat is his "universal." (Even *Open City* is conceived in terms of passivity: heroism is presented not as the capacity to act but as the capacity to suffer; the priest and the Communist are one, and the activity of the underground leads not to victory but to sainthood.) From this hopelessness—too inactive to be called despair—Rossellini gains his greatest virtue as an artist: the feeling for particularity. In the best parts of *Paisan*, it is always the man who dies, and no idea survives him unless it is the idea of death itself.

One more point may make this contrast clearer. In the three good episodes of *Paisan* (Sicily, Florence, the Po River), there is very little effort to individualize the characters; each displays only as much of himself as his situation requires (the most important exception to this is the conversation I have already mentioned between the Italian girl and one of the Americans in the Sicilian episode). And since the situations are abnormal, the activities of the characters do not in any full sense represent them: they remain strangers. Certain of them stand out because they are more continuously prominent in action, but there are important characters who appear only momentarily—for instance, the German soldiers in Sicily or the partisan leader Cigolani in the Po

* "The Italian Church and Fascism," by Guido Piovene, *Horizon*, March 1948.

River episode. But the reality of these figures does not depend on "characterization"; they come to the screen full-grown, and are as real in ten seconds as they could be made in half an hour—they are *visibly* real. (The stranger one sees on the street is no less real and no less individual because one does not know him.) In American films, on the contrary, the characters are likely to be emphatically individualized, and precisely because they are basically abstractions: without character traits and personal histories, they would disappear.

But the rejection of ideas is also a rejection of principles. Rossellini has no intellectual defenses, and when he attempts to go beyond the passive representation of experience, he falls at once into the grossest sentimentality and falsehood. The monastery episode, in which three American chaplains (one Protestant, one Jew, one Catholic) are taught some lesson—humility, perhaps; certainly not tolerance—by a group of Italian monks, is so outrageously vulgar that it must surely be the product of a calculated dishonesty, probably for political reasons. And the dishonesty is made all the plainer by the fact that a view of the Church such as no politically sophisticated Italian could seriously advance in his own name is here presented through the eyes of three simple-minded Americans (what little intelligence they display among them is all given to the Catholic); by this device, Rossellini tries to preserve his "neutrality." (A similar tenderness for the clergy appears also in all the other Italian films I have seen: *Open City, Shoeshine,* and *To Live in Peace.* Piovene suggests that the key factor in Italian "bad faith" is a refusal to deal honestly with the issue of the Church.)

But the sentimentality goes beyond any single issue. The "message" of *Paisan*—after all, it does have a "message"—is that the whole meaning of war (indeed, the whole meaning

227

of history) is suffering and death. Moral and political differences are obscured: the death of a Fascist equals the death of a partisan, and, as Siegfried Kracauer points out, the American liberators look much like the German conquerors; even the German officer of the Po River episode is presented sentimentally (and therefore with relative success; Rossellini's complete failure with the sadistic German officer of *Open City* is evidence of his inability to deal with real moral distinctions). This view of war is always valid: Falstaff is more nearly right than Prince Hal, and Thersites than Ulysses. But it is also a view that has a special attraction for a defeated Fascist nation, and Rossellini cannot restrain himself from taking a special advantage of it; there must always be one more push—and it always destroys his position, for if death and suffering are not *in themselves* the greatest of misfortunes, then we are back in the field of politics and morals, and it is Prince Hal who is right. Thus, in the Sicilian episode, after the Italian girl is dead, there must be the final scene to show how cruelly she has been misunderstood. In Naples, it is not enough that the Negro and the Italian child are both suffering; it must be shown that *even* an American Negro is shamed before Italy's misery. In Rome, it is not enough that the prostitute and the soldier are both unhappy; the prostitute must be the *very same girl* that he remembers from his first days in Rome and has looked for in vain; and at the end we must see him throw away her address with a sneer: "Just the address of a ——."

A number of Americans collaborated with Rossellini on this film, and their influence is apparent—not least in its sentimentality. But the strength of this American element is a sign not so much of the corrupting influence of America as of the accomplished corruption of Italy: only the fact of defeat is Rossellini's own; beyond that, he must nourish himself at the table of the victors. And there is a significant difference that betrays the nature of this relationship. American sentimentality is rarely without a note of aggressiveness: I am a small man *and* I shall inherit the earth (this must be one of the things that impress Europeans as hypocrisy). But Rossellini transforms this into complete passivity: I am *only* a small man and I have suffered terribly.

From this point of view, the six episodes can be plausibly interpreted as representing the fantasies of the eternally defeated as he tries anxiously to read his fate in the countenance of a new master. In Sicily, the Italian girl is rejected: the American does not know that she was really his friend, and the one who could testify for her is dead. In Naples, the American finds his heart overflowing with pity: he *understands;* he, too, has suffered. In Rome, the Italian girl is rejected again: she is a whore; she has not waited. But in Florence the American nurse presses the dying partisan's head to her breast; and in the monastery, the arrogant victor is humbled before the simple goodness and wisdom of those who have chosen to exempt themselves from history (see Piovene again). Finally, on the Po, the American is at last both loved and loving, directing the Italians in their struggle and then losing his life in a protest against their murder.

(*1948*)

Day of Wrath:
The Enclosed Image

CARL DREYER's basic problem as an artist is one that seems almost inevitably to confront the self-conscious creator of "art" films: the conflict between a love for the purely visual and the tendencies of a medium that is not only visual but also dramatic. The principle that the film is a medium based on movement has often been used to justify a complete preoccupation with visual patterns, as if the ideal film would be one that succeeded in divorcing movement from content, but it is this principle itself that raises the problem, for the presentation of human beings in movement necessarily leads to the creation of drama; thus the maker of "art" films, unless he limits himself to complete abstraction or to generalized poetic symbolism, tends to raise aesthetic demands that he cannot satisfy within the framework he has set. Only in the earlier parts of *Day of Wrath* can Dreyer be said to have solved this problem. And the solution, though brilliant, is essentially unstable; the weaknesses of the film's later parts grow out of the virtues of its beginning.

The film opens with the playing of "Dies Irae," a dreadful, insistent hymn prolonged to the point where it comes to seem a kind of outrage; it is music that does not aim at the listen-

231

er's pleasure or require his consent. In effect, this music establishes the existence of a world whose graces pretend to no connection with the needs of human beings, a world that may find it proper in the realization of its designs to burn a woman alive for being a witch.

There is only the most unemphatic indication that such a world is supposed to have existed in Denmark early in the seventeenth century. It is not a historical world—though it exemplifies certain historical ideas—and the primary tendency of Dreyer's direction is to keep it from becoming historical, to preserve it self-enclosed and static. Everything leading up to the execution of the witch Marthe is presented like a pageant: each movement is graceful and dignified, each figure in some particular fashion beautiful, each shot "composed"; and the camera focuses always on the leading figures of the pageant itself, following their slow and predetermined movement with an entranced solemnity that permits no glance at the actuality which has brought them into being. Not a single shot is spent on documentation, and though the whole "issue" is between good and evil, these concepts, too, exist only as parts of the spectacle: "evil" is the figure of an old woman whose function is to be thrown upon a fire after completing certain movements of flight, suffering, struggle, and despair; "good" is the process by which this ceremony is carried out.

No dramatic conflict surrounds the witch herself—her one mistaken effort to bargain for life remains no more than an expected stage in her destruction—and there is only the barest beginning of the drama that is to take place after her death. Her very sufferings are given an explicit quality of formality: three screams mark the three decisive moments—capture, confession, death; when she lies bound to the ladder and impotently shaking her fist, one's attention is drawn to a pattern of leaf-shadows that moves across her face. And all problematical aspects of the subject—questions of justice and authority, the reality of witchcraft, the existence of God and the Devil—are avoided or postponed: it is shown, for example, that the pastor Absalon, who is the leading figure in the witch's condemnation, is himself in an ambiguous situation, but this is not permitted to become a dramatic problem until after her death; and the activities that constitute the witch's crime, though formally indicated, remain vague—only later on is it shown that she might have been regarded as actually dangerous.

Yet this formalized and narrow spectacle creates a degree of excitement beyond anything one experiences during the later, more dramatic portions of the film; by the time the witch falls screaming upon the fire, the tension has come close to a point at which it might be reasonable to leave the theater. The chief source of this tension seems to be in the interplay between Dreyer's general approach to art and certain of the specific tendencies of his medium.

Dreyer's initial impulse, in his deliberate exclusion of the historical and dramatic, is to deprive events of the quality of reality; it is this, indeed, which accounts for his concern with the past: since the past can be contemplated but not changed, it exists from one point of view as an aesthetic object ready-made—one can experience it "pure." But he practices his aestheticism on events that possess *a priori* an unusual emotional importance, and in one of the most realistic of all mediums. In the screen's absolute clarity, where all objects are brought close and defined unambiguously, the "reality" of an event can be made to inhere simply in its visible presence; so long as the internal structure of a film remains consistent, all its elements are in these terms equally "real"—that is, completely visible. Thus at his best—which means, in this film, when he is creating his own images and not imitating the creations of seventeenth-century painting—

233

Dreyer is able to give his aestheticized vision of the past all the force of reality without impairing its aesthetic autonomy; in the absence of a historical-dramatic reality, the purely visible dominates and is sufficient: the witch is an object of art, but she is also—and just as fully—a human being (she is *there*), and she is burnt; the burning is so to speak accomplished by the camera, which can see the witch without having to "interpret" her.

The effect is something like a direct experience of the tension between art and life. In a sense, the image *as* image becomes a dramatic force: the issue is not, after all, good against evil or God against Satan, but flesh against form; stripped as it is of all historical or social reference, the spectacle is of a woman burnt to serve beauty. It is a spectacle not to be understood—the image itself is all the meaning—but to be endured; and the enormous excitement that surrounds it, the sense almost of a prolonged assault on one's feelings, results largely from the exclusion of all that might be used to create an appearance of understanding. Even to see the witch as a victim of injustice would provide a certain relief by placing the events on the screen within some "normal" frame of response. But no such opportunity appears, nothing *in* the film is allowed to speak for the audience or to the audience (two of the characters cannot bear to watch the burning, but this is not what is wanted: it is merely a sign of their weakness). It is as if the director, in his refusal to acknowledge that physical movement implies dramatic movement, were denying the relevance of the spectator's feelings; one is left with no secure means of connecting the witch with reality, and yet she is real in herself and must be responded to; as responses are blocked, the tension increases.

In this blocking of responses, it is again important that Dreyer's aestheticism leads him to the past. The historical past, being real, embodies a multitude of possibilities; the aesthetic past is created by eliminating all possibilities but one, and that is the accomplished one. Thus time becomes fate: the image is distant and untouchable because its form was fixed long before we come to see it; the witch *will* be burnt because witches *were* burnt. The feelings of the spectator really are in a way irrelevant: he is watching what has ceased to exist, and there is no one to "care" what he feels. He has his feelings nevertheless.

In the later parts of the film, in order to relieve the tension that has been established, it became necessary to permit a reassertion of those historical-dramatic elements which have been so rigidly suppressed. But the basic style of the film is already fixed, and this need to introduce new elements results in incongruities, passages of boredom, and dramatic incoherence.

The dramatic plot which begins to work itself out after the witch's death concerns the adultery of the pastor's young wife Anne and his son Martin; Anne becomes a witch, ensnaring her lover and later killing her husband by the power of evil. The ambiguity of the pastor's position, too, is involved with witchcraft: his sin was to conceal the fact that Anne's mother was a witch. Thus witchcraft is no longer pure image, it is a way of behaving, and the question of its reality is no longer to be avoided. A psychological answer is impossible: Dreyer is already committed to keeping the past *in* the past. But the supernatural answer, which is the one he chooses (and with a hesitation that only makes matters worse), is just as bad: once the question of witchcraft is raised, no one can be expected to believe in its reality.

The attempt to impose belief by purely aesthetic means is inevitably a failure, both dramatically and visually. There is a scene in which the pastor walks home at night through an "evil" storm that is the height of visual banality; then his wife, at home with her lover, is shown saying, "If he were

235

dead—"; then back to the pastor, who suddenly straightens up in the howling wind and says to his companion, "I felt as if Death had brushed me by." And there is a continual effort to use the camera for symbolic comment that eventually becomes clear enough but is never convincing: when Anne first tries her "power" in order to call Martin to her side, Dreyer repeats on her face the shifting pattern of leaves that appeared on the face of the old witch before she was burnt; when the lovers walk in the fields, the camera keeps turning upward to the trees above their heads. In general, there is an attempt to equate the outdoors, the world of nature, with evil (the pastor's mother, who is the one firm moral pillar, is never seen outside the rigidly ordered household she controls); but the camera cannot create a religious system.

The purely dramatic failure is most obvious in the film's conclusion, when Martin turns against Anne and thus leads her to confess her witchcraft. Martin's defection is not made to seem an adequate reason for Anne's confession, and Martin's action itself is entirely without motivation: the very skill with which the director now tries to transmute visual patterns into drama (as earlier he had tried to make dramatic patterns purely visual) becomes a kind of irrelevancy. But even in this later section of the film there is still much that is successful. When Anne resolves to kill her husband, a virtual transformation of character is accomplished by the manipulation of lighting. And whenever the aesthetic image does not come into direct conflict with the dramatic structure, it can still take on some of the purity and completeness of the earlier scenes—for example, in the procession of choir boys at the pastor's funeral—except that now the image is felt as an interruption of the action.

At bottom, the film is an aesthetic paradox: out of the pure and enclosed image Dreyer creates a sort of "pure drama," in which the point of conflict is precisely the exclusion of drama; but this in turn creates a tension that the image alone cannot resolve; the dramatic nature of the medium must reassert itself in the later portions of the film, and Dreyer is involved again in the initial contradiction.

(1948)

Re-Viewing
the Russian Movies

*A curse on all Marxists, and on all
those who want to bring into all the
relations of life hardness and dryness—*
LEV DAVIDOVICH BRONSTEIN
(1896); quoted by Bertram D. Wolfe
in *Three Who Made a Revolution.*

SIX of the famous movies of the Russian Revolution have
been shown recently in New York. Five of them are among
the most celebrated products of what we have all agreed to
call the great age of the Soviet cinema: Pudovkin's *The End
of St. Petersburg,* Dovzhenko's *Earth,* and Eisenstein's *Potemkin, Ten Days That Shook the World,* and *The General
Line.* The sixth, *Tsar to Lenin,* is a collection of authentic
pictures of actual people and events taken by perhaps a hundred different photographers—newsreel and military camera-
men and amateurs, including the Czar himself and members
of his circle.

I had seen most of these movies at one time or another,
but none of them for at least fifteen years, and I went this
time looking very consciously for the pathos and irony of that

239

enormous historical failure which now weighs so dangerously on us all. Irony, God knows, was easy enough to find; every glimpse of the enthusiasms of that revolution brings forth all at once the whole wearisome joke of human aspiration and wickedness—we shall be having it dinned into our ears, in just this form, until we die. There was more irony than the most avid of paradox-mongers could possibly want. Only to see the word "comrades" or the word "workers" in a subtitle was enough. Before I was through I could no longer even understand why our age insists on finding the idea of irony so attractive. I would have given up all ironies, and the sense of tragedy and the sense of history along with them, just to have stupid, handsome Nicholas grinding his heel once more into the face of unhappy Russia.

Pathos was another matter. For pathos there must be victims, and in five of these six movies the glare of triumphant righteousness is so blinding that one can't see any victims at all, only a few martyrs of the working class, their lives well expended, and a few bourgeois or monarchist anachronisms, swept properly into the dustbin of history. No death is without meaning; even that baby hurtling in its carriage down the Odessa steps in *Potemkin* is part of the great plan, and the spectacle is exciting but not saddening. Of course it could be said that Eisenstein and Pudovkin and Dovzhenko were the real victims, ultimately betrayed by the revolution they celebrated; but that idea, if it is important at all, becomes important only on reflection. It is hard to feel the pathos of their lives when you see them playing with corpses; if they had got the chance, they would have made a handsome montage of my corpse too, and given it a meaning—their meaning and not mine.

I do not say that these films of the famous Russian directors left me unmoved, but what I felt was all the wrong things, anger more than anything else. And it is just the best elements that arouse the greatest anger. When Eisenstein photographs the slow raising of the bridge in *Ten Days That Shook the World,* with a dead woman's hair stretched over the crack between the two sides as they come apart, and a dead horse hanging in its harness higher and higher above the river as the bridge goes up, the whole slow sequence being further protracted by the constant cutting in of other shots in "rhythmic" contrast, these controlled elements that once marked Eisenstein's seriousness as an artist become now the signs of an essential and dangerous frivolity which, one suspects, was a part of what made him an artist in the first place (and which is exhibited also in the intolerable pedantry of his theoretical writings). And when Pudovkin in *The End of St. Petersburg* cuts rapidly back and forth from scenes of fighting at the front to scenes of excitement in the stock exchange, one's anger is mingled with shame: this sequence is mentioned with honor in the histories of the cinema.

To be honest, I must say that I had come with some hope of finding that the pretensions of the great Soviet cinema were false. Since I had never, in fact, quite accepted those pretensions, it may not count for much to say that these films seemed to me, in aesthetic terms, as successful as ever. But I do mean that they belong with what we are accustomed to call great films, which is to say that they are crude, vulgar, often puerile, but yet full of sudden moments of power. The scene of the Odessa steps, for instance, deserves all the praise that has been given to it, and perhaps even justifies a recent attempt by Timothy Angus Jones (*Encounter,* January 1955) to establish *Potemkin* as an "epic," especially when one recalls that epic is often an expression of barbarism and superstition. It was not at all an aesthetic failure that I encountered in these movies, but something worse: a triumph of art over humanity. It made me, for a while, quite sick of the art

241

of the cinema, and sick also of the people who sat with me in the audience, *mes semblables,* whom I suspected of being either cinema enthusiasts or Communists—and I wasn't always sure which was worse. (In fact the audiences were unusually silent at most of these movies, and for all I know may have been suffering the same emotions as I was.)

It has been said often that the great achievement of the early Soviet cinema was its grasp of the impersonal, of the drama of "masses" and "forces." It was a new art, for a new age, in which the individual was seen to have his truest being as part of the mass. The real hero of these movies is history. But if there is one thing we should have learned from history— and from the history of the Russian Revolution above all—it is that history ought to be nobody's hero. When it is made into a hero, it is not even history any more, but falsehood. There is something peculiarly appropriate in Eisenstein's and Pudovkin's fondness for architectural and statuary symbolism. Eisenstein represents the rising of the workers, for instance, with a famous montage of three stone lions, one asleep, the second with its head lifted, and the third rising to its feet; by projecting these images in rapid succession, he creates the impression of a single lion stirred into action. This is another example of montage that is mentioned with honor in the textbooks, usually with the information that the three lions were not even photographed in the same city, a fact which is supposed to cast light on the question of whether the cinema is an art. The use of the stone lion is, indeed, a clever and "artistic" idea, but it is also fundamentally cheap, and in both respects it is characteristic of Eisenstein, and of the Soviet cinema generally. What we want most, that cinema rarely gives us: some hint of the mere reality of the events it deals with. The important point about the lions is that all the "art" of their use depends on the fact that they are not alive.

Against the films of Eisenstein and Pudovkin, *Tsar to Lenin* has at least the advantage of not being a work of art or even, in the usual sense, a documentary. This is not to say that it is completely artless. The material, gathered over a period of years from a multitude of sources, was carefully arranged and, no doubt, carefully selected. The sequences are presented as much as possible in chronological order, and there is a spoken commentary by Max Eastman (the pictures themselves, of course, are without sound). At one point there is even a rudimentary "montage," contrasting the homely and unassuming Kalinin with the aloof and splendidly uniformed Czar. I don't suppose, either, that the process of selection rested solely on the objective interest of the material. It is notable, for instance, that the only pictures of an execution show the shooting of Communist prisoners by soldiers of Kolchak's army; on the Bolshevik side there is only a photograph of the room in which the Czar and his family were killed, and a brief glimpse of the head of the Cheka, identified by the commentator as "the incorruptible Dzerzhinsky." (What can it mean to call a political mass murderer "incorruptible"?) Again, in contrast to *Ten Days That Shook the World,* where the existence of Trotsky is never even acknowledged (except for a brief shot of an unnamed figure with the familiar pointed beard shown vaguely "plotting" against Lenin), this film takes perhaps special care to document as fully as possible Trotsky's role as a Bolshevik leader and as commander of the Red Army; the face of that "bloody-minded professor" is the most persistent image in the film. Nor are we spared the ineffable vulgarities of Communist rhetoric; indeed they are more oppressive here than in the other films because the commentary is spoken and we must endure to hear Max Eastman expressing the sentiments of 1937 in the very tones of 1937. "Kerensky had completely ignored the fundamental demand of the masses." "Lenin explained his purpose to the masses." "Kolchak was totally incapable of understanding the situation." "Trotsky proclaimed: 'Kerensky is a tool of the landlords and capitalists! All power to the Soviet!'" This is the language we once listened to with patience. I would have felt sorry for Max Eastman—who after all made no montages of corpses— if I had not been feeling more sorry for myself. Still, perhaps it would be no better if the sentiments were those of 1955. The commentator is one of the diseases of our time and must be endured; he will be there at the end of the world to say into a microphone: "This is the end of the world." But his greatest power lies not in what he says but in his tone of healthy intelligence; Max Eastman has at any rate a certain nervousness in his speech which makes one wish to forgive him.

What matters chiefly in *Tsar to Lenin* is simply that the pictures it presents are in the most primitive sense true. This is not "history" any more than it is art: it is no more than a fragmentary record of appearances. But after all the ideology and all the art, that may be the best we can hope to have; if it does not contain the truth of history, whatever that may be, it does allow us to know the pathos of history, the mere fact that enormous things have happened and human beings have been involved in them. The crowds that throng the cold Russian streets in this movie are the crowds that really saw the Czarist government fall. They are not "the masses" and they do not enter upon the screen in pleasing and meaningful patterns established by a director seeking to express "the masses." Watching them, it is easy to accept the remark of a British observer, quoted by Eastman: "Nothing like these crowds was ever seen before in Europe"—whereas Eisenstein's crowds make you think most of how brilliantly he has "handled" them. You can look at a face in these crowds and say: that man was really there. Is this important? It must be important.

There was even a brief shot of a man I had met: Victor Chernov, a member of Kerensky's government. When I was a child I sat once at the dinner table while the exiled Chernov talked in Russian with the grownups. He seemed to me a wonderfully big and strong man, with a great voice and beautiful white hair. I knew nothing, really, of who he was or what he had done, and I could not understand a word that was said. I stared at him for that hour or so and thought: he was there, he was part of it. Chernov died only a while ago in New York—by then, I suppose, a commonplace figure among the Social Democrats—but I never saw him again except in this movie, where he looks still like a big and strong man. Kerensky himself is still alive somewhere in New York and no doubt I could arrange to meet him if it were important to me. Maybe it ought to be important. He "completely ignored the fundamental demand of the masses," we are told, and so played his part in what has happened to us; one could ask him what he thought he was doing. But he has already written his answer, I believe, and I have never bothered to read it. What answer he might give could bring us closer to the thing we want to know? It is enough to have him fixed on the screen; a small, not quite handsome man smiling down upon a crowd in St. Petersburg, or holding a bouquet that some admirer has pressed on him, or finally, an exile in Paris, composing his features for the camera in an absurd pose of depth and resolution. The selection of pictures is manifestly unfair to him, but what we see is Kerensky nevertheless—another man who was there. (With Eisenstein, in *Ten Days That Shook the World*, he is portrayed—by an actor—as a posturing fool who dreams of being a dictator; once he is shown brooding at his desk below a bust of Napoleon. He has had the last laugh on Eisenstein at any rate.)

There is also Nicholas II. Rather short, it seems, but very handsome with his neat features and beautiful beard, dignified, clean, inhumanly composed. My mother was born on the day his grandfather was assassinated, and eight or nine years later she was taken to America; my father, a young man of twenty or so, left Russia two or three years after Nicholas came to the throne; but Czar of Russia is still the name of an enemy, upholder of superstition and maker of pogroms. And yet he was not always thinking about how to oppress the Jews, or even about how to oppress the Russians. We see him here at play with his friends and his family. Once there is some kind of romp in a field, with the young man trying to catch the girls and making them fall down in the grass; the Czar does not himself engage in this sport, but looks on, one hand behind his back. Another time there is an incomprehensible ball game, with innumerable balls lying about on the ground; now and then somebody picks up one and seems to throw it at somebody else, but there is a certain awkwardness about the whole thing and it looks like a very dull game. Once the Czar goes swimming with his men friends; they are naked and when the Czar stands up in the shallow water, exposing his behind, Max Eastman says, "This is the first time in history that a king has been seen as he really is." At other times the Czar is shown in his imperial role, reviewing his guard; walking in solemn procession with a robed priest; visiting the front. In a number of these scenes the Czarevich is beside him, a thin pinched boy, learning how to be a Czar. Once the Czarevich appears by himself, perhaps no more than nine years old, dressed in a Cossack uniform with a little sword; an officer lifts him onto a horse

and he is allowed to ride around a little; Max Eastman remarks, "The Czarevich was probably the best-spoiled child
in the world." Well, the Bolsheviks did not spare the rod:
a little later there is a picture of the Czar with his whole
family—four daughters, the Czarina, and the Czarevich—and
Eastman announces in the loud flat tone of one who has understood and assimilated all: "Eighteen months later all
seven of them were shot in a cellar in Ekaterinburg!"—he
calls it "Yuhkadderinburg." The Czar and his family, like
Kolchak later on, were "totally incapable of understanding
the situation," and history exacts a penalty for such incapac-
ity, even of young boys with hemophilia. Though Eastman
does not mention it, the Bolsheviks also shot in that cellar in
Ekaterinburg the Czar's servants and his doctor and when
the shooting was over the executioners trampled on the
bodies and smashed them with the butts of their rifles. No
doubt if there had been no revolution and the Czarevich had
become Czar, he would have been a bigot and a despot like
his father. Also, no doubt, he would have died young, of
hemophilia.

Of Lenin and Trotsky I had hoped for more than the mere
sense of their presence. I think I was even looking for something that could be called "the face of revolution," and of
course it wasn't there; only Eisenstein ever gives us anything
like that, and what he gives is a falsehood. Yet one cannot
pretend, either, to see these two figures "pure"; the revolution
does envelop them like a cloud, and we look at them now
through its thirty-eight-years' thickness of disaster. When
Lenin poses informally for the camera in a sunny courtyard,
smiling, relaxed, his hands in his pockets and a workingman's
cap on the back of his head, it is easy enough to see that he
must have been a man of grace and charm, only it is no
longer easy to be interested in his grace and his charm. I

247

found him more "real" in his embattled postures: for instance when he harangues a crowd in the street, a black figure full of dangerous energy "explaining his purpose to the masses"; we do not hear his voice, of course, but the movements of his face are enough; we know in what language and what tones these "explanations" were offered. Trotsky's energy is less "elemental" than Lenin's, sharper and more nervous. We see him rushing around to his fourteen fronts, and the commentator reads us passages from his proclamation: "Without Czarist officers, bureaucrats, and capitalists, our country will live a peaceful and happy life. . . . Death to the hirelings of foreign capital!" Trotsky's little pedant's face is like the point of a weapon. His followers used to speak of him affectionately as "the Old Man," but that was when he was in exile and could no longer kill anybody.

They broke their eggs, and they made their omelette. But history was waiting for them too, just as if they were no better than the little spoiled Czarevich with his hemophilia. There is one very brief shot of the Great Muzhik who was to inherit: a heavy dark man standing at the very edge of a group, looking as if he is not quite sure where he fits in. Eastman says: "Nobody then dreamed. . . ." No, nobody did. Perhaps even Lenin and Trotsky were totally incapable of "understanding the situation."

What it means to break eggs we can perceive in the scene of the shooting of prisoners. That the victims are Communists and the executioners anti-Communist is of no importance. It could have been the other way around, or it could have been another war in another country: the firing squad is a leitmotif of modern history as the gallows was a leitmotif of the history of earlier times. Europe is covered with these graves where ten, twenty, or a thousand people lie dead together in pits that they themselves dug before they were shot.

The prisoners, twelve or fifteen of them, lie on their bellies

on the ground under the guns of their captors; the land seems
to stretch out flat and empty for limitless miles behind them.
From what one can see of their faces, they are all quite
young. Their shoes are collected from them, presumably for
the use of Kolchak's soldiers. One of the prisoners raises his
head and says something mocking to whoever is taking the
picture. Max Eastman says in a tone of exaltation: "The Red
soldier laughs!" Then the prisoners stand quietly, three at a
time, at the edge of the grave. When they are shot, their hats
fly ludicrously into the air and they fall backwards into the
grave ungracefully and with astonishing speed; it is hard to
believe, at first, that there is all there is to it. After each shooting the executioners walk up to the grave and look in to make
sure the victims are dead; once or twice an additional shot is
needed. Two of the prisoners wish to stand with their backs
to the firing squad, but for some reason that is not proper
and there is a pause while one of the executioners gently
takes hold of their arms and turns them around. When it is
the turn of the prisoner who had laughed, there is still something like a smile on his face, and Max Eastman again breaks
the silence: "The Red soldier is *still* laughing!" But in a moment there are those little puffs of smoke from the rifles and
the laughing soldier is in the grave with the rest of them.

To watch the suffering and death of real people in a movie
is an ambiguous experience, and it would be a kind of moral
outrage to make that experience an object of art criticism.
All that must be said is that in this movie scene of the death
of twelve or fifteen young men, nothing triumphs and nothing is "understood"; it is a record of something that happened. Even the one prisoner's laughter in the face of the
firing squad, if it was a triumph at all, was his own triumph;
it did not matter in the last moments of his life that the revolution was going to succeed, and as we watched the scene
now it does not matter that the revolution failed. What is

249

offensive about Max Eastman's comments is that they are too ready to claim this man's death for something beyond itself; for the workers, or the revolution, or for the two great breakers of eggs, or simply for the human spirit—it doesn't matter what particular claim is made. I do not say that such claims may not be valid, but they are valid only at a distance, not *while* the man dies; the death we watch belongs to the man alone.

Yet it is not fair to complain of Max Eastman. One need only think of what one of the great Russian directors might have done with a scene like this in order to appreciate how utterly vulgar art and belief can be, sometimes, when measured against the purity of a real event. There are innumerable examples of such vulgarity in the Russian cinema, moments when the director, taken up with his role as an artist who controls and interprets—few artists have put a higher value on that role than the early Soviet film directors—forgets what is really at stake and commits an offense against humanity. I have already mentioned examples from the work of Eisenstein and Pudovkin. Let me offer another from Dovzhenko's *Earth*, a movie about the collectivization of agriculture.

Dovzhenko is celebrated as the great "lyricist" of the Soviet cinema, and to judge by this film—I have seen no others of his—the title is largely deserved. *Earth* is beautifully photographed and composed, full of dreamy evocations of the slow, patient life of the Russian peasantry skillfully contrasted with the more urgent movement of the "new life" of progress, optimism, and tractors. There are wonderful closeups of peasant faces, at once appealing and frightening in their rigidity and incomprehension. One scene of a peasant household getting up in the morning could hardly be surpassed in its presentation of both the squalor of peasant life and its indestructibleness. And throughout the film there is the sense of limitless land and limitless time, and of the constant possibility of violence. One begins to understand from this film the overheated and equivocal fascination which the peasants held for the Russian intelligentsia; if these dumb and alien figures were to be accepted as human at all, then the temptation was great to make of them something quintessentially human. I thought I could understand also, for the first time, what it must have meant to the Jews to live among these peasants in continual expectation of their rage. It must be added that Dovzhenko's picture of the peasants and the countryside is often grossly sentimental—the "beautiful" death of the old peasant Semyon at the beginning of the movie is the clearest example of this—and that the painfully restrained tempo of his direction produces long passages of almost unbearable tedium. Nevertheless Dovzhenko shows himself a serious artist responding sensitively to his material. Compared to this, Eisenstein's *The General Line,* another film about the collectivization of agriculture, is the work of a skilled hack and a philistine.

But Dovzhenko's virtues are all connected with a certain passivity. He is most successful in presenting the life of the peasants when he is willing to accept it as something irremediably "given" and devote himself to recording its meaningful appearances; even his sentimentality, though it is partly dishonest like all sentimentality, is not so much an active falsification of the material as a willfully excessive surrender to it. Whenever he assumes a more active posture—which is to say, whenever he becomes fully an "artist" in the sense in which the Soviet film directors understood that term—his work takes on as glassy and inhuman a brilliance as Eisenstein's. In *Earth,* this quality is to be seen most clearly in the funeral of the young peasant Vasili, the leader of the "progressive" peasants who has been murdered by a resentful "reactionary."

At the desire of Vasili's father, who has at last understood what his son was trying to do, the body is carried to its grave by a procession of energetic young people singing songs of the "new life." We have seen these young people often: strong forearms, open collars, "healthy" and rather empty faces lit up with purpose and conviction—every "movement" puts them on its posters to symbolize the "new life" that will make us all twenty again. They carry Vasili's body as if it were a banner. As the open coffin passes beneath the trees, branches laden with fruit brush the face of the corpse. While the procession moves on its way, a woman back in the village is taken with labor and goes indoors to have her baby: one man is dead, another is born. At the grave, one of the young men makes a speech in which he says that Vasili "gave his blood for the new life" and that Vasili's death has "sealed the death warrant of our enemies"; to the dead man's father he says: "Do not be sad and do not worry—Vasili was a hero!" In the meantime the murderer, seized with remorse, has been running across the field to catch up with the procession; at last he bursts out on a hill beyond the crowd and screams his confession: "I killed him! I am the murderer! I killed Vasili!" But not a head turns; they are all listening to the funeral oration. The murderer, like all enemies of the people, simply does not exist; he has become, in Orwell's word, an "unperson," and even his remorse is of no interest to anybody. Thus failing to attract attention to himself, the murderer continues his mad flight into the distance, diminishing to a tiny insect-like figure at the very bottom of the screen, dancing back and forth in a ridiculous frenzy, while above him rises the vast landscape of fruitful Russia.

(Left unfinished.)

PART 5   PREVIOUSLY UNCOLLECTED ESSAYS

Kafka's Failure[*]

IT IS CURIOUS that Max Brod should have felt it necessary to suppress certain passages in Kafka's diaries as "too intimate." What could be more "intimate" than *The Metamorphosis*, say, or *In the Penal Colony*? To admit authorship of these fantasies was to admit everything. If this does not seem obvious, it must be that we are still confused by the astonishing literalness and immediacy of Kafka's communication: not many writers have committed themselves to paper so fully, and yet this very fullness, this rigidly disciplined refusal of all concealment or evasion, is what most stands in one's way when one reads him for the first time. And doubtless it is this same quality that has called forth the clouds of Kafka exegesis, those dreary "interpretations" so hopelessly below the level of their subject—as though one burrowed into Kafka's profundities to escape the dreadful nakedness of his surface. Look once directly at that surface—not an easy thing to do, perhaps, with our insistence that every important work of art must conceal a usable doctrine—and one

* Review of *The Diaries of Franz Kafka*, ed. Max Brod, Schocken Books.

255

begins to see how much of Kafka's art is direct and shameless self-revelation.

It is, to be sure, a strange kind of self-revelation, entirely devoid of what for most men is the essential element of personal life: the details, what actually happened. But in this one case at least, the details really do not matter. Kafka gives us directly what the facts of his biography, however "intimate," could have revealed only indirectly; the "secret" Kafka labored so painfully to set down was not the content of his experience—how commonplace that was, after all— but its form. Thus: if he had conscientiously written the story of his engagement, it would have seemed that it was really possible for him to get married, just as he himself in the course of the engagement must have felt that it was possible; but he could not have written a story except on the assumption that marriage was not possible, and this assumption, even if it required a complete suppression of the facts, would have been correct. There is a perpetual discontinuity between Kafka and the world of other human beings (every "interpretation" is at bottom an attempt to conceal this), but the contours of his personality fit perfectly the contours of his art. In a sense, Kafka's personality is the final product of his art. The "real" Kafka is a certain way of writing (one might almost say: a certain kind of syntax).

Still, this is obviously more than the exact truth; that is, it is true only because he is dead and has become his books. While he still lived, there were always the "possibilities" of which he wrote so desperately (". . . . under what stone do they lie?")—he could not be *absolutely* sure they did not exist. (Perhaps Dora Dymant was a possibility realized.) The issue was never resolved except on the aesthetic level, and it remained to torment him at every moment in that half-life of the "normal" world which, even if he came to think of it (and rightly) as no life at all, was still in the most literal sense the life he had to lead. In this area of his existence, the details, such as they are, do have some relevance, and it is to this area that the diaries primarily belong. Kafka's fiction is from one point of view the record of his success; the diaries are the record of his failure, of the fragmentary and disjointed life that never came to anything.

Of Kafka one asks, not: what kind of man could have written these books?—but rather: how could the man who wrote these books have walked the streets? There is obviously no answer to such a question. And yet the diaries are relevant. If they bring us no closer to Kafka, they are of interest as one more element in what will never be a coherent picture; they give—as he puts it—"a kind of inkling of the way a life like this is constituted."

It is surprising to find in the earlier passages, despite the constant recurrence of despair, a sort of common-sense hopefulness; Kafka has not yet come to realize that the "possibilities" will recede infinitely—perhaps, after all, there is only some temporary impediment keeping him from life. Even his drive to write seems still to fall within a recognizable framework: one can see him, at moments, as a young man with strong "literary aspirations." He is capable of banality: "If the French were German in their essence, then how the Germans would admire them!"—later, he will have no energy to spare for this kind of thing. He seeks people out, talks with them, observes, is attracted or not. ("There are still one or two houses in which I have something to do. . . .") He becomes acquainted with a troupe of Yiddish actors visiting Prague and writes pages and pages about them, noting down the details of their appearance and mannerisms, the complicated plots of their plays, scraps of the Talmud; he becomes a close friend of the actor Löwy, falls in love with one of the actresses. The whole episode forms the brightest section of the diaries, and represents a sustained attempt on Kafka's part to circumvent his situation; in effect, it seems to have been an effort to entrap his father from behind, from the Jewish East—but, like all of Kafka's stratagems, it was conceived too far above the level of his enemy. (The father had this to say of his son's friendship with Löwy: "Whoever lies down with dogs gets up with fleas.") Apparently whatever important consequences the episode had were literary. And, thinking back over Kafka's account of it, one is not surprised that this should have been so: the brightness of the episode (like Kafka's personal "sociability," which still deceives Max Brod) is superficial—Kafka's concern with the actors remains fundamentally conceptual and lifeless, as if they belonged not to ordinary experience but to some stimulating intellectual regimen; all his detailed notations do not really evoke them as human beings.

This failure, not so much to understand other human beings as to experience their presence freely, can be seen throughout the diaries: they are peopled with wraiths; the discretion that leads Brod to identify so many of the chief characters by their initials is oddly appropriate. (In 1922, Kafka writes: "The gesture of rejection with which I was forever met did not mean: 'I do not love you,' but: 'You cannot love me.' . . . It is consequently incorrect to say that I have known the words, 'I love you'; I have known only the expectant stillness that should have been broken by my 'I love you,' that is all that I have known, nothing more.") Only in the travel notes, where Kafka can permit himself a relatively relaxed susceptibility to his surroundings, does one find the quality of "true" experience—for example, in a rather charming glimpse of Max Brod in Paris, young, "healthy," and slightly ridiculous. (It should be added that anyone would look ridiculous next to Kafka, once we have decided that it was not Kafka himself who was ridiculous.) In the diaries proper, the only really vivid portrait is of a lunatic, who obviously does not raise the problem of a personal relationship (". . . . how refreshing it is," Kafka writes, "to speak with a perfect fool").

But as Kafka records his personal failure—more and more desperately as time goes on—there is a corresponding effort towards success on the level of art, the only level where success was possible. The diaries offer only a glimpse of this struggle, in a certain number of fragments and false starts, but it is enough to give one a sense of how writing defined for Kafka the limits of his being. The man with "literary aspirations" disappears—indeed, as soon as one looks at him—and there emerges in his place a man whose existence is contained in a certain relationship to language, and for whom writing is as necessary as breathing but as painful as the breathing of one dying of tuberculosis. The least fragment of his art becomes a total assertion of his living presence, like the small movement with which the sick man announces that he is still there. If the personal failure was complete, the artistic success was, in a sense, absolute; one wonders, even, why anything more than fragments was necessary.

There is, certainly, a connection between the two levels of Kafka's existence—it can even be said that the connection is perfectly clear, that one cannot possibly miss it: one level is but the mirror image of the other—and yet it stretches across a gap of infinite dimensions. The failure and the success are not merely opposite "aspects" of Kafka's life: each is complete, each makes its own universe. Now and then we catch a glimpse of him making the leap from one to the other—for instance, when he writes, "This morning, for the first time in a long time, the joy again of imagining a knife twisted in my heart"—but even this tells us, not how the leap was made, but only that there was a leap.

259

Perhaps in the final pages of the diaries the two universes touch at last—when there can no longer be any question of success or failure, but only a despairing summation: "It is enough that the arrows fit exactly in the wounds that they have made." Disease and approaching death bring everything into a terrible harmony, the facts and the art together; when he writes down his temperature—"March 17: 99.3°"—it is like a line of poetry. But for him it was still suffering; that must be remembered. He writes, in 1920: "A segment has been cut out of the back of his head. The sun, and the whole world with it, peep in. It makes him nervous, it distracts him from his work, and moreover it irritates him that just he should be the one to be debarred from the spectacle."

(*1949*)

The Dying Gladiator[*]

HEMINGWAY'S SUPREME VIRTUE—I think it might almost be said, his only virtue—has been the clarity and immediacy of his relation to language. In his best work he achieves an almost absolute congruence of form and content whereby the rhythms and tone of his prose seem as much the creators of his experience as its expression. To be sure, this near-perfection is the product of certain gross simplifications, but in general the simplifications belong to the writer's personality rather than his ideas—Hemingway has always tried to protect himself from ideas—and are in that sense "natural" and therefore convincing; he has often (though not always) had the good fortune to see only as much as his prose is designed to express, and because of this he could make it appear that he had seen all that was relevant.

In most American writing, style means only more or less grace of language, or certain recurrent idiosyncrasies; at best, as with Faulkner, it is a form of rhetorical commentary,

[*] Review of *Across the River and into the Trees,* by Ernest Hemingway, Scribners.

261

the willful imposition of meaning upon the "given." (This is not to say that Faulkner does not have his own "universe," but only that it has more than one level.) With Hemingway, despite his self-conscious seeking for "real" experience, the world itself comes sometimes to seem contained in language: the "real" is the way he writes as much as the things he writes about; or, to state it differently, certain "realities" seem to derive their existence largely from the peculiarities of Hemingway's vocabulary and sentence structure. In this inextricable unity of language and perception (when he achieves it), as well as in the somewhat morbid construction of vision that makes it possible, Hemingway of all American writers is the closest to Kafka. Like Kafka, he gets his strongest and most characteristic effects by a perverse tone of innocence: "They shot the six cabinet ministers at half-past six in the morning against the wall of a hospital." ("Waking one morning from troubled dreams, Gregor Samsa found himself changed in his bed to a monstrous insect.") Like Kafka, he exercises sometimes an almost magical power over his readers, and, in the apparent ease with which he can be imitated, constitutes a dangerous temptation to other writers. Hemingway is the more accessible of the two because the premises on which he works are more popular, but the cult of Hemingway, though it numbers its adherents in the hundred thousands, is in its way no less esoteric than the cult of Kafka. Both Hemingway and Kafka belong to the small class of writers, not necessarily the greatest, who by the purity and brilliance of their technique transform the universe.

For such a writer, language—his own particular language—is everything. Let him for a moment cease to care about the precise weight of each word that he sets down, let him indicate by the smallest gesture that he may not be entirely in earnest, that the words are not really elements of his being but only instruments that he manipulates, and the

Hope and Wisdom*

IF THE GENTILE often fails to understand Jewish humor, it is because the Jewish joke rests upon knowledge he does not share and assumptions he is not prepared to recognize.

The line that divides Jew from Gentile also defines the moral complexities of our world. The acceptance or exclusion of the Jew—the precise area of acceptance and the precise area of exclusion—characterizes the moral structure of a society with particular sharpness, not because the Jew is a saint (or a sinner), and not simply because it is a bad action to exclude the Jew, but, in a more complicated fashion, because of the Jew's "omnipresence," and because everyone, friend or enemy, regards the Jew's existence as a moral rather than a practical issue. (That is why it matters so little whether the Jews "really" have power or "really" are cheats.)

The Jews have developed, during all those years in their half-world of history, one special competence: they know

* Review of *The Old Country*, by Sholom Aleichem, Crown Publishers.

the nature of society. They know without thinking and without formulation; the knowledge is as habitual to them—and as necessary—as the mechanic's knowledge of his tools. Often enough they have misunderstood the incidental (but not unimportant) values of the larger world; often enough they have been duped by their own compulsion to hope; but in the back of their minds they have always known the basic facts. Marx was no surprise to them: how could they not have understood capitalism? Freud was no surprise to them: who knew better how the mind moves against itself? Even Hitler, the final horror, was not precisely unexpected: to the logical mind that cared about the problem one murdered Jew implied six million.

Their knowledge is not theirs exclusively, but they come to it earlier and more inevitably, having fewer illusions and fewer of the graces of security to shake off. They are not better than others, or worse, or wiser, or more intelligent. They are *older*.

Like old men, they are pessimists. Whatever the ultimate affirmations of the Jewish religious tradition (and the religion is significantly lacking in personal promises), individual Jews are strongly aware of the need to live in this world from day to day; and in this world, though never without hope, they expect the worst. Like old men, they can be sour or anxious or wise, depending on how they accommodate themselves to their knowledge of the possibilities. And they express themselves best in complex and ironical humor, that characteristic expression of mature pessimism, in which all the sad conclusions are assumed and nothing remains but to arrange them over and over again in new poetic configurations.

In America the Jewish joke means: I make believe I am a gentleman, but the joke is I am just a miserable Jew. And

266

this means: the attempt was a bad idea and it is too late to do anything about it.

In the ghetto of eastern Europe—Sholom Aleichem's world—the joke was different.

The ghetto was dark and dreary and narrow, and it had its own vices—after all, no one really enjoyed it—but it had its own mind, too. There, where almost everyone was hungry and the smallest processes of survival demanded every day new prodigies of manipulation and exertion, the individual was protected from demoralization by the suffering community. Everyone was worth something, everyone could raise his voice in the synagogue or argue about the interpretation of the Talmud. Poverty was no shame and Jewishness was no shame.

There developed in the ghetto a special type of worldly wisdom, in which a pervasive pessimism existed side by side with persistent (and unreasonable) hope and a certain indulgent acceptance of misery and evil. With what seems almost equal tolerance the Jews accepted God's injustice and their neighbors' cruelty, having suffered exceptionally from both. (The Jews have jokes about Gentiles, but they have never produced anything like the Gentiles' jokes about Jews.) And they were sure of their own value, as they have not been since.

The ghetto was conscious of its idiosyncrasies and felt very strongly the tension of its relationship to the larger world, but it also had to take its position very seriously. The ironies and absurdities of ghetto experience could not become entirely clear until the ghetto itself began to break up. Sholom Aleichem was not a folk artist; he was an "enlightened" Jew who looked at the ghetto in terms of the larger world. His audience stretched from Ukrainia to New York— the whole length of the path of migration—precisely be-

267

cause he expressed the dilemma of the generations that felt the inadequacy of the ghetto and had to make a choice: the ghetto was wrong in every detail, but it was "essentially" right.

"No," Sholom Aleichem writes, "the Kasrilevkites have never heard of canals or water works or electricity or other such luxuries. But what does that matter? Everywhere people die the same death, and they are placed in the same earth, and are beaten down with the same spades. Thus my Rabbi, Reb Israel, used to say—when he was happiest, at a wedding or other celebration, after he had had a few glasses of wine and was ready to lift up the skirts of his long coat and dance a *kazatsky*. . . ."

In the end, this is what all great humor says: death makes us all ridiculous together, even Rothschild, so Reb Israel is not the most ridiculous because he stays in Kasrilevka and dances a *kazatsky* when there is a wedding or other celebration.

For Sholom and Aleichem, the Jewish joke meant: I have to live like a miserable wretch, and I *am* a miserable wretch, but the joke is that I am also a king among men—a Jew. This means: considering the circumstances, I have not done badly.

"As we say on Yom Kippur," say Tevye the Dairyman, "the Lord decides who will ride on horseback and who will crawl on foot. The main thing is—hope! A Jew must always hope, must never lose hope. And in the meantime, what if we waste away to a shadow? For that we are Jews—the Chosen People, the envy and admiration of the world."

(1946)

Essence of Judaism*

FOR MOST JEWS of the West, it is not Palestine, but the
Pale of eastern Europe that stands at the center of the idea
of being Jewish. That is where they came from—they or
their parents—emerging into the modern world from a
background of experience that has no real parallel anywhere. They left the ghetto for very good reasons indeed,
and there is probably no one who would want to go back
even if it were possible. But the world outside the ghetto
turned out to be uncomfortable too—uncomfortable for
everybody, perhaps, but for Jews especially and in a special
way, mostly because the world was reluctant to receive
them, but also because the Jews themselves had lived too
long on the fringes of western society to accept its pretensions completely and allow themselves to be submerged; the
ghetto was still a good point of reference. And by 1933,
when the ominous possibilities of the "Jewish problem" began to crystallize, it was natural that some Jews should begin to think of the virtues of the ghetto. For the ghetto did

* Review of *Burning Lights*, by Bella Chagall, Schocken Books.

269

have virtues, and whatever might be said against it, it was almost enough for a Jew in the years after 1933 to say that the life of the ghetto was at least not the life of modern capitalism.

Certainly it is unreasonable (though not easily avoidable) to feel oneself a Jew merely because of the Nazis, but it is true that the Nazis made the matter of being a Jew a little simpler. The case of the dead Jews of Europe is quite clear: people are never massacred for their vices. In the mind of the victim, at least, a certain moral advantage is established; it is no longer even conceivable that the anti-Semites might be right. And thus the experience of being a Jew takes on a new value.

This book of Bella Chagall's childhood memories, begun in 1939 and written in Yiddish, a language she had not spoken since she left her parents' home, is interesting less as a picture of life in the Pale than as a document in the Jewish experience of the past fifteen years. In 1939, when death was in the minds of Jews everywhere, this is how it seemed to her that her childhood had been: secure and happy, orderly, full of love—a life punctuated by the observances of unchanging piety, one Sabbath after another, one Holy Day leading into the next, each with its special excitement and preparation, its special foods (there is enough food in the book to make one faint with desire), its prescribed quality of emotion and religious exaltation. But there is none of the enormous complication of Jewish life, the pervasive sense of alienation from the larger world, the ironic disparity between the largeness of Jewish conceptions and the realities of Jewish life. For this one must go to other writers, for whom the ghetto was real life and not merely an emotional center. Bella Chagall's ghetto is the ghetto she needed in 1939.

But for all its quality of unreality, this book—like many

sentimental books—does give some softened image of what a lover of Judaism might choose to call the "essence" of its subject—the "idea" of Jewish life, what it was supposed to be and what for brief periods it may actually have been: a life in which every detail was an element in the master-pattern, a life with some of the intensity and formal clarity of a work of art.

(*1947*)

The Working Day at the Splendide[*]

AT THE HOTEL Splendide, where all the waiters speak French, the basic relationship of our society is seen naked and pure. The man on the assembly line at General Motors is after all in a very complex position; in a sense he really is just as important as the president of the company—he too is "essential," he too can think of himself as a man who makes automobiles rather than a man who sells his labor to General Motors at so much an hour, and he is not absolutely compelled to admit that the difference between his rewards and the rewards of the president of the company is an accurate reflection of his value. There is no such complexity about the Hotel Splendide. The Splendide is an institution that ministers to the comforts and vanities of the rich, precisely so that the rich may enjoy the sensation of their own importance. It is exploitation idealized, without even the irrelevancy of a tangible product to cloud the image: the efficient operation of the Splendide produces not an automobile but a feeling of well-being in the breast of someone who has a lot of money. And if the receiver of comfort is to be

[*] Review of *Hotel Bemelmans*, by Ludwig Bemelmans, Viking.

273

distinguished by the fact that he has money, the giver of comfort is to be distinguished above all by the fact that he does *not* have money. For in the absence of an aristocracy—and nothing about the Splendide is clearer than the absence of an aristocracy—there is no good reason for anyone to work in such an institution, except to make money. No concealment is possible: one man serves another because he gets paid for it.

The waiters at the Splendide would talk to themselves as they went to and from the kitchen, formulating dreadful insults not to be spoken in the dining-room; at the limits of patience, they could spit in somebody's food before serving it; they could celebrate discreetly when a guest died. Their satisfactions were fugitive and peripheral; one waiter derived pleasure from brushing the back of his hand against the behinds of fat women. Server and served dwell in an atmosphere of hateful intimacy and mutual exploitation, and the feelings of the server are painful and confused: he hates the best people, but at the same time he feels that they *are* the best, and he looks down his nose at the second-best; after a while his only relief is to spend his vacation at some other hotel ordering somebody else around.

While Ludwig Bemelmans was assistant manager of the banquet department at the Splendide, one of his subordinates, a man who had been a waiter all his life, began to crack up. At a magnificent dinner, when the guests included Otto Kahn, Bernard Baruch, Secretary Lansing, and other giants, this old waiter stood on the balcony biting his nails, and when the assistant manager came up, he said, "Give me two machine-guns, one on this side and the other over on the other side. I'll cover the doors and get them as they try to get out, just like with a hose up and down—brrrrr—and the other gun can spray the speakers' table—brrrrr—brrrrr—brrrrr, Table No. 1—brrrrr, Table No. 2—aim for

274

the plates, shoot through the table, hit them in the stomach so they suffer a while. Here are our enemies. *Ecrasez l'infâme! Liberté, égalité, fraternité!"* The assistant manager sent the man home to take it easy.

Now Mr. Bemelmans never really entertained the idea that two machine-guns might be an appropriate response to a banquet. He has no real passion about the Splendide, and therefore no real vision of its meaning. He breaks his experience up into segments, one thing after another, and there is never the power of feeling and imagination to make the segment embrace the whole. (Think of Chaplin.) If the picture of the whole does emerge, it is only by a process of inference from the particulars; so far as Mr. Bemelmans is concerned, you are free to think of the Splendide as an accidental and queer institution on the margin of society. He himself is *in* the picture; he has still the snobbery of one who knows how food should be served: in his mind the abomination of the Splendide gets overshadowed by the greater abomination of somebody bringing in a service of cheap red dishes for a Jewish wedding, and when the management takes the red dishes over and calls them the "ruby service" (with an extra charge), it is to him as if the Splendide had allowed itself to be corrupted.

Mr. Bemelmans has a special and individual talent; it is very easy to be charmed by him. But one feels in the end that his humor is always a technique for taking lightly what is serious, that he is concerned less with understanding the object before him than with feeling that he has seen through it, that his humor is a personal way out. He is therefore neither as funny nor as profound as his material requires him to be. True humor is least of all a way of taking things lightly; on the contrary, it is a way of taking things particularly hard, for it looks always at our saddest humiliations and it does not compromise. The Splendide is a terrible place, and terribly

275

funny; Mr. Bemelmans has had to reduce it, because he is not capable of dealing with the terrible. In this he is like his fellow-humorists of the *New Yorker*, who have had to turn self-consciously solemn now that their universe can no longer be seen through but demands to be understood; the true humorist is not so embarrassed in the face of death and suffering—death and suffering are his subjects.

(1946)

Sadism for
the Masses*

MR. LEGMAN, ALARMED by the overwhelming predomi-
nance of motifs of violence on the lower levels of our popular culture (murder mysteries, comic books, etc.), argues: (1)
That these motifs are to be understood as response to the
censorship on sex, indeed as its very instruments. "There is
no mundane substitute for sex except sadism"; consequently
an ever-increasing supply of fantasy-violence is needed to
keep us from feeling the enormity of our frustration, and
we find our society involved in "the insurmountable schizo-
phrenic contradiction that sex, which is legal in fact, is a
crime on paper, while murder—a crime in fact—is, on paper, the best seller of all time." (2) As an alternative or
supplement to the above: that manufactured fantasies of violence are needed to divert us from our just grievances.
Thus, in a tone of revolutionary truculence: "Next after fire,
the murder-mystery is society's most valuable servant. Without it, there might be some changes made." (3) That repeated exposure of adults and children to cultural images of

* Review of *Love and Death*, by G. Legman, Breaking Point.

violence may be expected to result in the practice of violence.

In support of the first point, interesting enough on its face, Mr. Legman has little to offer except repeated examples of how censorship forces deletion of sexual preferences but passes over the grossest presentations of violence without protest. These examples demonstrate the existence of the phenomenon he is discussing and very clearly indicate its importance, but they are of no help in explaining it. To the suggestion that the impulses of violence expressed in popular culture may themselves be in some way native to the human personality, Mr. Legman replies only: "No animal kills for pleasure alone"—a statement of which one may doubt both the truth and the relevance. Nor does he deal with the fact that those young people whose cultural interests are most fully comprehended in comic books and similar types of art are also likely to be most active sexually (see Kinsey).

The second point is common coin in the discussion of popular culture, but it is time we asked whether, in the crude formulation it usually receives, it really offers any illumination. In what sense does "society" actually make use of culture as a "servant"? What is the relation to this "society" of those who consume popular culture—or, for that matter, of the critic himself? And, after all, is an examination of comic books the most reasonable method of demonstrating that our lives are difficult? Mr. Legman gives us only his sullen conviction that some kind of conspiracy is going on.

For his third point, Mr. Legman relies heavily on scare statistics: five hundred million comic books are printed every year; one Canadian tree out of—is it three?—goes into the manufacture of paper on which will be printed pictures and descriptions of violence; an American child now seventeen has probably been exposed to a minimum of eighteen million separate images of fighting, torture, and murder. And so on: one could invent these figures and still be sure they were substantially correct. But it is not so easy to decide what they mean: we cannot assume that the intensity of an experience is to be measured by how many individuals expose themselves to it how many times. Mr. Legman has again made the mistake of thinking that a strong statement of the existence of a phenomenon implies its significance. (Figures on American consumption of chewing gum—also, surely, a form of "compensation"—are likely to be equally "alarming.") It is possible, for instance, that the tremendous dissemination of comic books is mainly a technological triumph (Mr. Legman himself mentions the principle that bad art drives out good). The real problem—aesthetic as well as sociological—may be what happens to *one* reader confronted with *one* image of violence, and on this there is little information, since those who write about comic books do not often read them for pleasure. (My own child, discussing adult objections to the comics, asked: "What's wrong with things being exciting?" This seems to me a question that must be dealt with.)

The most interesting element of Mr. Legman's pamphlet is its tone, which is one of the grossest demagoguery. "In our culture the perversion of children has become an industry." "That mystery writers are murder-pimps would be hard to gainsay." "That the publishers, editors, artists, and writers of comic-books are degenerates and belong in jail, goes without saying. . . ." ". . . two comic-book companies staffed entirely by homosexuals and operating out of our most phalliform skyscraper." "Hollywood homosexuals"—"Parisian fairies"—"pansy intellectuals"—"bought psychologists" . . . there is no end to the hatreds of this crusader against violence; he has learned more from the comic books than he thinks.

I agree that one may reasonably be distressed by the culture represented by the comic books, but it is a mistake to base our criticism of that culture on suppositions about its specific moral effects. To treat Superman as we would not treat Henry Miller is only philistinism in reverse, and like all philistinism contains the threat of censorship; indeed, Mr. Legman's pamphlet makes almost no sense at all unless one reads it as a demand for censorship of themes of violence, though he eventually denies this intention. (He proposes instead that the censorship on sex be *lifted;* with this proposal I am in full agreement, but Mr. Legman is deceived in thinking it would have any effect either in relieving our sexual frustrations or in raising the level of our culture: its most probable result would be a flood of pornographic comic books no less violent than the present "clean" ones.) The "immorality" of the comic books consists in their being ill-conceived, ill-executed, and vulgar; but in these terms Mr. Legman's pamphlet is possibly just as "dangerous" as any of the materials it discusses.

(*1950*)

"Gerty" and the G. I.'s[*]

THE CHIEF THING Gertrude Stein tried to do was to write as if she had kept her innocence. Everything had to be seen simply and sharply, as a new thing and a wonder. If the vision was direct enough, it did not matter whether it was profound: she was not trying to make progress. That is why she could write so much that was nonsense and so much that was banal (". . . the girls tend to be tall, taller than they used to be but not the boys not taller than they used to be, I suppose there is a physical reason for this, I do suppose so") and still be a fine artist.

She had to leave America, where the pressures of middle-class earnestness were too strong; she had to work very hard with the language, and cultivate her egotism to follow her own way strictly, shutting out many of the important intellectual currents of her time that meant much to others but had nothing to do with her purpose—so that when she was successful she could write like a twelve-year-old girl full of

[*] Review of *Brewsie and Willie* by Gertrude Stein, Random House.

281

intelligent and sensitive curiosity and very brilliant, more brilliant than any girl ever was at twelve. (Twelve is about right, I think: all the essential knowledge has been gained, but the adult world of sex and misfortune and ideas is still part mystery and part stupidity.)

Her relations with the people of the United States were not quite like those of any other bohemian expatriate. She aroused considerable irritation—you are not supposed to go and live your own life in France while the rest of us must stick it out with the Book-of-the-Month Club and the American Labor Party—but in the end hundreds of American soldiers who had never read her books sought her out in France and called her "Gerty" and found her a great old girl. For her part, though she could not live in America she was always very seriously concerned with America and with being American, and she was certainly very happy to see the soldiers and to find that they had heard of her.

"Brewsie and Willie" is the result of that curious lovers' meeting between her and the American soldiers after the invasion of France. She formed a very high opinion of the soldiers—they were sure of themselves, she wrote in "Wars I Have Seen," no longer provincial as they were in the last war—and in "Brewsie and Willie" she tried to set down what they were like and what she herself had to say to them, in a number of conversations among soldiers, and to her countrymen in general.

Her private world here got mixed up with our public world, and it is fair to say of "Brewsie and Willie" what it would not have been fair to say of the more personal "Wars I Have Seen": that she did not look deep enough or drink hard enough.

Her soldiers are very real in the things that concern them—jobs, morals, security, the threatening future—and in the way they talk, outwardly relaxed and inwardly worried, fumbling earnestly for answers, painfully conscious of their own inadequacies. ("Listen, said Brewsie, you see, said Brewsie, you see I don't think we think, if we thought we could not articulate the same, we couldn't have Gallup polls and have everybody answer yes or no, if you think it's more complicated than that . . . thinking is funnier and more mixed than that . . . oh Willie, I get so worried, I know it is just the most dangerous moment in our history, in a kind of a way as dangerous more dangerous than the Civil War. . . .") But their decency is too pure, and they are more honest in their thinking and more childlike in their attitudes than most Americans really are; she saw that they sucked candy and tried hard to get things straight in their minds, but she did not see how knowing and cynical they could be also, and how acquisitive and cruel. She endowed them with her own innocence—but Gertrude Stein's innocence was a literary method for the creation of Gertrude Stein's world, and in giving her innocence to the soldiers, whom she had made quite recognizable and *public*, she was patronizing them and distorting them. "G. I.'s and G. I.'s and G. I.'s and they have made me come all over patriotic"—she fell in love, and she allowed herself to be taken in by the myth of a special American decency and good-heartedness.

And there is her final message to Americans at this "most dangerous moment in our history": Don't exhaust the country's raw materials. Learn to be individuals. Find out why there was a depression. Worry hard and think hard. This is sound advice—except that the raw materials seem to have preyed upon her mind unduly—but I hope it is not merely ill-natured to say that it doesn't help much. It was the price of Gertrude Stein's art that she paid too little attention to the serious preoccupations of her time; in politics she was

283

stupid and uninformed—she could apologize for Pétain like any good-natured and unintelligent *bourgeoise.*

The funniest thing is that in reading "Brewsie and Willie" one even feels a twinge of that unreasonable philistine irritation she aroused so often when she deserved it less. For she has escaped again; worry and think, she said, and then died, expatriating herself so effectively this time that we cannot hope to reach her with our murmur: yes, that's what we *have* been doing, worrying and thinking.

(1946)

The Art of the Film[*]

The Art of the Film is an expert's account of the possibilities of film technique, written to stimulate "film appreciation" through public enlightenment. The dust-jacket says that Mr. Lindgren has made a "special study" of film technique and appreciation, and the unaffected seriousness with which he pursues his educational aim may be seen in the book's glossary, which includes definitions of such terms as acetic acid, camera, censor, cinemagoer ("one who attends cinemas regularly"), film, studio, and writer ("technician who writes script of a film, or any part of it"). There are informative chapters on the separate aspects of film-making—photography, sound, music, etc.—and a few more general chapters, including a final one on the question of whether films can be art, which reaches the correct conclusion that they can but contributes nothing to the discussion. In spite of its pedestrianism—a common failing among English film critics, who have succeeded in making the films as legitimate an object of cultured interest as archaeology, penal reform, or

[*] Review of The Art of the Film, by Ernest Lindgren, Macmillan, and Chaplin: Last of the Clowns, by Parker Tyler, Vanguard.

285

bird-watching—the book is a useful compendium of information, and especially valuable for its emphasis on the film's development toward greater verisimilitude and on its character as a medium of communication.

But there is a basic error in the idea of "appreciation" itself, an idea that presupposes a homogeneous culture in which a progressive refinement of taste will lead almost automatically from bad art to good art. (This error, too, is characteristic of English intellectuals, who have not yet had to face the problem of middlebrow culture squarely—precisely because the general cultural level in England is so high.) It is more than the development of taste that leads one to prefer Kafka to Somerset Maugham; indeed, the cultivated taste left to itself is perhaps a little more likely to choose Maugham. And in the films, though it is obviously desirable to respond as fully as possible to the aesthetic complexities of technique, these "pure" values are at least equalled in importance by the medium's immense power of communication, which always raises aesthetic problems that go beyond the boundaries implied by the idea of "appreciation"; the film "connoisseur" tends to go wrong in so far as his concern with the "cinematic" causes him to ignore these problems. Mr. Lindgren protects himself by taking the values of middlebrow culture—the "human values," as he calls them—for granted; he can thus "appreciate" both Jean Vigo and Noel Coward. (In this country, where the problem presented by middlebrow culture is at its sharpest, the errors of serious film criticism are often extreme: one of the most sensitive of American critics has overvalued such trash as *The Best Years of Our Lives* and *Key Largo;* another critic writing in one of the little magazines, has suggested that the films of Maya Deren are superior to Chaplin's *Monsieur Verdoux* and Eisenstein's *Ivan the Terrible.* These are contrary errors, but they come from the same source: a refusal to acknowledge the essential *aesthetic* importance of film content.)

Parker Tyler's book, a series of free associations revolving around the word "Chaplin," hardly falls within the realm of film criticism at all. Mr. Tyler puts the films to peculiarly personal uses that often lead him to brilliant flashes of insight, but in the present case he is handicapped by the independent brilliance of Chaplin himself, whose dominating presence makes Mr. Tyler's disorderly observations appear commonplace when not irrelevant.

Mr. Tyler's free-floating application of psychoanalysis has the effect of reducing the complexity of Chaplin's art to a mechanical structure in which every element can be translated into some simple "meaning." Thus the machine that swallows Chaplin in *Modern Times* becomes a womb; an incident in *The Gold Rush*, when a starving prospector imagines Chaplin is a chicken and chases him with a knife, becomes a "paradigm of the child's fear of the father-devourer"; in *Shoulder Arms*, when Chaplin pantomimes the stars and stripes in order to identify himself as American to a French girl, the stars and stripes together represent a bed, the star alone represents a vulva, the "straight-shooting stripe" represents a penis; a photograph of Chaplin impersonating a woman is labelled "identification with the love-object." And so on, until psychoanalysis in Mr. Tyler's hands ceases to be a method of investigating and describing a man's relations with reality but becomes a kind of "system" in itself, an arbitrary code of correspondences that one can *choose* to employ; the penis might just as well be a symbol for the stripe, and "identification with the love-object" is only a way of saying "Chaplin impersonating a woman."

(*1948*)

287

EPILOGUE: AFTER HALF A CENTURY

ROBERT WARSHOW'S *The Immediate Experience* is one of those books whose discovery, early or late, can create so specific a feeling of personal gratitude for its existence that it is almost a surprise to learn that others know how good it is. That is how I account for my recurrent feeling—despite recognizing that individual essays within the book have been repeatedly anthologized, in college textbooks on writing, in celebratory collections of essays—that the book remains neglected. Partly the feeling is that the writing is so lucid and so peculiarly valuable that *everyone* should read it who cares about coming to terms with her or his relation to our culture; partly the feeling is that the writing is so consistent and urgent that its collection advances claims upon attention going beyond anything to be expected from a sequence of essays so many of which are devoted to mere movies—even though no one in our culture has written better about movies than Robert Warshow. A paradoxical expression of the feeling is that one wishes at once to make a present of the book to friends and to strangers, and at the same time to keep it private, as if playing for time to work out one's own

289

relation to it. My effort in this Epilogue is to begin to understand, in some measure to realize, both of these wishes, taking myself as an emissary from another time, a time specified by the association of the appearance of the earliest of the essays in this book with the arrival in my life of the not unfamiliar crisis of reconstituting one's education.

From the fall of 1948 through the summer of 1951 I bought, or rather seized and laid trembling money on the counter for, each number of the quarterlies *Partisan Review* and *Hudson Review* and *Sewanee Review* as they appeared in the elegant little bookstore in Westwood Village, several square blocks of shops adjacent to UCLA that were mostly too expensive or irrelevant for me and the other graduate students I knew to enter. Supplemented by the new periodical *Commentary*, which as I recall the bookstore did not carry, this was almost the only reading I allowed myself in those years to take me away from the regime of philosophical studies I had found my way to after graduating from Berkeley a year earlier, having majored in music and read no philosophy. I had spent most of the intervening year in New York, the last months avoiding my composition lessons at Julliard, very often, afternoons and evenings, at the movies. In *Hudson* and *Sewanee* one could expect essays by all the major names associated with the New Criticism (it is easy to remember, for example, finding Empson on Wordsworth, and R. P. Blackmur on Eliot and Flaubert, and Allen Tate on Poe), and in *Partisan* as well as in *Commentary*, the figures of those who will later be called the New York Jewish intellectuals and who were at the height of their powers—a given issue could contain fiction by Saul Bellow and Isaac Rosenfeld (even if rather more Chicago than New York), a piece on painting by Clement Greenberg, an essay by Lionel Trilling, and something odd, perhaps on movies, by a certain

290

Robert Warshow. The trembling anticipation I note was distinctly, but only partly, directed to the pleasures I knew the reading would afford me. It was equally directed to my daily reminders that these pleasures were not welcome in the profession of philosophy, at any rate not then and there, when English and continental analytical philosophy were its dominant modes, together with American pragmatism. Contrariwise, my consciousness was alerted to the fact that philosophy, in any form, was essentially absent from the cultural commitments, literary or political, of any of the quarterlies. I was having too much trouble recognizing the subjects I was being expertly taught as essential to what I had imagined I wanted from the study of philosophy—something, let's say, that spoke to my crisis in giving up music—to welcome having to face the fact that my America was one in which philosophy and the life of literature were forbidden to each other.

Robert Warshow was the principal writer constituting my strict diet of extra-curricular reading who was asking what America is, and specifically what his relation to American culture is. This explicitly meant not only following his sense that film, and popular culture more generally, were key manifestations in which to read this relation, but also his awareness at the same time that his upbringing and education had given him no way in which to articulate this sense with honesty and interest and conviction—the culture's power to reveal itself, even at its most blatant, could not break free of its capacity to keep itself concealed. Perhaps Warshow's knack for interesting himself in what Lionel Trilling in his Introduction calls "objects unworthy of his attention" contributes to the notion (mine at any rate) that Warshow, or his sensibility, was of a younger, or I might say later, generation than most of the writers with whom he was appearing.

This youthful cast of mind, marked by a fresh, irritated, but undisappointed sagacity, seems to go with other distinguishing characteristics of his writing, among them the fact that he cites few major literary figures as touchstones of ideas. His official reason for this is that while the likes of T. S. Eliot and Henry James (whom he names but does not, I believe, discuss or quote) are great artists, unlike those who create the comic strip *Krazy Kat* and write Broadway plays and make Hollywood movies, the latter say things he (also) wants to hear, or rather things he (also) can and must understand his relation to; this relation manifests the way he lives, his actual life of culture. He concludes that to say what he finds in these more everyday concerns he needs to write personally, but it seems clear that the reverse is equally true, that he wants to attend to them because that attention demands of him writing that is personal, and inspires him to it. And why would this way of writing seem to him of such importance?

He expresses his sense of the necessarily personal in various ways in his opening essay ("The Legacy of the 30's")—namely, a sense of the writer's having to invent his own audience (p. 9), of the writer's having to invent all the meanings of experience (p. 16), of the modern intellectual's "facing the necessity of describing and clarifying an experience which has itself deprived him of the vocabulary he requires to deal with it" (p. 9). What experience has caused this devastation?

Before giving his answer, I note the magnitude of the claim. It expresses an isolation (he is without an audience) so extreme as to deprive him not only of meaningful speech (as if he is effectively aphasic) but also of that access to recognizable experience of his own that is the cause of meaningful speech. Something of this sense of inexpressiveness or suffocation is how I would come, two decades later, to

292

characterize a fundamental philosophical motive of Wittgenstein's *Philosophical Investigations*, to teach us to return to ourselves the language that philosophy, in response to modern culture, would repudiate, the ordinary language in which we can recognize our desire. ("Ordinary language philosophy" has proven to be an unfortunate title for this mode of philosophizing, because it has been taken to contrast with extraordinary, or sometimes with literary, language. What it contrasts with, rather, is a fixated *philosophical* language which precisely would preempt the extraordinary from disturbing customary experience.) The sense of being unexpressed, or as Warshow also puts the matter, of lacking "an adequate emotional and moral response to experience" (p. 17), is an intimate tie of this mode of philosophizing with the motivation to psychoanalysis. I take it as a significant gesture of the *Investigations* that Wittgenstein begins with a description or memory (from Augustine's *Confessions*) of a child learning language; and I take it as a mark of Warshow's philosophicality that the only conversations in which he actually depicts himself engaged are ones with his then eleven-year-old son, Paul (in "Paul, the Horror Comics, and Dr. Wertham"), and there is even a footnoted transcription of an exchange when Paul was four.

It is hard to perceive such matters (the relation to American culture, the relation to one's own speech) as the bases for marking an affinity I felt with Warshow's work that distinguished my sense of it from what I was learning from his more renowned companions in the pages of those quarterlies. And even when I came to be moved, out of my own work, to take up the presence of film (for philosophical reasons, and consciously as well for the claims its powers placed upon the description of experience), and even to assign Warshow's path-breaking essays on the gangster film

293

and the Western in the first seminar I offered on the aesthetics of film, at Harvard in 1963, it was another dozen years before Warshow's example manifested its fuller effect upon me—something which took the form of adducing, in what eventually appeared in an essay appended to my book *Pursuits of Happiness* ("Film in the University"), the fascinating coincidences of concepts that thinking about film had produced between the writing of Warshow and the writing of Walter Benjamin (whom I am assuming Warshow had not read).

In that essay I emphasize that both refuse to exempt themselves from the common response elicited by film, yet both insist that film poses a revolutionary problem for criticism and aesthetics. Both demand the legitimization of film as an object of (philosophical, theoretical) study, a study that must modify the concept of art, hence of what we mean by the popular and what we mean by the exclusive. And the more I explore the writing of Benjamin, the more interesting I find the occasional conjunction of it with the wildly different pages of Warshow. I had not, for example, in my first thoughts of the conjunction, recognized that something like Warshow's sense of the loss of access to his own experience was what produced the centrality for Benjamin of Baudelaire's access to the experience of the modern.

Is this sufficient ground for insisting on so unlikely a conjunction, which might prompt, if not disbelief, exaggeration? I bring it up now mainly as a spur to ask whether the current extreme prestige of Benjamin and the comparative neglect of Warshow, even within the realm of the academic study of film, is a reasonable measure of their comparative value. The point of this gesture is not to suggest that something needs to be done about this disparity but to ask what it betokens about our relation to our own experience. Here is

294

a place from which to give Warshow's answer to the question
I postponed, concerning the cause of the devastation of culture (of audience, of language, of experience) and the consequent sense of isolation within which Warshow understands the serious American intellectual of his time to have
to work.

Warshow calls the cause the "mass culture of Stalinist
liberalism" (p. 16), a development to which he attributes the
corruption of American radicalism and the "vulgarization of
intellectual life" (p. 3), whose sign is that "alienation from
reality" which is "the characteristic experience of our age"
(p. 9). Warshow writes as one to whom becoming a socialist
had been the expected step of having grown up in New York
with a life-long socialist immigrant Jewish father, hence one
for whom, while "the *issue* of Stalinism" is settled (though
the danger is not)," "the *experience* of Stalinism remains
[with its "peculiar complexity"] . . . the most important of
our time" (p. 6). And of our place. "The Communists could
never completely set the tone of thinking in Europe" because in Europe the Communist movement, while "at once
more serious and more popular" than in America, "was still
only one current in intellectual life." In this country, by contrast, "there was a time when virtually all intellectual vitality
was derived . . . from the Communist party," whether you
existed within its "wide orbit" or "maintained yourself in opposition," resulting in "a disastrous vulgarization of intellectual
life" (p. 3). Robert Warshow's father, like Walter Benjamin's,
was a businessman, but Benjamin's was much more successful in amassing wealth, alienated from Berlin high bourgeois
life only (*only*) because he was a Jew. Benjamin separated
from him as a result of perpetual, mutual grievances. Yet for
all the incommensurabilities in the weaves of the sensibili-
ties of Benjamin and of Warshow, the issue of the Commu-

nist movement, and in particular of what Stalinism can be taken to signify, was as unsettled an issue in Benjamin's writing, in its way, as it was in Warshow's, in its different way. It was the issue over which Benjamin and his old friend Gershom Scholem were fatefully at odds.

Still, why insist on what is incommensurable, also, in importance? The conflicts within an incontestably great European intellectual such as Walter Benjamin become part of subsequent intellectual history in the West; the conflicts of a talented young American thinker, whose early death stopped short his exploration of his gifts, die with him—unless perhaps given life in the work of some later such young. I have a variety of reasons for the insistence. First, I want to emphasize not so much that Warshow is as immediate for us as Benjamin is, as that Benjamin is no less remote than Warshow is, that each is writing from memories that should not deprive us of our differing memories, that an inescapable autobiographical moment in philosophizing ("we," as I remarked a long time ago, is still first-person) is inseparable from an autopolitical task, letting the polis reflect upon itself, define itself. In Benjamin's case, film has to bear up under a proof of its usefulness to social aspiration; in Warshow's case film's powers are seen, for example in transforming Charles Chaplin's Tramp into Monsieur Verdoux and thence (in *Limelight*) into Calvero, to test whether our reception of socialist aspiration can bear up under the observations of irony: the former requires high theory, for which Warshow was engaging to prepare himself, the latter requires high criticism of individual objects, to which, in the case of movies, Benjamin never turned himself.

Second, Warshow's revulsion and anger at the devastation of national radical politics by the absorption into an international popular front creates passages some will find hard in the critic's portrait of Julius and Ethel Rosenberg's exchange of stilted messages in prison and in his contempt for Arthur Miller's *Death of a Salesman*, which half a century later was chosen for celebration by a production in China. But these passages of Warshow's, in the candor and complexity of their expression, are measures of the effort of imagination called upon to reach the reality of an old story, and of what is perhaps the continuing story—of the movement of so many American intellectuals from left to right, and of the mutual contempt of older and newer lefts.

Third, the conjunction is meant to counter an impression perhaps left by the understandable editorial decision, in originally collecting Warshow's writings, to use as the book's Author's Preface (rather than, say, as an Appendix) Warshow's project statement for a Guggenheim Fellowship application to prepare a study of movies. Together with the subtitle (I assume also an editorial decision)—"Movies, Comics, Theatre & Other Aspects of Popular Culture"— the decision encourages the sense that Warshow was identifying movies as a part of a wider and quite well known phenomenon named popular culture, whereas it strikes me as closer to what Warshow evidently regards as his unheard-of efforts, to say that they explode what we think we know of the natures of movies and of popular culture, manifested, for example, in the fact that the viewing of a pair of Chaplin films inspires from Warshow sustained and powerful and moving instances of the criticism of human creativity (what Henry James wickedly calls "appreciations" of it), whereas looking through comic books produces from him intelligent and concerned thoughts about how we are to protect the integrity of each, evidently necessary, side of a loving but tricky generational impasse. The tact and range of such exercises convey the promise of, and provide instances of, a sophistication of intellectual life whose luster, as idea and achievement, has not dimmed.

By the fall of 1951, a fellowship took me to graduate study at Harvard and an even more exclusive concentration on philosophy. While I still had not found a voice in philosophy, I could allow myself some association with the dissident voices within it that traditions inevitably create. Although Pascal, Nietzsche, and Kierkegaard, for example, were still not part of an accepted philosophy curriculum, they were not exactly dismissed as philosophy when discreetly inserted in term papers. Then, a short decade after Warshow's death in 1955, another radicalism emerged in connection with a revived civil rights movement and, bewilderingly rapidly, a catastrophic chain of misjudgments concerning Vietnam, precipitating a new culture of popular music that defied familiar forms of criticism. New Criticism and the New York intellectual life could seem now, suddenly, impertinent, an impertinence that some will take to be confirmed theoretically in the late 1960s by the onslaught of the French transfiguration into English-speaking academic life of (largely) German philosophy. Was this reasonable? It could be said that old and new revolutions in philosophy (and their uneven effects on literary theory, and for that matter social science) were not being allowed time to work out their own implications and demises; even apart from wars, persistent thoughts derived from Vienna (logical positivism) and then from Cambridge (the later Wittgenstein) and from Oxford (Austin and the unfortunately named ordinary language philosophy) and later from Paris (with stunning indiscriminateness, sometimes of acceptance, sometimes of rejection) kept—keep—rubbing one another wrong.

I allude to these immediate forces active in the ways I work in order to note that one issue that has remained throughout their as yet uncharted and incalculable cultural effects is that of movies, almost as foreign to professional philosophy as it has always been. The issue had itself intensified at the beginning of the 1960s with the decline of Hollywood and the importing of the outburst of new, and a new awareness of earlier, filmmaking in Italy and France and Sweden and Japan. Foreign films were no longer foreign. And Warshow's words about movies, and more than movies, remain, the words' very distance (but distinction) bespeaking an intellectual conscience that is wary of saying less than it feels, or more than it knows. An admirable aspiration for philosophy.

My emphasis, intended to follow Warshow's, on his reclaiming and challenging his experience may still strike some as a craving for metaphysical presence. To convince oneself, on the contrary, that he wrote in recoil from metaphysical abduction, I recommend the exercise of tracking the term "experience" as it makes its inevitable appearance in each of his essays. From out of his sense, so far as he can determine it, of the powers that offer to substitute attitudes in place of his experience, he seeks it as a measure, for example, of his young son's restriction of experience, anxious over the poor preparation it affords for life's surprises (cf. p. 63); of the *New Yorker's* vulgarity in insisting upon the tasteful in the face of the unconscionable (cf. p. 75); of the memory at his father's funeral of the disappointment that constituted his father's experience (cf. p. 91); of Hollywood's power to discourage thoughtfulness (cf. p. 126); of the Westerner's imperviousness to experience (cf. p. 120); of Arthur Miller's slighting of experience (cf. p. 158) or freezing of it (cf. p. 170) in *The Crucible;* of Dreyer's blocking of it in *Days of Wrath* (cf. p. 234); of an American posture of affirmation that comfortably assumes one's adequacy to any experience (cf. p. 225); and goes so far as to attempt, noting

299

his probable insufficiency, to measure the experience, or rather the shutting off from experience (cf. p. 215), of the Jews in Europe who survived Hitler. To me this itinerary, along with the other turns I have cited, suggests an enactment of that responsiveness to events and to others as they present themselves (awake when everyone else has fallen asleep)—counting again, for ourselves, what the world has counted for us, presuming to assign the significance of our experiences for us—that marks philosophy as I care about it most.

STANLEY CAVELL

ACKNOWLEDGMENTS

THE ARTICLES printed in this collection originally appeared in the following magazines and are reprinted with permission.

THE NATION: "Hope and Wisdom"—August 10, 1946; "'Gerty' and the G.I.'s"—October 5, 1946; "The Working Day at the Splendide"—November 9, 1946.

COMMENTARY: "Poet of the Jewish Middle Class"—May 1946; "The Legacy of the 30's"—December 1947; "The Flight from Europe"—October 1948; "The Movie Camera and the American"—March 1952; "The 'Idealism' of Julius and Ethel Rosenberg"—November 1953; "The Liberal Conscience in *The Crucible*"—March 1953; "Paul, the Horror Comics, and Dr. Wertham"—June 1954; "Re-Viewing the Russian Movies"—October 1955.

PARTISAN REVIEW: "Woofed with Dreams"—November–December 1946; "Melancholy to the End"—January–February 1947 (appearing here as "E. B. White and the *New Yorker*"); "The Anatomy of Falsehood"—May–June 1947; "*Monsieur Verdoux*"—July–August 1947; "The Gangster as Tragic Hero"—February 1948; "*Paisan*"—July 1948; "*Day of Wrath:* The Enclosed Image"—December 1948; "The

Art of the Film"—1948; "Kafka's Failure"—1949; "Sadism for the Masses"—1950; "The Dying Gladiator"—1950; "An Old Man Gone"—May–June 1951; "Movie Chronicle: The Westerner"—March–April 1954; "A Feeling of Sad Dignity"—November–December 1954.

THE KENYON REVIEW: "Essence of Judaism"—Spring 1947.

AMERICAN MERCURY: "Father and Son—and the FBI"—June 1952.